ULTI/
HANDGUNS

PHOTOGRAPHS OF MORE THAN 500 WEAPONS

DAVID MILLER

Skyhorse Publishing

Skyhorse Publishing books may be purchased in bulk at special discounts for sales promotion, corporate gifts, fund-raising, or educational purposes. Special editions can also be created to specifications. For details, contact the Special Sales Department, Skyhorse Publishing, 307 West 36th Street, 11th Floor, New York, NY 10018 or info@skyhorsepublishing.com.

Skyhorse® and Skyhorse Publishing® are registered trademarks of Skyhorse Publishing, Inc.®, a Delaware corporation.

Visit our website at www.skyhorsepublishing.com.

10 9 8 7 6 5 4 3 2 1

Library of Congress Cataloging-in-Publication Data is available on file.

Design by Phil Clucas, MSIAD

Print ISBN: 978-1-5107-5666-3
Ebook ISBN: 978-1-5107-5691-5

Printed in China

Contents

Historic Pistols

Winkler

The Josef Winkler company was in business from 1915 to 1956, and was well-known in Europe for sporting arms, principally double barreled shotguns. The town of Ferlach has been a thriving center of gun making for centuries. This weapon is known in the US as a "parlor pistol," derived from the German name "zimmerschutzen," or "room shooting". This involved weapons with very heavy barrels and very small caliber, which were used for family entertainment (presumably in large houses!).

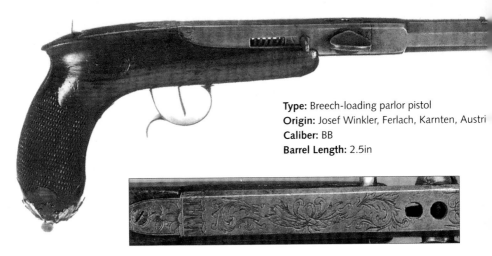

Type: Breech-loading parlor pistol
Origin: Josef Winkler, Ferlach, Karnten, Austri
Caliber: BB
Barrel Length: 2.5in

Werder

Werder, a gunsmith of Nurnberg, was the designer of the Werder rifle, which equipped both the Austrian and Bavarian armies in the late nineteenth century. He also designed a patented pistol Model 1869 for use by light cavalry regiments and the weapon shown here has the same act but with a much longer barrel, which is actual cut-down rifle barrel. Ammunition was loaded manually from the top using a mechanism resembling that of a Martini-Henry rifle.

Type: Breech-loading pistol
Origin: L. Werder, Nurnberg, Bavaria
Caliber: 11.5mm
Barrel Length: 15in

Box Lock

This half-inch caliber pistol has an ornate barrel shaped like that of a full-size ship's cannon and would have had a serious effect on a target at the very close ranges for which it was intended. The hammer for the percussion ignition system is mounted in a box in the middle of the frame hence the term box lock It bears a Belgian proof-mark, but there is no means of identifying the maker.

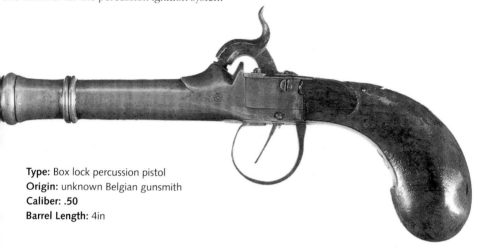

Type: Box lock percussion pistol
Origin: unknown Belgian gunsmith
Caliber: .50
Barrel Length: 4in

Double Barrel

Muzzle-loading pistols were too slow to reload in action so the double barreled weapon gave the firer a second chance at an adversary. Such "pocket" pistols were produced in large quantities by Belgian gunsmiths in the early nineteenth century and this is one of the better quality weapons to survive. The pistol is some 6.5in long and weighs 12oz, enabling it to be carried in one of the capacious pockets of coats then in style.

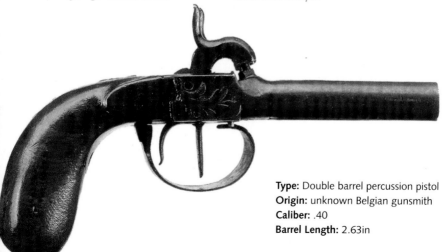

Type: Double barrel percussion pistol
Origin: unknown Belgian gunsmith
Caliber: .40
Barrel Length: 2.63in

Large Bore

This early nineteenth century percussion pistol has Liege proof marks, indicating that it was manufactured in this famous gun making city in Eastern Belgium, it is marked with the maker's name but the initials "FT" could be attributed to any of some half-dozen local gunsmiths. The massive .70 caliber ball would have weighed approximately 1oz, which on firing would have resulted in considerable damage.

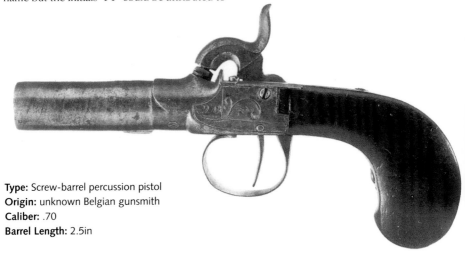

Type: Screw-barrel percussion pistol
Origin: unknown Belgian gunsmith
Caliber: .70
Barrel Length: 2.5in

Mariette Pepperbox

This pepperbox, made by Gilles Mariette, of Cheratte, near Liege, Belgium (1832-65), has five 8mm caliber barrels, which were rotated by hand. It was unusual in that in most pepperboxes the hammer struck the nipple behind the uppermost barrel, but in this desig by Mariette it struck the lowermost. The significance of this weapon is that it had five-shot capability and was the forerunner of the revolver.

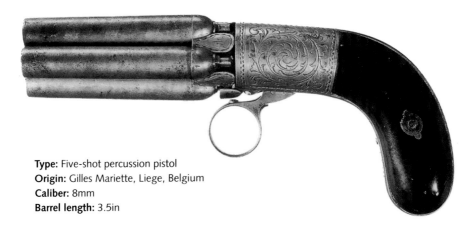

Type: Five-shot percussion pistol
Origin: Gilles Mariette, Liege, Belgium
Caliber: 8mm
Barrel length: 3.5in

Nagant Rolling-Block Pistol

The Belgian firm of Nagant, founded in 1859, made weapons fitted with the Remington rolling-block breech-loading mechanism under license, the first of which was a somewhat ungainly double barreled pistol for the Belgian gendarmerie (military police). The company also produced this, equally ungainly, single barrel version.

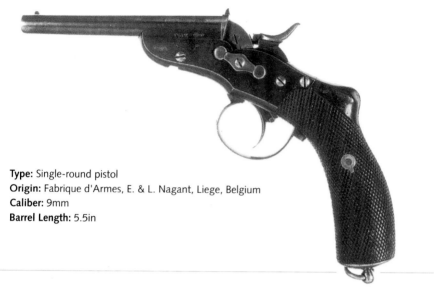

Type: Single-round pistol
Origin: Fabrique d'Armes, E. & L. Nagant, Liege, Belgium
Caliber: 9mm
Barrel Length: 5.5in

Pepperbox

This pepperbox is of a much higher standard than usual, with engraving on the metalwork and a fine rosewood stock. The five barrels are .75 inches in length and of .32 caliber, and the unit, which has fluted sides, is better engineered than in almost any other pepperbox. Despite all this, the maker has left no trace of his name or country of origin, although from the general style and the proof marks, he was almost certainly Belgian.

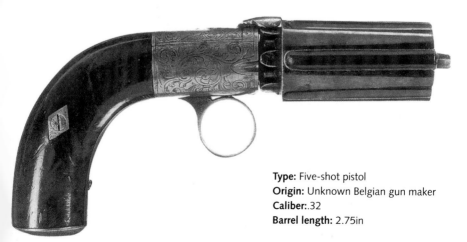

Type: Five-shot pistol
Origin: Unknown Belgian gun maker
Caliber: .32
Barrel length: 2.75in

Percussion Pistol

There are no identification marks on this well made and neatly designed percussion pistol, one of many thousands produced by skilled Belgian gunsmiths in the late eighteenth and early nineteenth centuries. The guns were exported to the United States in volume providing relatively inexpensive firearms in the days before America's homegrown gun industry became well established. The (probably steel) ramrod has been lost over the years and would normally have been located beneath the barrel.

Type: Percussion pistol
Origin: unknown Belgian gunsmith
Caliber: .50
Barrel Length: 5in

CONTINENTAL WEAPONS

The word "continental" in weapons terms almost always means that a firearm is known to have been made somewhere in continental Europe (as opposed to the US), but that, despite extensive research, neither the precise gunsmith nor the country of origin can be established. Quite why gunsmiths should have been so reluctant to put their names on their products is not clear but the fact is that many didn't, and many thousands of such weapons still exist as shown by these three pistols.

This percussion pistol is typical of weapons produced in Belgium in the late eighteenth and early nineteenth centuries, but the only marking on it is the serial number "14." It is a very simple weapon with a 3.63in barrel, firing a .52 caliber ball.

Box Lock Pistol

This flintlock pocket pistol does not have any maker's or proof marks, either, although both sides of the metalwork carry elaborate engravings. Note the very short barrel, which is of .50 caliber and only 1.63in long allowing it to be easily concealed in a coat pocket.

Type: Box lock/flintlock pocket pistol
Origin: Unknown Continental gunsmith
Caliber: .50
Barrel Length: 1.63in

Flintlock Pistol

A smaller flintlock pistol, this one similarly lacks any form of marking and the purist collector will note that while the barrel and body are original, a number of parts, including the ramrod and main spring are replacements.
This type of gun would be carried by the driver of a carriage to ward off highwaymen.

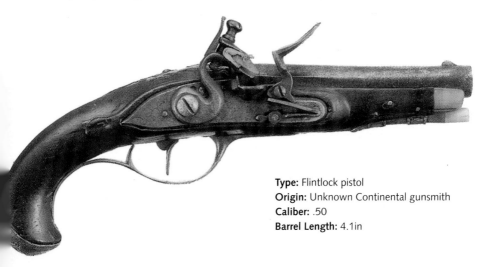

Type: Flintlock pistol
Origin: Unknown Continental gunsmith
Caliber: .50
Barrel Length: 4.1in

Flobert Tip-Up Pistol

In 1847 a Frenchman named Louis Flobert invented a cartridge which consisted of a ball in a case whose base contained a percussion cap with a rim of primer The charge was sufficiently powerful to propel the round over short distances for target shooting, but propellant was later added to increase the range. Flobert also manufactured rifles and pistols to use his cartridges, which were available in 4mm upwards The pistol we show was produced at his factory.

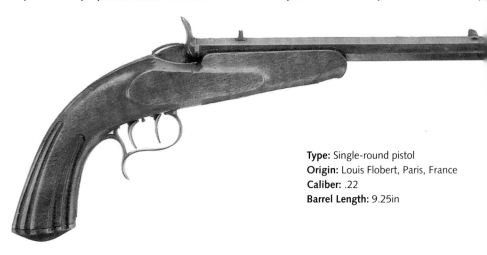

Type: Single-round pistol
Origin: Louis Flobert, Paris, France
Caliber: .22
Barrel Length: 9.25in

St Etienne Model 1822

When the percussion mechanism became widely accepted, many older flintlock weapons were converted to this way of firing, either by their original makers or by independent gunsmiths. Shown here is a pistol originally made as a Model 1822 flintlock at the St Etienne arsenal, but subsequently converted by an unknown hand to the percussion method It is a large military-caliber pistol with a part-octagonal barrel, and unusually, no ram appears to have been fitted.

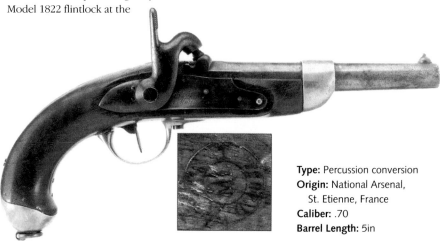

Type: Percussion conversion
Origin: National Arsenal,
    St. Etienne, France
Caliber: .70
Barrel Length: 5in

St Etienne Palm Pistol

Palm-pistols (also known as "squeezers") were popular in the nineteenth century as a form of personal protection. Made to resemble a cigarette packet, they were similar in mission and size to derringers, but with the major difference that whereas the derringer held one, or two rounds, palm pistols held five. The palm pistols shown here are similar to each other, each carrying five rounds. Muzzle velocity was very low and range probably no more than a few feet, although they are, somewhat optimistically, fitted with foresights.

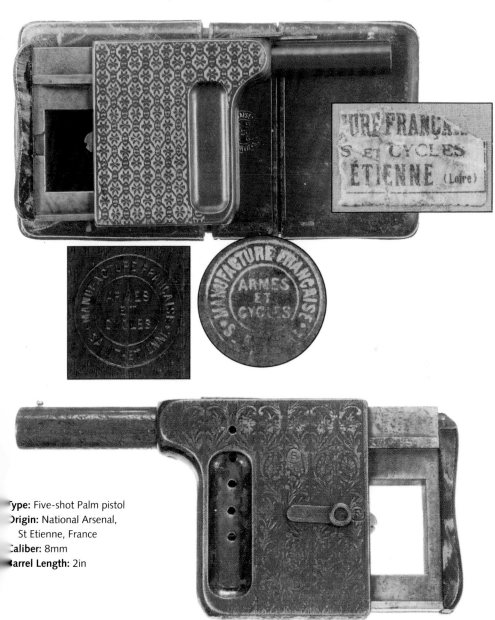

Type: Five-shot Palm pistol
Origin: National Arsenal, St Etienne, France
Caliber: 8mm
Barrel Length: 2in

Target Pistol

This handsome .22in caliber breech-loading German target pistol is marked with the name "J.H. Hampe, Gettingen" on the top of the barrel, but no gunsmith of this name is recorded by any of the authorities on the subject. The weapon is made in the old style of target pistol, with a long (11.2in) barrel and a gracefully curved stock. The frame is decorated with light scroll engraving. The grips are checkered walnut.

Type: Target pistol
Origin: unknown German gunsmith
Caliber: .22
Barrel Length: 11.2in

John Rigby Duelling Pistol

The Rigby family is known to have been in the gun making business in Dublin in the nineteenth century, but this dueling pistol, which bears that name, suggests that they may have been operating there in the eighteenth century, as well. The barrel is also marked "DC-479" which means that it was registered at Dublin Castle, the residence and main offices o the British Lord Lieutenant, who governed Ireland on behalf of the British Crown.

Type: Dueling pistol
Origin: John Rigby, Dublin, Ireland
Caliber: .60in
Barrel Length: 10in

Flintlock Pistol

This military style pistol bears the mark "Dunn" on the lockplate and "Dublin" on the top of the barrel. The gun's general design and features suggest the early eighteenth century and it is known that there was a gunsmith named Nathaniel Dunn working in Dublin in this period. The pistol has ornate brass fittings such as the trigger guard, butt end and ramrod tubes. The original wooden ramrod is still present but is missing its brass tip.

Type: Flintlock pistol
Origin: Dunn, Dublin, Ireland
Caliber: .68
Barrel Length: 8in

Naval Flintlock

An unknown gunsmith manufactured this eighteenth-century flintlock large bore pistol in Italy. It is fairly typical of a mid-eighteenth century European weapon. According to the markings, the lock was manufactured in Turin and the walnut stock in Capellaro. The barrel was originally longer, but has been cut short at some time in the pistol's life. The ramrod socket is a brass fitment as is the trigger guard and butt end cap.

Type: Flintlock pistol
Origin: unknown Italian gunsmith
Caliber: .64in
Barrel Length: 7.9in

Knap Percussion

This very handsome target pistol was made in the middle of the nineteenth century at Rheinfelden in Switzerland. It is unmistakeably representative of the middle-European style of "shutzen" target gun of the time. Its carved stock with checkered grip and ornate trigger guard are typical features. It is marked with the name "A. KNAP" who is known to have been an active gunsmith in that town at that time.

Type: Percussion target pistol
Origin: A. Knap, Rheinfelden, Switzerland
Caliber: 0.50in
Barrel Length: 9.5in

Blanchard

A target pistol from the mid-nineteenth Century, this one was made by Blanchard of London. The Blanchard family were originally from Paris and were famous for their precision made weapons, which were known for their accuracy and therefore were often used for dueling purposes. Finely made with microgroove rifling in the 8-inch barrel, it has a finely checkered butt, with a cap box inside, and the turned steel ramrod held in the wooden stock.

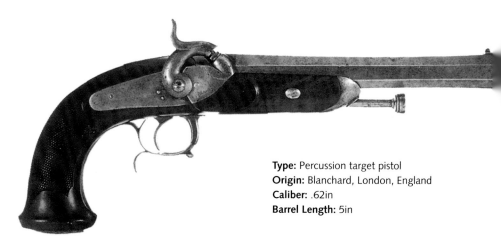

Type: Percussion target pistol
Origin: Blanchard, London, England
Caliber: .62in
Barrel Length: 5in

Brunn Double-Barreled Pistol

Before the advent of revolvers, one of the only ways to get more than one shot from a pistol without reloading was to have more than one barrel. A London gunsmith made this fine example, around 1790. It has two side-by-side barrels, and two separate triggers operating two complete flintlock mechanisms. The design of this pistol shows signs of European influence with the eccentric shaped trigger guard and cross-hatching on the grip.

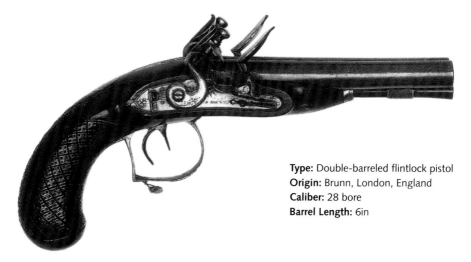

Type: Double-barreled flintlock pistol
Origin: Brunn, London, England
Caliber: 28 bore
Barrel Length: 6in

Bunney Cannon Barreled Pistol

As is obvious from the picture, the shape of this kind of pistol gave rise to the "cannon-barrel" description. This unusual and attractive flintlock example dates from around 1770 and is typical of the type. The polished bronze barrel can be unscrewed, giving access to the breech for reloading, while a sliding trigger guard safety gives the user some protection from accidental discharges. The flat-sided wooden handgrip is finely carved with scroll patterns.

Type: Single-barreled flintlock pistol
Origin: Bunney, London, England
Caliber: 24 bore
Barrel Length: 5.25in

Cogswell Pepperbox

Made by Benjamin Cogswell, 224 Strand, London, and engraved as such, this finely made percussion pepperbox has six barrels, each of 60 bore and each three-and-a half-inches long. The self-cocking hammer is top mounted. Note the large trigger guard and the shield around the nipples to prevent copper fragments from the cap hittin the user. The sides of the action are intricately engraved in a scroll pattern The company is still in business today as Cogswell and Harrison.

Type: Six-shot pistol
Origin: Cogswell, London, England
Caliber: 60 bore
Barrel Length: 3.5in

Collumbell Holster Pistol

Made in around 1740, by Collumbell of London, this is a solid example of a holster pistol of that time. David Collumbell was apprenticed to Gerrett Johnson in 1712, established his own company at King Street, Westminster, from 1734 to 57. He moved to Parliament Street in Westminster in 1763. He was appointec gun maker to the East India Company in 1761. The lock has the maker's name engraved on it, and uses a "swan-neck" cock. The stock is made from walnut, and comes complete with a brass butt cap.

Type: Single barreled flintlock pistol
Origin: Collumbell, London, England
Caliber: 20 bore
Barrel Length: 5in

Cooper Large Pepperbox

Joseph Rock Cooper was an English gunsmith, working in Birmingham, England, but with sales outlets in London and in New York City who held patents for six and twelve-barreled revolving pistols. The model seen here is a six-barrel pepperbox, each barrel being 5.9 inches long and .40 caliber, making it rather large for a weapon which was supposed to fit into the shooter's pocket. In this model the barrel unit was advanced mechanically by the trigger mechanism.

Type: Multi-shot pistol
Origin: Cooper, Birmingham, England
Caliber: .40in
Barrel Length: 5.9in

Deane Belt Pistol

This mid-nineteenth century pistol was designed and manufactured by G. & J. Deane of 30 King William Street, situated in the London Bridge area of London, England. It has a Damascus steel brown hexagonal barrel with the address "George & John Deane. (Makers to H.R.H. Prince Albert.)" The parts are engraved and there is a captive swivelling steel ramrod. The large caliber of this weapon would have created considerable recoil. It would have considerably damaged the target if the firer's aim was good.

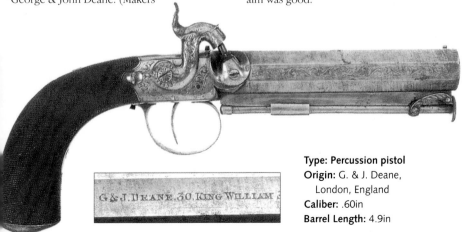

Type: Percussion pistol
Origin: G. & J. Deane,
London, England
Caliber: .60in
Barrel Length: 4.9in

Egg Flintlock

Durs Egg had reputation for high quality work. He was an appointed gun maker to various members of the British royal family, including the Prince of Wales and the Duke of York. This flintlock brass barreled holster pistol is dated 1796. It is a fine example of his work. It is a solid usable firearm rather than a highly decorated presentation piece. It has a walnut stock with a brass butt cap, trigger guard, and a wooden ramrod with a brass tip.

Type: Percussion pistol
Origin: D. Egg, London, England
Caliber: 24 bore
Barrel Length: 7in

EIG M1842 Cavalry Pistol

The East India Company ran India almost as if the company was an independent state, to the extent that it even formed, trained and equipped its own armed forces. The East India Gun Company made this heavy military pistol for its own forces.

The gun is dated 1871, and has Birmingham proof marks on the lock. It has several issue marks stamped on the stock, including one that reads "1885 Bentley and Playfair." Indian issue marks are also engraved on the barrel.

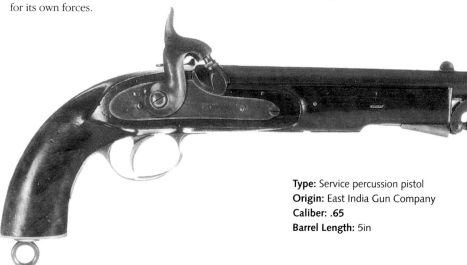

Type: Service percussion pistol
Origin: East India Gun Company
Caliber: .65
Barrel Length: 5in

Fisher Flintlock Traveler's Pistol

This typical flintlock pistol has the names "Fisher" on the lock and "Bristol" on the barrel. It is known that a gunsmith of that name was active in Bristol, England in the 1820s. A stylish gun, its sideplates are shaped and engraved, the stock is of light walnut, and the barrel is made of brass. The ramrod is finished in contrasting dark stained hardwood and has a brass ferrule.

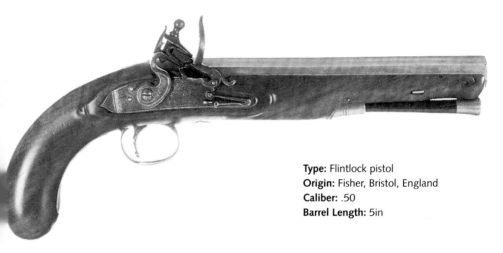

Type: Flintlock pistol
Origin: Fisher, Bristol, England
Caliber: .50
Barrel Length: 5in

Galton Flintlock Pistols

This handsome pair of flintlock pistols is housed in a specially made case, together with the original bullet mold, although the powder flask appears to have come from another weapon. The two closed lids on the case are compartments in which to store lead balls. Other tools, like the nipple wrench and screwdriver are noticeably absent. These pistols were made by Galton and there were several gunsmiths of that name active in London and Birmingham between 1750 and 1812.

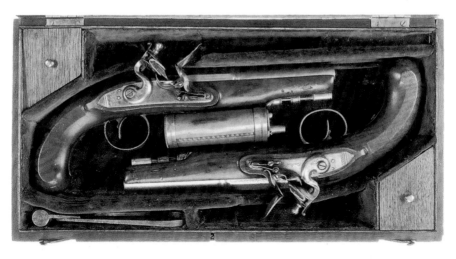

Hollis & Sheath Percussion Pocket Pistol

Hollis & Sheath were gunsmiths, based in Birmingham and London in the middle of the nineteenth century. This attractive percussion cap pocket pistol is about six inches long. It has a detachable barrel, which is threaded in front of the firing nipple. It is also equipped with a foresight, an engraved action, and a hammer. It was designed to be hidden about the firer's person to be used as a "last-ditch" defense against the robbers and footpads that frequented the back streets of nineteenth-century London.

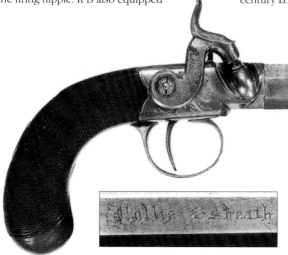

Type: Percussion pistol
Origin: Hollis & Sheath,
    London, England
Caliber: .40
Barrel Length: 4in

Ketland Flintlock Pistol

This flintlock pistol has a brass barrel, iron mechanism, and a walnut stock. The lock is marked "W/KETLAND/&Co." Several generations of this family were employed in the weapons business from the mid-eighteenth to mid-nineteenth centuries. It was based in Birmingham and London. The family also had close ties with the United States and two brothers, John and Thomas Ketland, were resident in Philadelphia from 1797 to 1800. They supplied a large number of weapons to the Commonwealth of Pennsylvania.

Type: Flintlock pistol
Origin: William Ketland & Co,
    Birmingham, England
Caliber: .60
Barrel Length: 7.75in

Ketland Dragoon Flintlock Pistol

Another product of the Ketland family, this dragoon pistol is undated, but bears the "GR" (George Rex or King George) royal cipher in front of the cock. This would date it to some time midway between 1714 and 1830. Various parts of this weapon are replacements, including the cock, hammer and ramrod, and the barrel has significant signs of corrosion in the vicinity of the touch hole. Despite this, the gun is still of considerable value as an antique.

Type: Flintlock pistol
Origin: William Ketland & Co,
　　　　Birmingham, England
Caliber: .70
Barrel Length: 9.0in

Manton Traveler's Pistols

Joseph and John Manton were brothers who traded Independently. They were two of England's finest gunsmiths of the early nineteenth century. Shown here is a pair of so-called "Travelers Pistols." These were handy but effective weapons, designed for self-protection from robbers and brigands, while travelling on the unpoliced roads of the time. Each pistol has a full-length walnut stock, finely checkered butt and Birmingham proof marks. The barrels show the distinctive markings of the manufacturing process that was known as "Damascus twist."

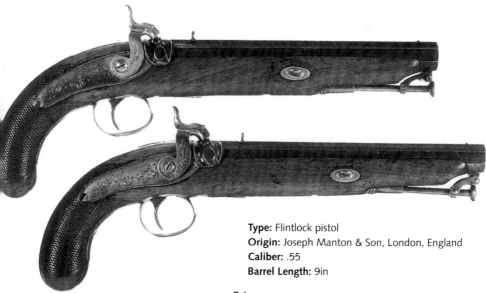

Type: Flintlock pistol
Origin: Joseph Manton & Son, London, England
Caliber: .55
Barrel Length: 9in

21

Mewis London Blunderbuss Pistol

This pistol is marked "Mewis & Co." A gunsmithing company of that name was in business in Birmingham, England in the late eighteenth century. The gun was proofed in Birmingham and has London retailer's marks indicating that it was supplied to a London trader. The effect of such a blunderbuss weapon would have been devastating against a human being or an animal at short range. In common with many blunderbusses the barrel is made from brass.

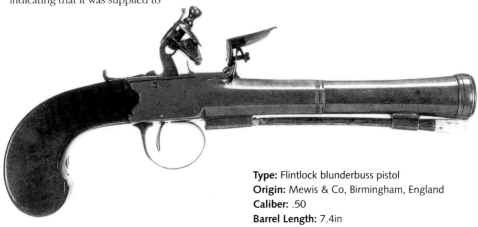

Type: Flintlock blunderbuss pistol
Origin: Mewis & Co, Birmingham, England
Caliber: .50
Barrel Length: 7.4in

Nock Flintlock .45 Pistol

The Nock family were active gunsmiths from the 1770s to the 1860s. They had numerous government contracts, particularly with the Royal Navy. Many of their weapons are also marked "Gun makers to His Majesty," suggesting that they were in the privileged position of supplying weapons to the Royal Household. This weapon is marked "London," but has Birmingham proofs suggesting that while Nock's premises were in London, they had either a factory in Birmingham, or that the gun was supplied by a subcontractor.

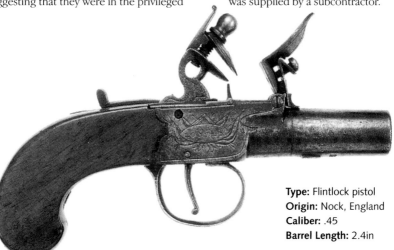

Type: Flintlock pistol
Origin: Nock, England
Caliber: .45
Barrel Length: 2.4in

Richards Over/Under

The over/under pistol was one of the early attempts at obtaining a compact multi-barrel weapon without the breadth involved in the double barrel design. The preloaded barrels swivelled to use the same flintlock firing mechanism, meaning that the second shot was not instant. As with many weapons of this period this pistol was manufactured and proofed in Birmingham, but sold in London, England. The inscription on the side of the action confirms this.

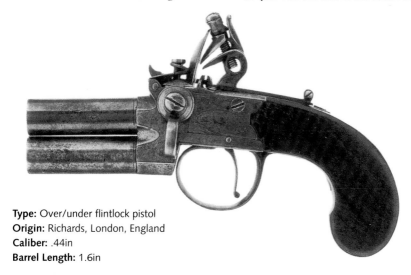

Type: Over/under flintlock pistol
Origin: Richards, London, England
Caliber: .44in
Barrel Length: 1.6in

Saunders Queen Anne

This style of pistol is often referred to as the "Queen Anne" type, although most pistols of this sort were produced after that Queen died in 1714. It has the cannon barrel shape, and has a "three stage" barrel. Made by T. Saunders, a contemporary London gunsmith, it has a finely engraved lockplate, and a serpent engraving in the stock on the opposite side. The stock is walnut and has a hefty brass butt cap.

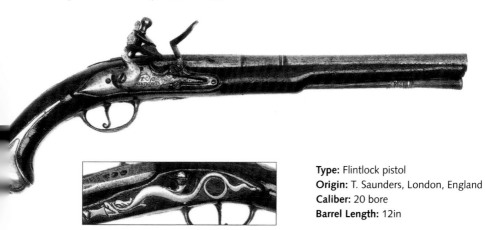

Type: Flintlock pistol
Origin: T. Saunders, London, England
Caliber: 20 bore
Barrel Length: 12in

Scottish Dress Pistol

In the seventeenth century, the Scottish gunsmithing tradition was to make pistols completely from metal. The stock was made from brass, or steel. In the early Victorian years, there was a popular romantic view of Scotland, partly inspired by the novels of Sir Walter Scott. Unlikely versions of "Highland Dress" became popular at parties, and wearers often completed their outfit with pastiches of "traditional Highland weapons." This pistol dates from around 1840, and was intended for this market.

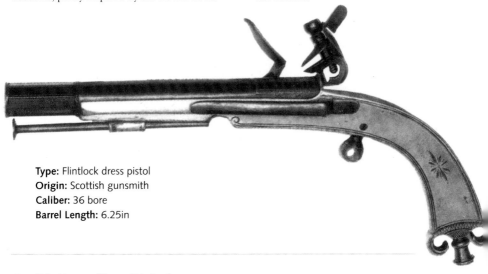

Type: Flintlock dress pistol
Origin: Scottish gunsmith
Caliber: 36 bore
Barrel Length: 6.25in

Smith Boarding Pistol

This is a short barreled pistol with a solid walnut stock, checkered butt and back action lock. It fires a hefty projectile but the short hexagonal barrel means that the accurate range would be short. Pistols like this were often known as "boarding pistols." Ostensibly, the gun was designed for use by naval officers in close-quarter actions. This one comes complete with a spring-loaded bayonet under the barrel, which is released by sliding the trigger guard lock.

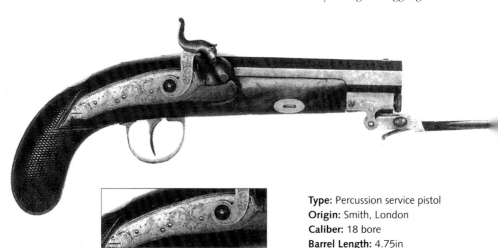

Type: Percussion service pistol
Origin: Smith, London
Caliber: 18 bore
Barrel Length: 4.75in

Thomas Holster Pistol

This is a long pistol, typical of those used by cavalrymen and mounted troops. Dated around 1775, it has an early-style rounded lock with silver wire inlay. The pistol also has a wonderfully patinated walnut stock with inlaid engraved teardrop panels.

Trigger guard, ramrod mounts, and butt cap are made from brass. It has a wooden ramrod with a brass tip. These were popular throughout the eighteenth century, both for their lightness and their attractive appearance.

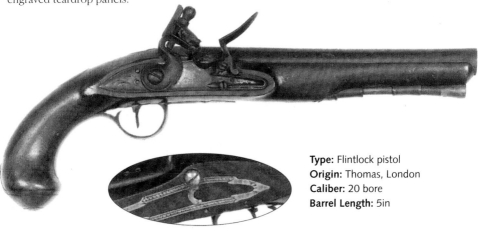

Type: Flintlock pistol
Origin: Thomas, London
Caliber: 20 bore
Barrel Length: 5in

Tipping & Lawden Four-Barrel Pistol

This stunningly engraved four barreled pistol indicates how, by the middle of the nineteenth century, the world was becoming a smaller place, at least as far as manufacturers were concerned. The original patent for this design was held by Christian Sharp (born in 1811).

Sharp was involved in gun making in Connecticut, but Tipping & Lawden of Birmingham, England manufactured this weapon under licence. In addition, the rosewood box is from Bombay, India.

Type: Four-barrel pistol
Origin: Tipping & Lawden, Birmingham, England
Caliber: 7mm
Barrel Length: 3in

Tipping & Lawden Model 3 Four-Barrel Pistol

Four barrel pistols were weapons designed for self defense. They could be easily concealed about the firer's person until required for use. Thus, as in the previous entries they were normally very small, so the comparatively large size of this Tipping & Lawden Model 3 comes as something of a surprise. Nonetheless the gun is designed to fit in a pocket, having smooth contours to the frame, a concealed trigger, and no trigger guard to snag on the pocket lining.

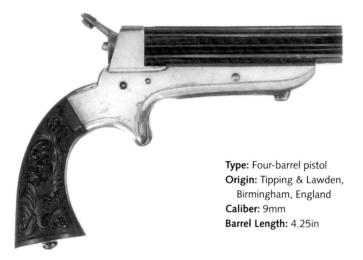

Type: Four-barrel pistol
Origin: Tipping & Lawden,
   Birmingham, England
Caliber: 9mm
Barrel Length: 4.25in

Tower Sea Service Pistol

This is a solid British flintlock military pistol from the period 1740 to 1840. It has a heavy stock, and a rounded butt cap. The markings show that it was assembled in the Tower of London Armoury, although the components would have been most likely supplied by a range of contractors. It has "GR" (for George Rex or King George) on the side plate and the date 1805 stamped into the butt. The steel ramrod is a replacement as the originals were wood tipped with brass.

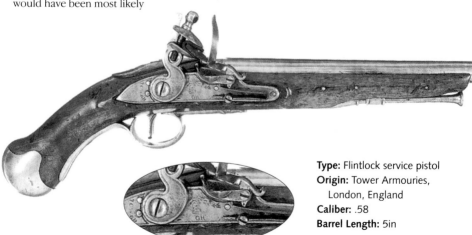

Type: Flintlock service pistol
Origin: Tower Armouries,
   London, England
Caliber: .58
Barrel Length: 5in

Allen & Thurber Single-Shot Pistol

This odd-looking single-shot pistol is one of a batch of some three hundred manufactured by Allen & Thurber, one of the companies in which Ethan Allen (1806-1871) was involved. These pistols were produced in the late 1840s and early 1850s. They were intended for competition use, for which they were fitted with an adjustable rear sight. The cast steel barrel is threaded and detachable at the breech. Its octagonal part is marked "Allen & Thurber, Worcester."

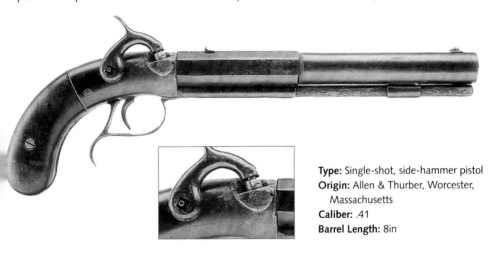

Type: Single-shot, side-hammer pistol
Origin: Allen & Thurber, Worcester, Massachusetts
Caliber: .41
Barrel Length: 8in

Ames Model 1842 Navy

Ames were better known for their swords than for firearms, but they did get a contract to produce 2,000 of this military percussion pistol. The Model 1842 was the first major government-issue percussion pistol to be made from new, rather than being a conversion. With a heavier stock than its army counterpart, the Model 1842 Navy had a brass barrel band and butt cap, while the hammer pivot and spring are actually on the inside of the lockplate.

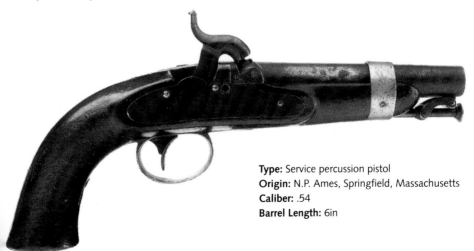

Type: Service percussion pistol
Origin: N.P. Ames, Springfield, Massachusetts
Caliber: .54
Barrel Length: 6in

Aston Model 1842

In 1845, Henry Aston won a contract from the war department to provide the army with 30,000 of these Model 1842 pistols. It thus became the first percussion pistol to be generally adopted by the United States forces, as opposed to converted earlier guns. The gun was a solid arm, which was used by many combatants in the Civil War. It is marked US and H. Aston & Co. on the sideplate. The gun has brass fittings and it has a swivelling steel ramrod.

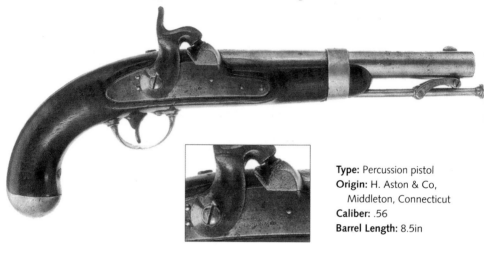

Type: Percussion pistol
Origin: H. Aston & Co,
   Middleton, Connecticut
Caliber: .56
Barrel Length: 8.5in

Colt First Model Derringer

This was the first single-shot pistol to be manufactured by Colt. It was in production from 1870 to 1890, during which some 6,500 were completed. The all-metal weapon was loaded by releasing the barrel using the small round catch (which can be seen below the hammer) and swinging it to the left and then down. The empty cartridge case could then be removed and replaced by a full one.

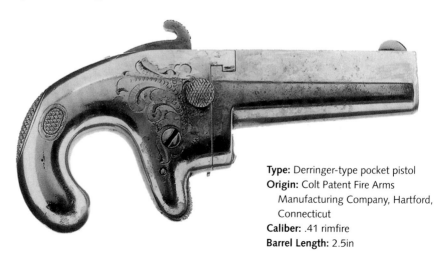

Type: Derringer-type pocket pistol
Origin: Colt Patent Fire Arms
   Manufacturing Company, Hartford,
   Connecticut
Caliber: .41 rimfire
Barrel Length: 2.5in

28

Colt Second Model Derringer

This gun was produced between 1870 and 1890 in parallel with the First Model. The main difference between them was its larger butt, complete with varnished walnut grips. To load the gun, the barrel was put at half cock and the breech swung up. The empty rimfire cartridge case was ejected automatically when the breech was opened. Firearms of this type were carried as a back up a revolver visible in a holster.

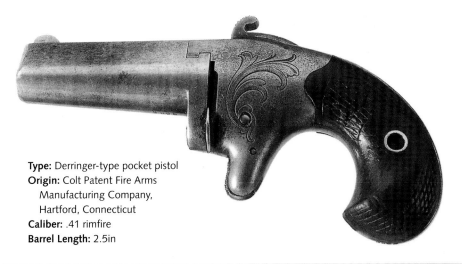

Type: Derringer-type pocket pistol
Origin: Colt Patent Fire Arms
    Manufacturing Company,
    Hartford, Connecticut
Caliber: .41 rimfire
Barrel Length: 2.5in

Colt Third Model Derringer

Colt's Third Model Derringer was designed by Alexander Thuer, and, as a result, is often known as the "Thuer Derringer." Like the previous two models, it was chambered for .41in rimfire and had a 2.5in barrel, but in this case, it pivoted to the right for loading. The weapon was in production from 1875 to 1912 and it is not surprising that there should have been minor changes, as seen here.

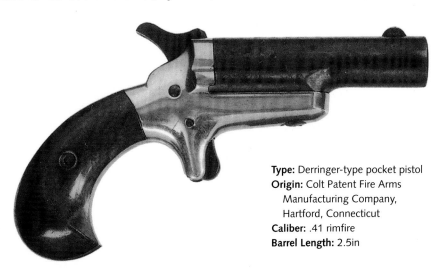

Type: Derringer-type pocket pistol
Origin: Colt Patent Fire Arms
    Manufacturing Company,
    Hartford, Connecticut
Caliber: .41 rimfire
Barrel Length: 2.5in

Deringer Pocket Pistol

Henry Deringer, Senior and his son, Henry Deringer, Junior, were gunsmiths in Philadelphia from the early 1800s until the latter's death in 1869. After the death of Henry Deringer, Junior, the company struggled on for ten years and then went out of business.

The company produced a number of rifle and pistol designs, but its most famous product was this large caliber, very small sized, single-shot, pocket pistol which was widely imitated under the generic name.

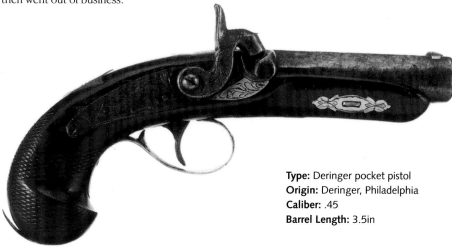

Type: Deringer pocket pistol
Origin: Deringer, Philadelphia
Caliber: .45
Barrel Length: 3.5in

Deringer M1842 Navy

Henry Deringer received a contract on July 1, 1845 to produce 1,200 of this pistol for the US Navy. He purchased the original manufacturing equipment from Ames who had already produced 2,000 items of the same pattern pistol from 1842 onwards.

Although they were existing suppliers of the US government (Deringer had built the Model 181 flintlock musket under license) the company's workmanship proved to be unreliable on this occasion. Only three hundred examples of the gun were accepted.

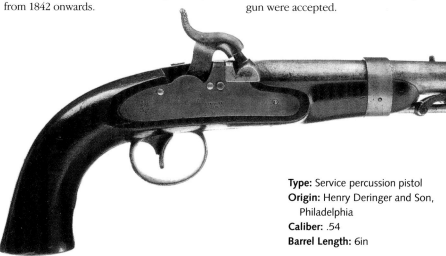

Type: Service percussion pistol
Origin: Henry Deringer and Son, Philadelphia
Caliber: .54
Barrel Length: 6in

Hammond Bulldog

A single shot self-defense weapon in the deringer class, this crudely finished breech-loading pistol fired a powerful .44 cartridge and was patented in 1864. The Connecticut Arms and Manufacturing Company operated only from 1863 to 1869. They were located in Naubuc, Connecticut, probably for the duration of the war. The gun would be effective enough at close range, and pistols of this nature became popular with many soldiers in the Civil War, who bought them to carry as concealed last-ditch back-up weapons.

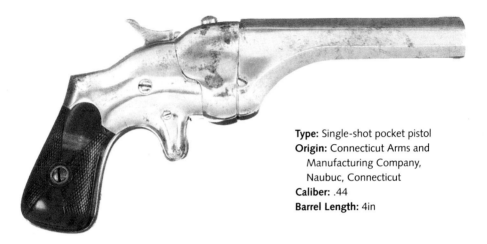

Type: Single-shot pocket pistol
Origin: Connecticut Arms and
    Manufacturing Company,
    Naubuc, Connecticut
Caliber: .44
Barrel Length: 4in

Harper's Ferry Model 1805 Flintlock Pistol

The United States government established an "Armory and Arsenal" at Harpers Ferry in 1799 to take advantage of the waterpower supplied by the Potomac and Shenandoah rivers, which meet there. Between 1801 and the outbreak of the Civil War over 600,000 muskets, pistols, and rifles were manufactured there. One of these guns was this Model 1805. This model was the first military pistol to be manufactured at a US government arsenal. A total of 4,086 were produced between 1806 and 1808.

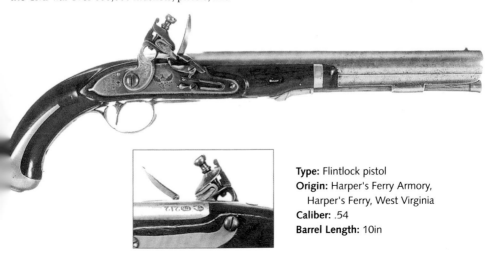

Type: Flintlock pistol
Origin: Harper's Ferry Armory,
    Harper's Ferry, West Virginia
Caliber: .54
Barrel Length: 10in

Henry Saw-Handle Flintlock

A pistol of this shape, with the stock spur extending horizontally back over the grip is often known as a "saw handle" pistol. The spur was intended to help keep the muzzle down, and the straight top edge was supposed to improve instinctive aiming. This one has a Model 1807 lock, and may either have been a target pistol or one of a pair of dueling pistols.

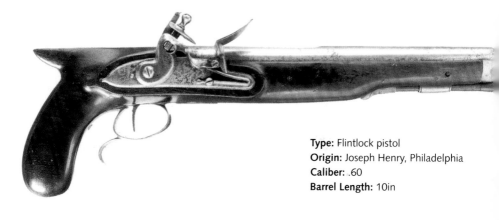

Type: Flintlock pistol
Origin: Joseph Henry, Philadelphia
Caliber: .60
Barrel Length: 10in

Hopkins & Allen Vest Pocket Derringer

Hopkins & Allen was established in 1868 and stayed in business until 1917. During that time, the company produced a large number of weapons, under its own name, and others such as Blue Jacket, Monarch, and Universal. This heavily engraved derringer-type pistol was marketed as a Hopkins & Allen weapon. It fired a single .22in round, but its very small size (it was a mere 1.75in long) meant that it could remain concealed until the last possible momer

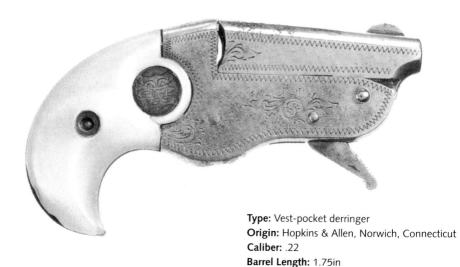

Type: Vest-pocket derringer
Origin: Hopkins & Allen, Norwich, Connecticut
Caliber: .22
Barrel Length: 1.75in

Johnson Model 1836 Pistol

This is a Model 1836 pistol manufactured by Robert Johnson to meet a government contract for 3,000 weapons at $9.00 each. It is of an obsolete design, but was made to a very high standard. This particular example was made in 1841 and it has lasted particularly well. In 1841, gun manufacture was already moving to percussion cap arms, this gun was one of the very last flintlock weapons contracted by the US government.

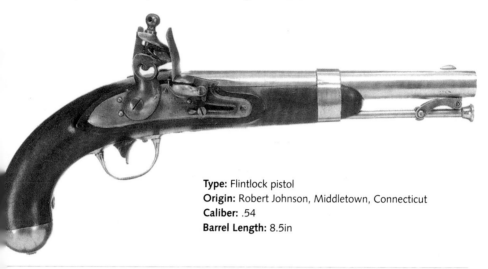

Type: Flintlock pistol
Origin: Robert Johnson, Middletown, Connecticut
Caliber: .54
Barrel Length: 8.5in

Lindsay Twin-Shot Pistol

One of the more unusual attempts to get more than one shot out of a percussion arm, this 1860 pistol was designed by John P. Lindsay. It had two charges and two projectiles, one aligned behind the other in the same barrel. The twin hammers were designed to fire them sequence. The Lindsay mechanism was also tried on a musket, but it was not successfully adopted. Only hundred examples of this pistol were made.

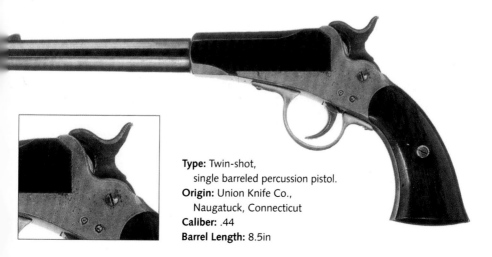

Type: Twin-shot,
  single barreled percussion pistol.
Origin: Union Knife Co.,
  Naugatuck, Connecticut
Caliber: .44
Barrel Length: 8.5in

Marston Three-Barrel Pistol

William W. Marston made a variety of multi barreled handguns, most of them pepperboxes. The design shown here is not strictly a pepperbox, in that the barrels do not rotate. The gun has three barrels mounted one above the other, so it does not fit neatly into any other category. The unit tipped forward for loading. Once loaded, each barrel was fired in turn, the indicator on the right of the weapon showing the firer which barrels remained unfired.

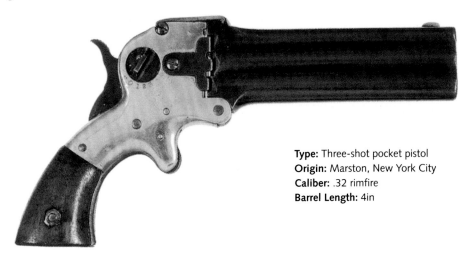

Type: Three-shot pocket pistol
Origin: Marston, New York City
Caliber: .32 rimfire
Barrel Length: 4in

Minneapolis "Protector" Palm Pistol

In the nineteenth century, many inventors attempted to produce the ideal "last-ditch" protection weapon. There were single- or double-shot guns but the weapon shown here housed ten cartridges in its circular magazine. Originating in France, where it was patented by Jacques Turbiaux, this weapon was held in the palm of the hand and was loaded and fired by clenching the fist. This weapon was manufactured in the United States under licenc by the Minneapolis Fire Arms Co. of Minneapolis, Minnesota.

Type: Radial pistol
Origin: Minneapolis Fire Arms Co.,
Minneapolis, Minnesota
Caliber: .32 Short rimfire
Barrel Length: 1.6in

National No. 2 Derringer

Moore's Patent Firearms Company was established in Brooklyn in the nineteenth century. It changed its name to the National Arms Company in 1866. Among its products was the National No. 2 Derringer (seen here). The gun had a spur trigger and was reloaded by pressing the release catch and swivelling the barrel to expose the chamber. Colt bought the National Arms Company in 1870, following which this weapon was marketed as the Colt No. 2 Derringer.

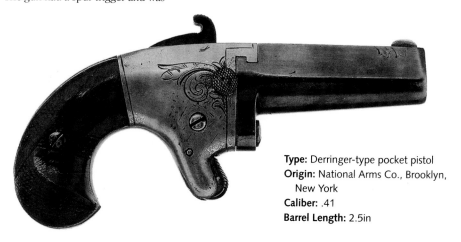

Type: Derringer-type pocket pistol
Origin: National Arms Co., Brooklyn, New York
Caliber: .41
Barrel Length: 2.5in

Palmetto M 1842

William Glaze and Benjamin Flagg set up the Palmetto Armory in Columbia, South Carolina. Between 1852 and 1853 they made 1,000 of these standard Model 1842 percussion pistols for the South Carolina Militia. Many of these weapons saw service with the Confederate forces during the Civil War. This one has both the date, 1852, and a C.S.A. stamp on the lock. The steel swivelling ramrod is missing on this example but the pivot lug can be seen under the barrel.

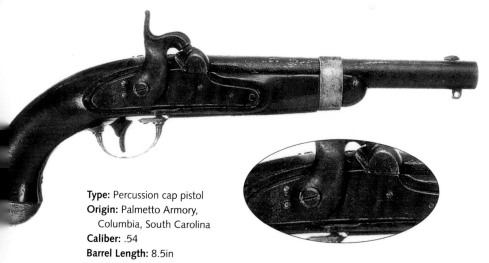

Type: Percussion cap pistol
Origin: Palmetto Armory, Columbia, South Carolina
Caliber: .54
Barrel Length: 8.5in

Simeon North Pistols

Simeon North (1765-1852) is one of America's forgotten heroes. He owned a farm in Berlin, Connecticut, but had a lifelong fascination with engineering. In particular, he was fascinated by the idea of producing equipment with standardized parts so that spares could be fully interchangeable. In 1813, he obtained a contract to produce 20,000 pistols and, for the first time ever in a government contract, it was specified that the parts were to be fully standardized.

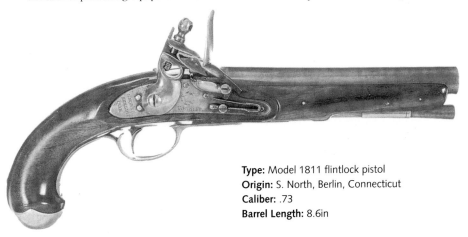

Type: Model 1811 flintlock pistol
Origin: S. North, Berlin, Connecticut
Caliber: .73
Barrel Length: 8.6in

Type: Model 1826 flintlock pistol
Origin: S. North, Berlin, Connecticut
Caliber: .54
Barrel Length: 8.6in

Remington Vest Pocket Pistol

Produced to an in-house design, the Remington Vest-Pocket Pistol was a single-shot, derringer-type firearm. It was aimed at the self-protection market, which was so important in the nineteenth century. The basic model fired the .22 round and had a 3.25 or 3.5 inch barrel, but there were also .30, .32, and .41 versions, with either 3.5 or 4 inch barrels. The ornate engraved version shown here is .22 caliber. It has a rosewood grip and is nickel-plated.

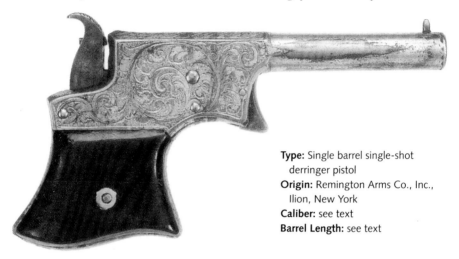

Type: Single barrel single-shot derringer pistol
Origin: Remington Arms Co., Inc., Ilion, New York
Caliber: see text
Barrel Length: see text

Remington Double Derringers (Over-and-Under)

Anyone in a "last-ditch" situation wanted to be sure that they had the best chance of repelling an attack. Most multi-barrel derringers were either complicated, large and heavy, or both. But the twin barrel version seemed to offer a compromise. These Remington "over-and-under" derringers became popular and were manufactured from 1866 to 1935. During this time, over 150,000 examples were completed. All known versions were in .41 caliber, but the guns had a variety of finishes.

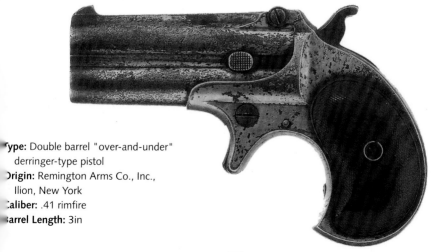

Type: Double barrel "over-and-under" derringer-type pistol
Origin: Remington Arms Co., Inc., Ilion, New York
Caliber: .41 rimfire
Barrel Length: 3in

Remington-Elliot Five/Four-Barrel Derringer

Sales of the Zig-Zag weapon were very sluggish, so Elliot analysed its shortcomings and decided that the solution lay in having a static barrel group and making the trigger rotate instead. The outcome was a weapon which was produced in two versions. The Elliot Patent Number One in .22 caliber with five barrels, and the Elliot Patent Number Two in .32 caliber with four barrels. In collectors' circles these guns are known as "Elliots Ring-Trigger Pistols."

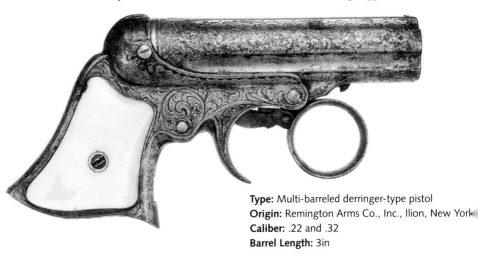

Type: Multi-barreled derringer-type pistol
Origin: Remington Arms Co., Inc., Ilion, New York
Caliber: .22 and .32
Barrel Length: 3in

Remington-Elliot "Zig-Zag" Derringer

Dr William H. Elliot was a prolific inventor who moved to Ilion where he contracted the nearby Remington Armory to produce his designs. His first weapon was the Remington-Elliot "Zig-Zag." This was a .22in caliber weapon, seen here.

Unlike revolvers, in which rotating chambers were aligned in turn with a single barrel, Elliot solution was to have a group of six barrels rotating as a unit. At the rear end, these were c with a zig-zag track.

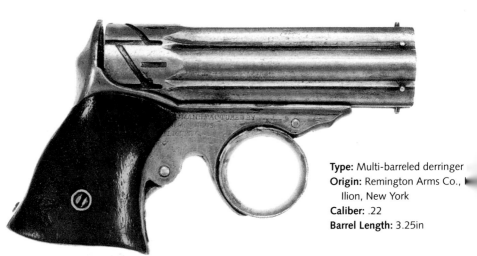

Type: Multi-barreled derringer
Origin: Remington Arms Co.,
Ilion, New York
Caliber: .22
Barrel Length: 3.25in

Remington Magazine Pistol

Another Joseph Rider design, this neat, "derringer-style" pistol was patented in 1871 and put into production in 1877, once Rider had perfected the design. The gun is more effective than it first appears. Five cartridges are held in the tubular magazine, and fed into the breech using the short lever next to the hammer. Production lasted only a few years, but the guns were not serial numbered and so actual production figures are not available.

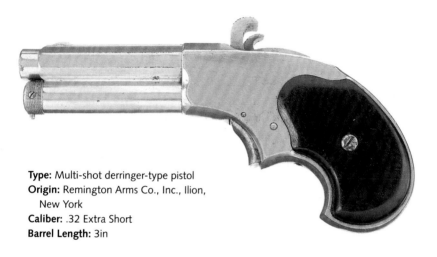

Type: Multi-shot derringer-type pistol
Origin: Remington Arms Co., Inc., Ilion, New York
Caliber: .32 Extra Short
Barrel Length: 3in

Remington Model 1867 Navy Rolling Block Pistol

At the end of the Civil War, Remington won a contract to provide the Navy with 5,000 Rolling Block breech-loading pistols of the Model 1866 pattern, followed by an order for a further 1,500 of the improved Model 1867 pattern. The most noticeable difference between the two was that the Model 1866 had a spur trigger, while the Model 1867 had the more conventional freestanding trigger inside a trigger guard.

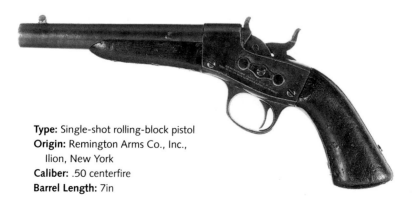

Type: Single-shot rolling-block pistol
Origin: Remington Arms Co., Inc., Ilion, New York
Caliber: .50 centerfire
Barrel Length: 7in

Remington Model 1871 Army Pistol

Remington won a government contract, which led to the supply of the Model 1871 Army pistol. A number were also made for the civilian market. The standard model has a blue or case-hardened finish, with walnut grips. The inspector's cartouche is clearly visible on the left side of the grip. The weapon has obviously been used during its 130-year life, but remains a thoroughly serviceable and handsome example of the gunsmith's trade.

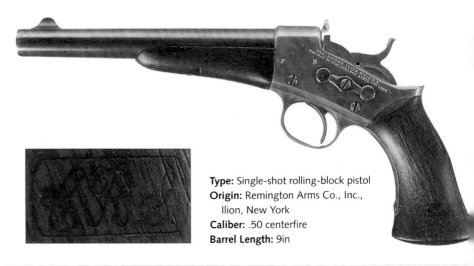

Type: Single-shot rolling-block pistol
Origin: Remington Arms Co., Inc., Ilion, New York
Caliber: .50 centerfire
Barrel Length: 9in

Remington-Rider Parlor Pistol

In 1859, Joseph Rider, who was then working at Remington's Armory, designed a very low powered, single-shot pistol. It was produced by Remington with some 1,000 being completed between 1860 and 1863. The gun is known as the "Remington-Rider Parlor Pistol," and was intended for indoor use only. It fired a tiny lead ball, in .17in caliber, and used only the fulminate from a percussion cap. This ensured that the muzzle velocity was so low that no damage would be done to people or furniture.

Type: Parlor pistol
Origin: Remington Arms Co., Inc., Ilion, New York
Caliber: .17
Barrel Length: 3in

Remington Rolling Block "Plinker" Target Pistol

On several occasions, Remington took surplus frames lying in the factory stockrooms to produce target pistols, which were also known as "plinkers." In 1887 they fabricated approximately 800 such pistols, basing the gun on the Model 1871 action with the barrel sleeved down to .22 caliber. "Plinking" refers to informal target shooting, using non-traditional targets such as tin cans, glass bottles, and water-filled ballons. The term refers to the sharp, metallic sound, known as a "plink."

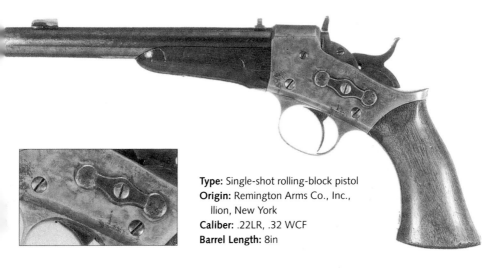

Type: Single-shot rolling-block pistol
Origin: Remington Arms Co., Inc.,
  Ilion, New York
Caliber: .22LR, .32 WCF
Barrel Length: 8in

Remington Model 1891 Rolling Block Target Pistol

In 1892, Remington began selling the Remington Model 1891 Rolling Block Target Pistol. This was a single-shot pistol, designed "for shooting galleries and target practice." They were made with left over M1871 Army-frame receivers, and 10-inch part-round/part-octagonal barrels. The guns were chambered for a variety of .22, .25, and .32 caliber rimfire and centerfire cartridges. Remington began advertising this pistol for $10.00 in their 1894 catalog. Factory records indicate that only 116 were sold between 1892 and 1899. This makes them a very rare collectors' piece.

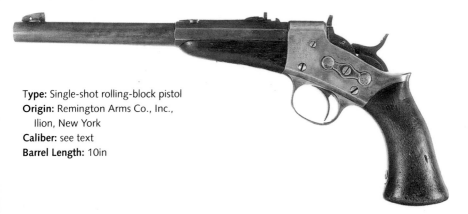

Type: Single-shot rolling-block pistol
Origin: Remington Arms Co., Inc.,
  Ilion, New York
Caliber: see text
Barrel Length: 10in

Remington Model 1901 Rolling Block Target Pistol

Remington continued to cater for the target-shooting fraternity with a series of rolling-block models. Introduced for "target and gallery practice" this well-made pistol also utilized surplus Model 1871 Army-framed receivers. It is nearly identical to the Model 1891 pistol but can be distinguished by the sights (a Lyman fixed blade front sight with an ivory bead, and a rear target sight, which is adjustable for both windage and elevation), together with the checkered walnut two-piece grips and fore-end.

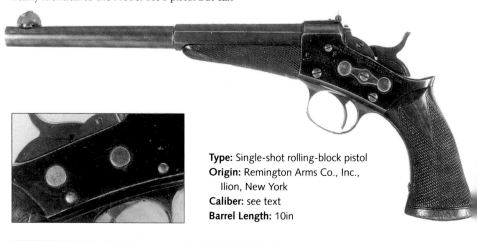

Type: Single-shot rolling-block pistol
Origin: Remington Arms Co., Inc.,
 Ilion, New York
Caliber: see text
Barrel Length: 10in

Robbins & Lawrence Pepperbox

The Robbins and Lawrence Company was based in Vermont. Among its employees were B. Tyler Henry and Daniel B. Wesson, both of whom went on to achieve greater fame elsewhere. The company produced this beautifully cased pistol some time between 1849 and 1852. It has a cluster of five barrels, which are rifled. The barrel cluster is hinged and tips forward for loading. The internal hammer strikes the nipple at the rear of each barrel in turn.

Sharps Pepperboxes

Christian Sharps patented a large number of designs, among them this weapon, which is actually a multi barreled pistol rather than a pepperbox. But, whatever its correct designation, it proved very successful and remained in production for many years, in the course of which it underwent the inevitable modifications and changes in model numbers. The Sharps pistol consisted of four barrels machined out of a single block of steel, mounted on a frame, which was usually made of brass.

Type: Multi-barreled pistol
Origin: Sharps, Philadelphia
Caliber: .22 short
Barrel Length: 2.5in

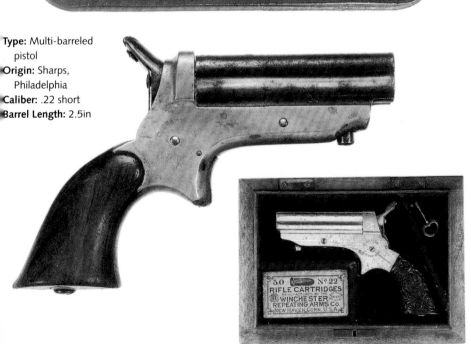

Sharps & Hankins Single-Shot Pistol

Christian Sharps was an inventor better known for designing rifles than pistols. In 1855, he established his own factories in Hartford, Connecticut and Philadelphia, Pennsylvania (the former becoming Sharps & Hankins in 1863).

There, apart from rifles, he produced designs for this pistol and a number of multi-barrel "pepperpots." His breech-loading percussion pistol was produced in various calibers. We show a .36 pistol with a large frame and a 6.4 inch

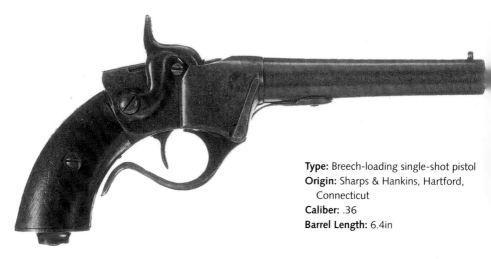

Type: Breech-loading single-shot pistol
Origin: Sharps & Hankins, Hartford, Connecticut
Caliber: .36
Barrel Length: 6.4in

Shattuck Unique Palm Pistol

C.S. Shattuck made this extraordinary vest-pocket pistol in the 1880s. Designed to look like a cigar case, the rectangular portion on the right of the weapon housed four .22 caliber barrels.

These were released by the knurled knob at the top and was then moved forwards and down on the pivot screw, whose head can be seen. The ammunition was fired by squeezing the trigger at the bottom of the weapon.

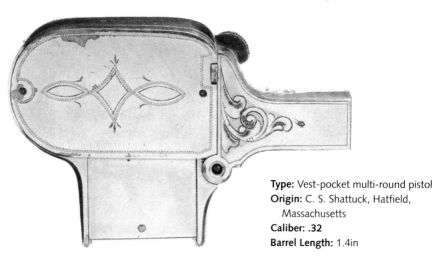

Type: Vest-pocket multi-round pistol
Origin: C. S. Shattuck, Hatfield, Massachusetts
Caliber: .32
Barrel Length: 1.4in

Smith & Wesson Volcanic Pistol

Horace Smith and Daniel Wesson formed their first partnership in 1852. They aimed to produce a repeating pistol, in which self-contained .40 caliber cartridges were stored in a tubular magazine and chambered using a manually-operated lever, which doubled as the trigger guard. The pistol was available with 6 inch, 8 inch, or 16 inch barrels. This example is the 8 inch long barreled version made at the Norwich factory.

Type: Lever-action repeating pistol
Origin: Smith & Wesson, Norwich, Connecticut
Caliber: .40
Barrel Length: 8in

Springfield Model 1817 Type 1

The Armory at Springfield, Massachusetts was set up in 1794 to produce military weapons. Some 400 Model 1817 flintlock pistols were produced at the Springfield Armory. This weapon dates from 1818, as proved by the date on the lock. Many of the locks at this time were imported from England or Belgium. The weapon is largely original including, unusually, the ramrod, which is made of hickory and has the characteristic swollen tip.

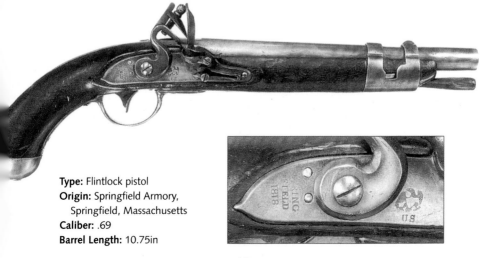

Type: Flintlock pistol
Origin: Springfield Armory,
    Springfield, Massachusetts
Caliber: .69
Barrel Length: 10.75in

Springfield M1855 Pistol Carbine

Designed for cavalrymen, this pistol was intended to be used as a handgun when mounted and, with the wooden shoulder stock attached, as a carbine when fighting on foot. It came complete with a cavalry-style hinged ramrod, and used the Maynard Tape Priming system. Many of these pistols saw service in the early days of the Civil War, but were soon superseded because they could neither compete with the new revolvers entering service, nor the purpose-made carbines

Stevens Pocket Rifles

One of the most successful Stevens products, this range of weapons can be thought of as either long barreled pistols, or (when fitted with their detachable wire frame stocks), lightweight carbines. They came in a range of models, and were chambered for many small cartridges. These included the .22S, .22L, .22LR, .22WRF, .2 Stevens, .32 S, and .32L. They were a neat, popular target shooting and varminting weapon and were also sold as "boy's rifles."

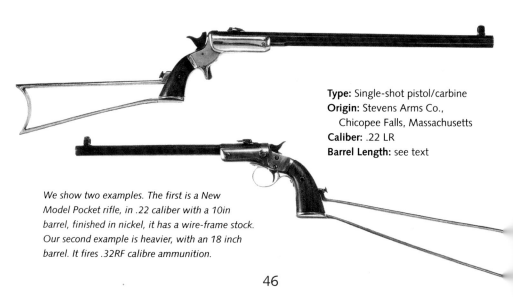

Type: Single-shot pistol/carbine
Origin: Stevens Arms Co.,
    Chicopee Falls, Massachusetts
Caliber: .22 LR
Barrel Length: see text

We show two examples. The first is a New Model Pocket rifle, in .22 caliber with a 10in barrel, finished in nickel, it has a wire-frame stock. Our second example is heavier, with an 18 inch barrel. It fires .32RF calibre ammunition.

Stevens No. 41 Tip-Up Pistol

From 1864 onwards, Stevens produced a series of vest-pocket pistols and derringers, leading up to this Number 41, of which some 90,000 were manufactured between 1896 and 1916. There were several models, chambered for either .22 or .30 Short and with either 3.5in or, as seen here, 6in barrels. It was described in the company catalogue as a "pocket pistol" but in this 6in version, at least, that seems to be something of an over-statement.

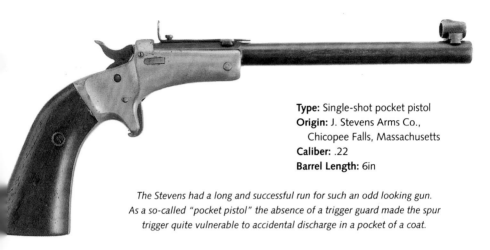

Type: Single-shot pocket pistol
Origin: J. Stevens Arms Co.,
   Chicopee Falls, Massachusetts
Caliber: .22
Barrel Length: 6in

The Stevens had a long and successful run for such an odd looking gun. As a so-called "pocket pistol" the absence of a trigger guard made the spur trigger quite vulnerable to accidental discharge in a pocket of a coat.

Stocking Pepperbox

Stocking & Co. of Worcester, Massachusetts made a single-action pepperbox with a mechanically-rotated cluster of six barrels. This was machined out of a single, long, solid block of metal. In common with many other designs, when the trigger was pulled the cluster was rotated and the spring-loaded bar hammer raised by a lever to the point where it disengaged and was driven down by the spring onto the nipple, firing the weapon.

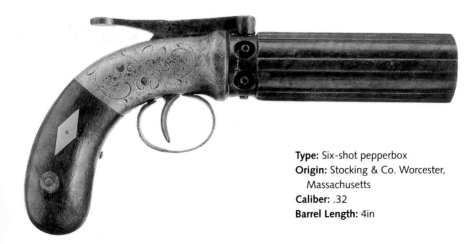

Type: Six-shot pepperbox
Origin: Stocking & Co. Worcester,
   Massachusetts
Caliber: .32
Barrel Length: 4in

Volcanic Pistols

Smith & Wesson persevered with the Volcanic pistols and their unique cartridge (the propellant and primer sat in the hollow base of the bullet), and by July 1855 they were trading as the Volcanic Repeating Arms Co. All the Volcanics of this period were made for the .41 caliber round, fed from the integral magazine under the barrel. We show a "Lever Action Navy Pistol," with a brass frame, six-inch barrel and flat-bottomed grip. The engraving shows an arm holding a dagger.

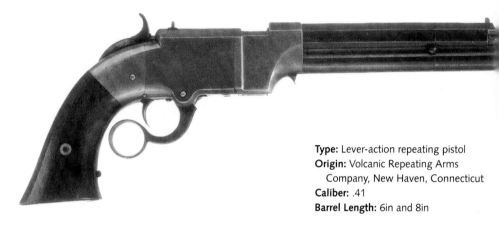

Type: Lever-action repeating pistol
Origin: Volcanic Repeating Arms
    Company, New Haven, Connecticut
Caliber: .41
Barrel Length: 6in and 8in

Volcanic Lever Action

The Volcanic Company was restructured as the New Haven Arms Company in 1857 to take over production of the Volcanic repeater. At the same time, Smith & Wesson severed their connections with the company. The origin of the weapon seen here is clearly established by the marking along the top of the barrel: "New Haven Conn, Patent Feb 14, 1853." This company eventually became Winchester, and the lines of this gun ca be seen in the famous rifles that followed.

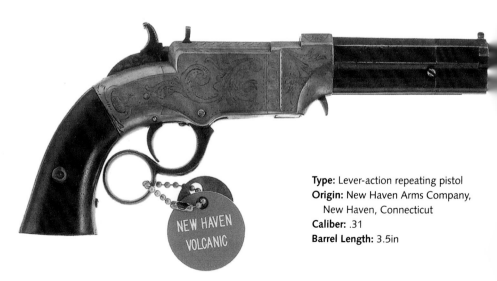

Type: Lever-action repeating pistol
Origin: New Haven Arms Company,
    New Haven, Connecticut
Caliber: .31
Barrel Length: 3.5in

Washington Arms Pepperbox

It is a curious fact that, despite all the research into gunmakers over the past seventy years, nobody seems quite certain where the Washington Arms Company conducted their business, although it is unlikely to have been Washington, DC. This company made single-shot pistols and good quality pepperboxes like the one shown here, which were very clearly inscribed with the company name, but with no indication of where it operated. This pepperbox has six barrels and operated on the double-action, bar-hammer percussion system.

Type: Six-shot pepperbox
Origin: Unknown
Caliber: .31
Barrel Length: 2.8in

Waters Model 1836 Flintlock Pistol

This handsome pistol was made by Asa Waters & Co. at their armory at Millbury, Massachusetts. It was part of a government order placed on September 22, 1836 for 4,000 pistols at US$9.00 each. As is clear from the pictures, this example has been very well maintained over the years and remains in very good condition. The Model 1836 came right at the end of the flintlock period and soon, the guns would be converted to percussion cap.

Type: Flintlock pistol
Origin: A. Waters & Co, Millbury,
Massachusetts
Caliber: .54
Barrel Length: 8.5in

Waters Flat Lock Pistol

This was one of a batch made by Asa Waters & Co. as a pattern for the Model 1842 percussion pistol, and assembled largely from parts left over from their Model 1836 flintlock pistol contracts. This one has a so-called "flat lock" and has had the ram pivot installed upside down. A lot of guns were converted to the percussion system by removing the frizzen and spring, and locating the nipple on a drum screwed into the barrel.

Type: Percussion cap conversion pistol
Origin: A. Waters & Co, Millbury, Massachusetts
Caliber: .54
Barrel Length: 8.5in

Wheeler Double Derringers

The American Arms Company was established in the early 1870s to produce pistols and shotguns. Among the weapons it produced were a number of derringers, whose design had been patented by Henry F. Wheeler. This design featured two vertically mounted barrels, and weapons were produced in a variety of calibers and lengths. The pistols had a nickel-plated brass frame, spur trigger, and blued barrels, which were rotated manually. Some 2,000 to 3,000 examples were manufactured between 1866 and 1878.

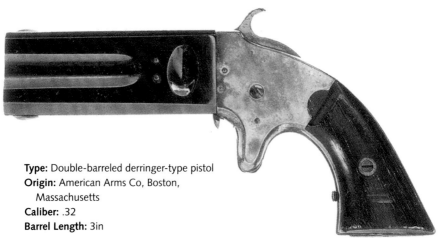

Type: Double-barreled derringer-type pistol
Origin: American Arms Co, Boston, Massachusetts
Caliber: .32
Barrel Length: 3in

Historic Revolvers

Model 1870 Austro-Hungarian Army Service

Leopold Gasser owned two factories, which produced vast numbers of handguns for both the Army and the civilian market. Gasser's first major success was the Model 1870, which was adopted as the standard cavalry weapon of the Imperial Austro-Hungarian Army. This had an "open frame" which meant that there was no bridge across the top of the cylinder. The barrel was attached to the frame by a heavy screw beneath the cylinder arbor.

Type: Six-round double-action, revolver
Origin: Leopold Gasser, Ottakring, Austria
Caliber: 11 mm
Barrel Length: 7.4in

Rast & Gasser Model 1898 Service Revolver

The Austro-Hungarian Army adopted the Rast & Gasser Model 1898 Service Revolver, seen here. This weapon had eight cylinders for an 8mm cartridge and the barrel group was secured to the frame by both a screw at the foot and a strap across the top of the cylinder. This weapon proved to be reliable, but as can be seen in the illustration, the grip was at right angles to the barrel making it uncomfortable to aim properly.

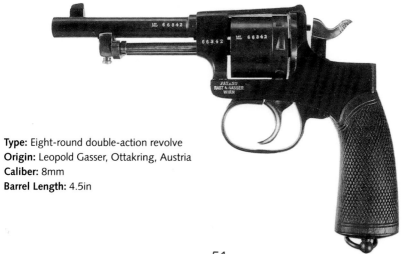

Type: Eight-round double-action revolve
Origin: Leopold Gasser, Ottakring, Austria
Caliber: 8mm
Barrel Length: 4.5in

British Bulldog Copy

Belgian gunsmiths produced a host of cheap copies of well-known weapons. The Bulldog concept originated in 1878 with the British firm of P. Webley & Sons. The company started to market a series of solid-framed revolvers with considerable hitting power, usually in .44 or .45 caliber for the civilian market. These guns were intended for use as a deterrent against thieves, but were also popular with civilian officials setting out for the remoter parts of the British Empire.

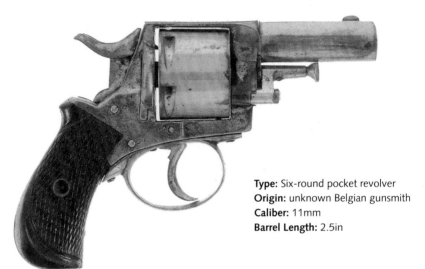

Type: Six-round pocket revolver
Origin: unknown Belgian gunsmith
Caliber: 11mm
Barrel Length: 2.5in

Francotte Pinfire Revolver

Auguste Francotte established his successful firm of Liege gunsmiths in 1805. The company is still in existence today, making a range of superb sporting and hunting weapons. This well made five-shot pinfire revolver was manufactured to a design of the Lefacheaux company of Paris, France, and carries Lefacheaux patent markings as well as the maker's marks. Compare it to the gun on page 57.

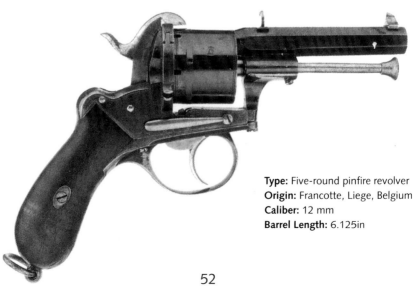

Type: Five-round pinfire revolver
Origin: Francotte, Liege, Belgium
Caliber: 12 mm
Barrel Length: 6.125in

Francotte Adams Percussion

This is a Francotte copy of the British Adams self-cocking percussion revolver, made under license (and marked as such). This is a fine, high-quality weapon, complete with engravings on the frame and (although worn) on the cylinder. It's almost identical to the English Adams weapons, with only minor modifications to the safety mechanism. Many of these guns found their way across the Atlantic at the time of the Civil War particularly to the Confederacy.

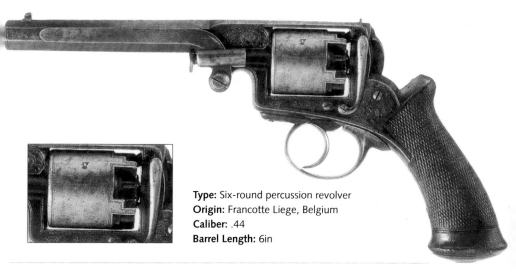

Type: Six-round percussion revolver
Origin: Francotte Liege, Belgium
Caliber: .44
Barrel Length: 6in

Liege 9mm Pinfire

This Belgian gun is a typical pinfire where the hammer is designed to impact a firing pin and drive it down into the case where it ignites the percussion cap inside the cartridge. It has Liege proof marks and plain ebony grips, while the nickel-plated frame and cylinder are extensively engraved. The model shown here is fitted with a bayonet, which clips on to a lug under the barrel and is supported by a muzzle ring.

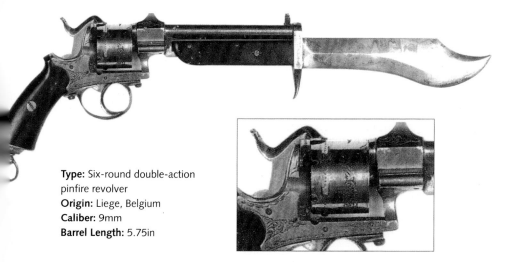

Type: Six-round double-action pinfire revolver
Origin: Liege, Belgium
Caliber: 9mm
Barrel Length: 5.75in

Nagant Patent Revolver

The Nagant Brothers designed a revolver for the 7.62 mm round, which incorporated an unusual feature. All revolvers had a gap between the rear end of the barrel and the front face of the chamber, through which a proportion of the propellant gasses escaped. Gun makers generally tried to reduce such losses by minimising the gap by precision engineering, but Nagant adopted a different approach. They designed a cartridge case with a narrowed neck and which totally contained the bullet. The case expanded on firing to create a gas-tight seal.

Type: Six-round revolver
Origin: Nagant, Liege, Belgium
Caliber: 7.62mm
Barrel Length: 4.5in

Pinfire Revolver

Another anonymous Belgian revolver, the only identification on it is the Liege proofing marks. This is large open-framed weapon in military caliber, firing a hefty 14.5mm pinfire cartridge. It is robustly made, with a decorative pattern engraved on the cylinder and frame. The butt has checkered wooden grips and comes complete with a lanyard ring.

Type: Six-round pinfire revolver
Origin: unknown Belgian gunsmith
Caliber: 14.5mm
Barrel Length: 6.35in

Revolver

This is a very handsome revolver, well made, and heavily engraved, but the gunsmith has refrained from making any marks which might identify him. There are no proof marks and the only script on the weapon states "Acier Fondu," the French for "cast steel." It is an open-frame design which bears a few similarities to the Gasser Model 1870 (see page 51). It is impossible to make a definite attribution.

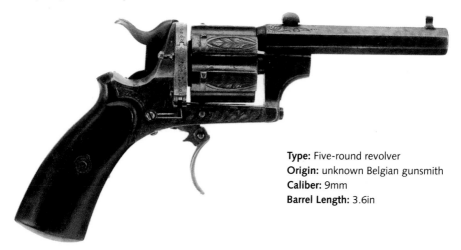

Type: Five-round revolver
Origin: unknown Belgian gunsmith
Caliber: 9mm
Barrel Length: 3.6in

Velo-Dog Revolver

"Velo-Dog" was a generic term for a type of small, cheap pocket revolver, which became fashionable in the late nineteenth century and was produced in Belgium. The name resulted from combining the term "velocipede" (the then current name for a bicycle) and "dog." Early cyclists seem to have been greatly troubled by fierce dogs and these little revolvers were designed to deter them using light bullets. The Model shown here is chambered for the specially-developed 5.5mm "Velo-Dog" round.

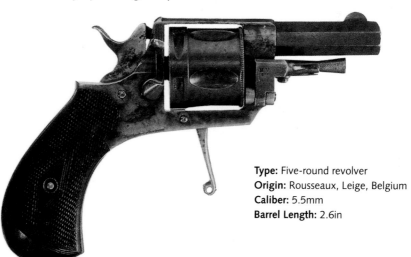

Type: Five-round revolver
Origin: Rousseaux, Leige, Belgium
Caliber: 5.5mm
Barrel Length: 2.6in

Converted Cartridge Revolver

This unidentified revolver has a European-style military frame that has subsequently been converted to fire .22 rimfire cartridges. It is probably for target shooting rather than military use. The barrel, sight, and cylinder are all replacements. The cylinder is relatively short compared to US revolvers of the same period and was probably originally fitted with one chambered for a large Continental caliber such as 11mm. The butt is rounded with a lanyard ring suggesting that the gun was originally intended for either naval or cavalry use.

Type: Six-round double-action revolver
Origin: unknown
Caliber: .22
Barrel Length: 8.25in

Open-Frame Pinfire Revolver

Many of the pinfire revolvers produced in France, Belgium or Germany were left unmarked, and are difficult to attribute to a specific manufacturer or even country of origin. This one copies the style of the Lefacheaux open-frame revolvers and is of reasonably high quality, with extensive engravings on the frame, cylinder, and round section barrel. The walnut grips are also finely carved and decorated. This gun is definitely intended for the civilian market

Type: Six-round revolver
Origin: unknown
Caliber: 9mm
Barrel Length: 5.25in

Devisme Percussion Revolver

Devisme was a Parisian gunsmith who produced a double-action percussion revolver before going on to work with centerfire cartridges. This is one of his percussion models, with an octagonal barrel hinged at the front of the cylinder.

Devisme was known for making high-quality items, but this model is superb even by his standards. The frame is engraved throughout. Even the screw heads have gold decoration, while the ebony grips are also finely carved.

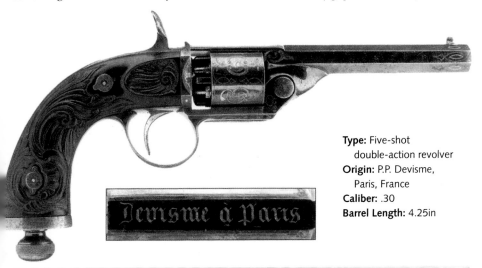

Type: Five-shot
   double-action revolver
Origin: P.P. Devisme,
   Paris, France
Caliber: .30
Barrel Length: 4.25in

Lefaucheux Model 1854 Pinfire Revolver

The pinfire cartridge was invented by a Frenchman, Casimir Lefaucheux, in 1828 and was in fairly wide use in Continental Europe by about 1840. Casimir's son, Eugene, designed a series of revolvers that made use of the pinfire principle. He produced many guns that were

used in the Civil War, like this fine example of a Model 1854. Plain and unadorned, it is a functional and effective weapon. Notice the recurved tang under the trigger guard, which allows the second finger to wrap around the guard.

Type: Pinfire revolver
Origin: E. Lefaucheux, Paris, France
Caliber: 12mm pinfire
Barrel Length: 6.125in

Lefaucheux Pocket Revolver

The gun shown here is a classic French pocket revolver of the 1860s. After the commercial success of his Model 1854, Eugene Lefaucheux went on to design civilian weapons like this pocket pistol, which had a folding trigger to avoid the gun being accidentally discharged in a pocket lining. The gun is intricately engraved on the cylinder and frame. Note how the hammer strikes the edge of the cylinder driving the pin into the cartridge igniting the primer.

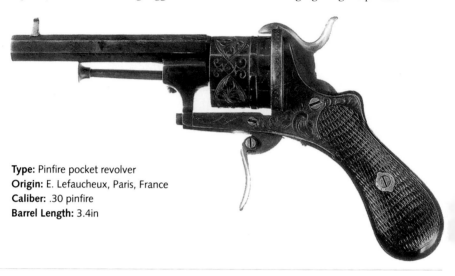

Type: Pinfire pocket revolver
Origin: E. Lefaucheux, Paris, France
Caliber: .30 pinfire
Barrel Length: 3.4in

Lefaucheux 20-Round Pinfire Revolver

Whilst most revolvers have cylinders housing either five or six rounds, there were constant attempts in the middle of the nineteenth century to produce weapons that fired even more. The extraordinary twenty-shot weapon seen here is chambered for 7.65mm pinfire and is an open-frame design with twin barrels and a cylinder. This houses twenty rounds in two concentric rows. The hammer has two tips and fires the rounds from each row alternately. It is marked "E Lefaucheux. Intr Brevette."

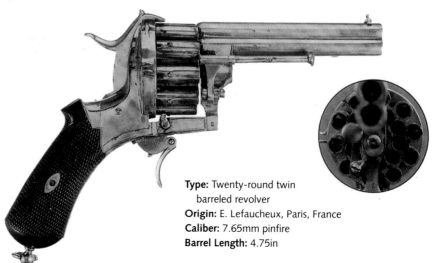

Type: Twenty-round twin barreled revolver
Origin: E. Lefaucheux, Paris, France
Caliber: 7.65mm pinfire
Barrel Length: 4.75in

58

Le Mat

The Le Mat, was patented in America by Jean Alexander Le Mat in 1856. It is a heavy gun weighing 58 oz. The frame, including the butt, is made in one piece, the lower barrel being integral. The cylinder is mounted on this lower barrel, which is smooth-bored, and is cylindrical. The upper barrel, which is rifled, is octagonal. The top flat of the barrel is inscribed "LEMAT AND GIRARDS PATENT, LONDON." The weapon was used by the Confederate Army during the Civil War.

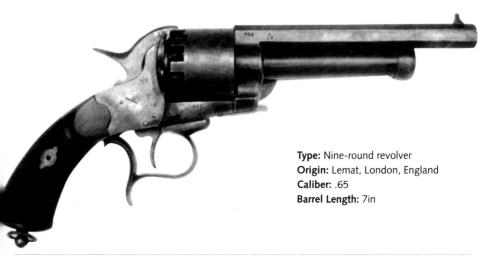

Type: Nine-round revolver
Origin: Lemat, London, England
Caliber: .65
Barrel Length: 7in

Noel Turret Pistol

One of the many ideas tried out on the road to the revolver as we know it today, was this pistol invented by Pierre Jules Noel of Paris, France. The weapon had a conventional 3.5 inch ribbed barrel and was chambered for the 7mm round. What set it apart was that the "turret" was vertical and turned by hand to bring each round into line with the barrel before being fired. It was not a success.

Type: Eight-round pistol
Origin: Noel, Paris, France
Caliber: 7mm
Barrel Length: 3.5in

MAS Service Revolver Modele 1873

The first centerfire revolver to be adopted by the French Army, the Model 1873 was produced at the French state arsenal, based at St Etienne. This origin is clearly marked on this frame, together with its year of manufacture, 1874. It was chambered for the French 11 x 17.5mm cartridge, the smooth-sided cylinder housing six rounds. Reloading was a complicated exercise, involving releasing the rod underneath the barrel, loosening the screw underneath it, drawing the axis pin forward, and then opening the loading gate.

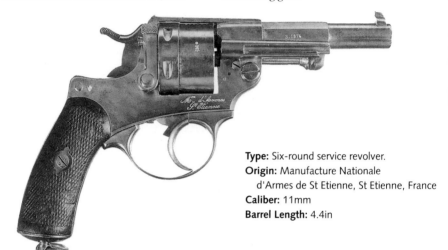

Type: Six-round service revolver.
Origin: Manufacture Nationale
d'Armes de St Etienne, St Etienne, France
Caliber: 11mm
Barrel Length: 4.4in

MAS Service Revolver, Officer's Pattern, Modele 1874

In essence, this gun was the Model 1873 revolver, but made to a considerably higher standard. It was better engineered and with a much higher quality of finish, as is evident when comparing this photograph with the previous entry. There were some minor differences. One is that that the cylinder was fluted, rather than smooth-sided, and it was marginally shorter. Note that the loading gate is a straw colored, rather than the blue of the remainder of the weapon.

Type: Six-round service revolver.
Origin: Manufacture Nationale
d'Armes de St Etienne,
St Etienne, France
Caliber: 11mm
Barrel Length: 4.4in

MAS Modele D'ordonnance 1892 (Lebel)

A number of efforts were made to develop the Model 1873 and Model 1874 revolvers, but although a few prototypes were produced in the 1880s they offered little improvement. Instead, a totally new weapon was designed, chambered for a new 8mm smokeless round, and known as the Modele 1892, Modele d'Ordonnance, or the 8mm Lebel. This six-shot weapon had a solid frame and a cylinder that swung sideways for reloading, with collective ejection by means of a hand-operated lever.

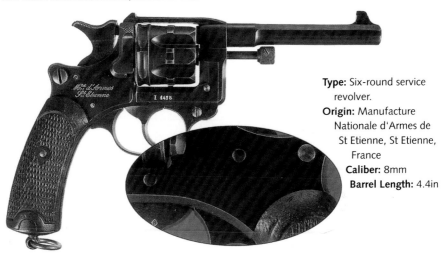

Type: Six-round service revolver.
Origin: Manufacture Nationale d'Armes de St Etienne, St Etienne, France
Caliber: 8mm
Barrel Length: 4.4in

French Pinfire Revolver

This small pocket revolver appears to be of French origin. It is intricately engraved with a leaf pattern and nickel-plated to a high standard, but bears no maker's name or proof marks. It is chambered for the 5mm pinfire cartridge and has a two-inch barrel and a folding trigger for safety. Its black ebony grips are also heavily carved .The ramrod is in the style of Lefaucheux.

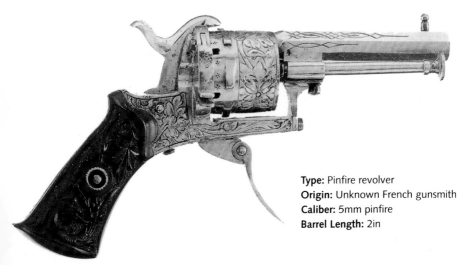

Type: Pinfire revolver
Origin: Unknown French gunsmith
Caliber: 5mm pinfire
Barrel Length: 2in

Reichsrevolver Model 1879

In 1879, the German government established various commissions to supervise the re-equipment of the army with modern, standardized weapons. One commission's work led to the Model 1879 Reichsrevolver ("government revolver") as seen here. It was a solid-frame revolver with a six-round, fluted cylinder and was manufactured by various gunsmiths under contract to the government. This particular weapon was produced by a consortium of three firms, all based at Suhl, one of the centers of German gun making.

Type: Six-round service revolver
Origin: Suhl, Germany
Caliber: 10.6mm
Barrel Length: 7.1 in

Reichsrevolver Model 1883 (Dreyse)

Shown here is the Model 1883, the better-engineered "officers" version of the previous gun, the Reichsrevolver. It is significant that officers were issued with a superior weapon with slightly improved features such as the more finely turned ejector rod and blued, rather than browned, metalwork. Dreyse, the firm set up by Johann Nikolaus von Dreyse, the inventor of the "needle gun" system, manufactured this particular weapon. Dreyse himself had died by the time this revolver was made.

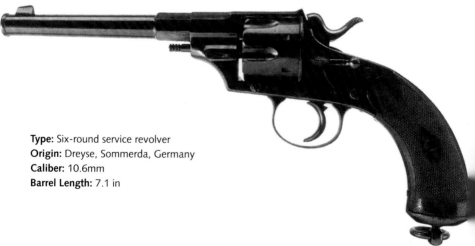

Type: Six-round service revolver
Origin: Dreyse, Sommerda, Germany
Caliber: 10.6mm
Barrel Length: 7.1 in

Ordnance Revolver Model 1882

In 1880, the Swiss Army was armed with revolvers chambered for the 10.4mm round and which resulted in a heavy weapon. So the director of the Bern weapons factory, Lieutenant-Colonel Rudolf Schmidt, designed a new 7.5 x 23R round and a revolver to fit it. Both were accepted and the weapon was placed in production as the Ordnance Revolver Model 1882. This was a conventional, double-action weapon with a hexagonal barrel and a six-round, fluted cylinder.

Type: Six-round double-action
   service revolver
Origin: Eidgenossischen
   Waffenfabrik, Bern, Switzerland
Caliber: 7.5mm
Barrel Length: 4.5in

Above: Weapon serial number 4396 is an early production Model 1882 with hard rubber grips. It is modified to accept a shoulder stock, although, as far as is known, the Swiss Army never officially acquired such stocks.

Adams Conversion Revolver

Robert Adams was an English gun designer who took out a large number of patents in the middle of the nineteenth century, which his brother, John was responsible for marketing. Their main business activity seems to have been licensing other companies to produce and market these Adams patents. The basic frame and mechanism of this neat, well-made revolver is Adams, but the barrel and cylinder have been added later, presumably convert the weapon to cartridge firing.

Type: Six-round, cartridge revolver
Origin: Unknown, England
Caliber: .50
Barrel Length: 3in

Beaumont-Adams Percussion Revolver

The Adams Brothers achieved some success with a series of self-cocking percussion revolvers, which could be fired only by exerting quite considerable pressure on the trigger. This made them relatively inaccurate, except at close range. This problem was overcome in 1855 when a Lieutenant Beaumont of the Royal Engineers invented a double-locking system. This allowed preliminary cocking without affecting the rate of fire. The resulting Beaumont-Adams revolvers were manufactured in two calibers, the smaller the two, in .44in, is seen here.

Hollis & Sheath Model 1851 Adams Dragoon

Hollis and Sheath were one of the many gunsmiths who manufactured Adams patent revolvers. The percussion weapon shown here is built to Adams' Model 1851 design, and is self-cocking only. While Adams self-cocking revolvers were less accurate than single-action types such as the Colts, their rate of fire made them useful for self-defense in a fast-moving close-quarters fight. The Adams designs also had integral top straps, which made them generally more robust than open-frame types.

Type: Five-round percussion revolver
Origin: Hollis and Sheath, Birmingham, England
Caliber: .38
Barrel Length: 7.75in

Percussion Revolver

This is a strange hybrid from an unknown British gunmaker. The self-cocking mechanism and butt shape is crudely reminiscent of the Adams style, but the octagonal barrel and open frame reflect Colt's early designs. There is engraving on the frame and the remains of an engraving on the cylinder. The trigger profile shows particular attention to keeping the finger firmly on the trigger in a close quarters fight.

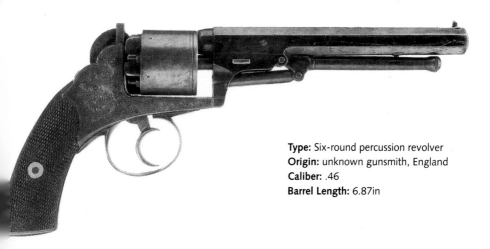

Type: Six-round percussion revolver
Origin: unknown gunsmith, England
Caliber: .46
Barrel Length: 6.87in

Tranter First Model

William Tranter was already a well-established gun maker by the time he patented the design of this double action revolver in 1853, two years ahead of Beaumont (page 64). Tranter's method used a double trigger system, where pressure on the lower trigger cocked the hammer. If carefully aimed fire was wanted, after the user cocked the hammer with this lower trigger, he would only need light pressure on the upper one to fire. In a close-quarters melee, where rapid fire was needed, the user just pulled both triggers at once.

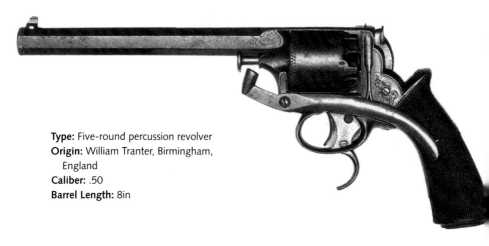

Type: Five-round percussion revolver
Origin: William Tranter, Birmingham,
   England
Caliber: .50
Barrel Length: 8in

Tranter First Model Pocket Revolver

Tranter revolvers were also made in small pocket sizes, using the same Adams frame and double trigger mechanism of their larger military brethren. Shown here is a First Model with the detachable ram missing. It was one made for a London dealer, and carries their markings "Wm. Powell & Son." Early Tranter models were based on Adams frames, as Tranter preferred to pay the fee for a well-proven and solid design, rather than go to the trouble of developing his own.

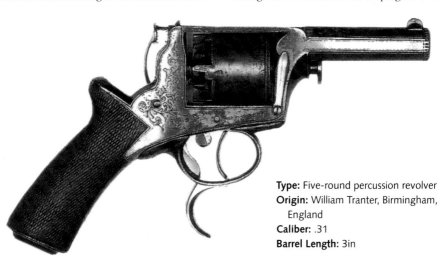

Type: Five-round percussion revolver
Origin: William Tranter, Birmingham,
   England
Caliber: .31
Barrel Length: 3in

Webley Longspur

James Webley patented this early Webley in 1853, three years before his death in 1856. Known as the Longspur, it was an open-frame design with the barrel assembly attached to the rest of the frame by the large flat-headed screw visible in front of the cylinder. There were three models of Longspur. The First Model had a detachable ram, the Second had a simple swivel ram, and the Third had the more complex ram shown here.

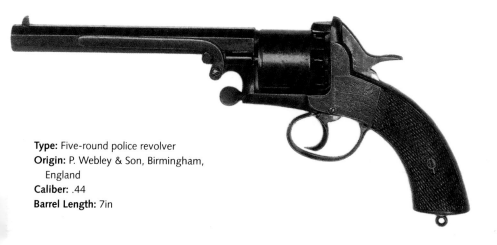

Type: Five-round police revolver
Origin: P. Webley & Son, Birmingham, England
Caliber: .44
Barrel Length: 7in

Webley R.I.C. Revolver No. 1

The R.I.C. No 1 revolver was produced by P. Webley & Sons specifically for the police force that maintained law and order in Ireland, the Royal Irish Constabulary. It proved, however, to be a most useful design and was adopted by many British colonial police forces. It was also sold commercially, as was the example shown here, which is stamped with the name of the retailer, "S.W. Silver & Co." It is a no-nonsense design, with a short, thick-walled barrel and a smooth-sided cylinder housing six rounds.

Type: Six-round police revolver
Origin: P. Webley & Son, Birmingham, England
Caliber: .455 Webley
Barrel Length: 4.5in

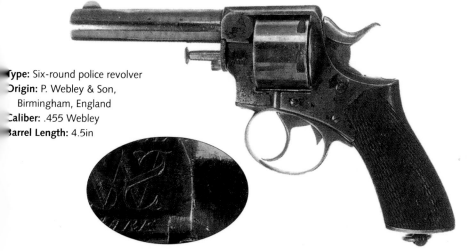

Witton Bros Tranter Patent Percussion

William Tranter was an English gunsmith who developed a fast-firing double-action mechanism to rival the Beaumont Adams. It was recognisable by a unique "double trigger." This is a later revolver, made by Witton Brothers. It has the Tranter signature lever ram alongside the barrel. This particular item was sold to the Confederate forces during the Civil War, although it never reached them. The Northern Revenue cutter "Harriet Jane" intercepted the shipment in February 1862.

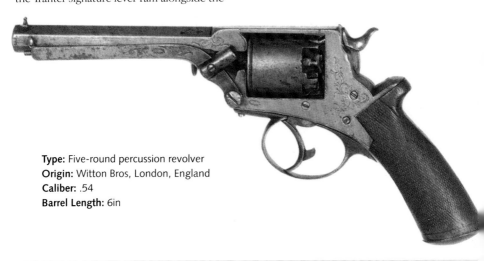

Type: Five-round percussion revolver
Origin: Witton Bros, London, England
Caliber: .54
Barrel Length: 6in

Allen & Wheelock Center Hammer Army Revolver

Although the firm of Allen & Wheelock was only in business for eight years, from 1857 to 1864, it produced a surprisingly large variety of firearms. This large revolver was chambered for the .44 cartridge and the smooth-sided cylinder housed six rounds. It had a 7.5 inch barrel, the rear half octagonal, the forward half round, and walnut grips. It was finished in blue, with case-hardene hammer and trigger guard. Only about 700 wei manufactured making this weapon, serial numbered 22, very rare.

Type: Six-round single-action percussion revolver
Origin: Allen & Wheelock, Worcester, Massachusetts
Caliber: .44
Barrel Length: 7.5in

Allen & Wheelock 2nd Type Sidehammer Revolver

This second variation of Ethan Allen's patent had a spring-loaded catch for the loading lever mounted on the rear of the spur trigger housing. The gun is marked "ALLEN & WHEELOCK WORCESTER, MASS. ALLEN'S PATENTS JAN. 13, 1857, SEPT. 7, 1858."

This text appears on the left side of the barrel. Approximately 1,000 each of the .28 and .31 caliber versions of this type were made. The guns have octagonal barrels and cylinder pins screwing into the frame from the rear.

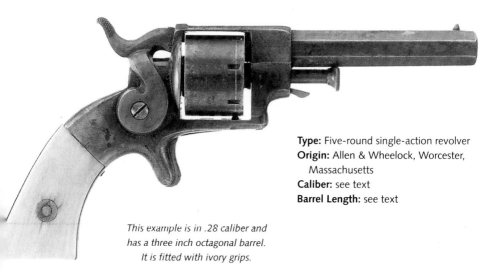

Type: Five-round single-action revolver
Origin: Allen & Wheelock, Worcester, Massachusetts
Caliber: see text
Barrel Length: see text

This example is in .28 caliber and has a three inch octagonal barrel. It is fitted with ivory grips.

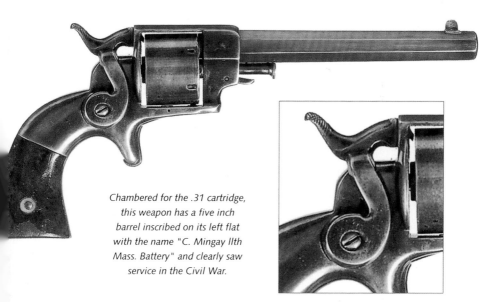

Chambered for the .31 cartridge, this weapon has a five inch barrel inscribed on its left flat with the name "C. Mingay llth Mass. Battery" and clearly saw service in the Civil War.

Inset right: A close-up of the characteristic hammer mounted on the right hand side of the frame. Guns from this limited production run are now extremely rare.

Allen & Wheelock "Providence Police" Revolver

The Providence Police Model is the fourth percussion revolver model made by Allen & Wheelock, and is the only one that does not carry the maker's name. It was manufactured between 1858 and 1852, supposedly for the Police Department of Providence, Rhode Island.

The model featured a three or four inch octagonal barrel, a smooth-sided cylinder housing six rounds, and a spur-trigger. The weapon seen here was serial number 84 of a total of around 700 examples manufactured and has the shorter barrel.

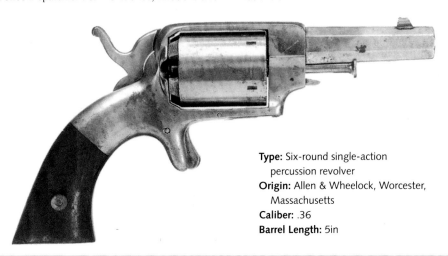

Type: Six-round single-action percussion revolver
Origin: Allen & Wheelock, Worcester, Massachusetts
Caliber: .36
Barrel Length: 5in

Brooklyn Bridge Colt Copy

Typical of the many copies that were made of the Colt Pocket models, and almost identical to Colt's production, this Brooklyn Bridge percussion revolver is believed to have been made in Belgium toward the end of the nineteenth century. The barrel is marked "Col

Sam'l New Model US Patented." Various companies in the Liege area specialized in production of these guns. They are a bit larger than Colt 1849 Pocket and the cylinder scene portrays the Brooklyn Bridge with New York Cit in the background, and ships on the river below

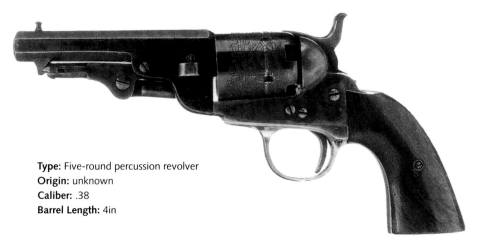

Type: Five-round percussion revolver
Origin: unknown
Caliber: .38
Barrel Length: 4in

Brooklyn Firearms Pocket Revolver

This weapon was Frank Slocum's attempt to circumvent the Rollin White cylinder patent. The revolver's cylinder contained five chambers, each covered by a forward-sliding sleeve. To load, the firer placed his finger-tip on the serrated section of an exposed sleeve and pushed it forward, placing the cartridge in the chamber, closing the sleeve, and moving the cylinder through one-fifth of a turn. The revolver was manufactured by the Brooklyn Fire Arms Co. and some 10,000 were completed between 1863 and 1865.

Type: Five-round tube loading revolver
Origin: Brooklyn Fire Arms Co.,
   Brooklyn, New York
Caliber: .32 rimfire
Barrel Length: 3in

Butterfield Army Percussion Revolver

Patented in 1855 by Jesse Butterfield, this design is reminiscent of the earlier "transition" revolvers. It had a unique priming system, where a tubular magazine held paper "pellet-style" percussion primers. When the single-action hammer was cocked, a pellet was slid over the cylinder nipple at the firing position. The US Government ordered the Butterfield in small numbers, but the contract was cancelled after only about 600 guns were delivered. A few saw service on both sides during the Civil War.

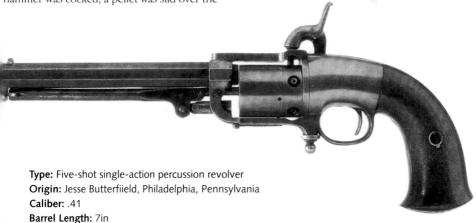

Type: Five-shot single-action percussion revolver
Origin: Jesse Butterfiield, Philadelphia, Pennsylvania
Caliber: .41
Barrel Length: 7in

Colt's Patent Fire Arms Manufacturing Company

The name of Colt is virtually synonymous with revolvers and "six-shooters" and this world-famous company has been in the firearms business since it was founded by Samuel Colt in 1836 in Paterson, New Jersey. The main factory moved to Hartford, Connecticut in 1850 but the head office remained in New York. The company's official name has changed several times over the many years that it has been in business. As a result, the style in which the name and location have been stamped on its products have become a matter of serious study among collectors and authors.

For the purposes of this book, and to avoid confusion, all Colt firearms are shown as being produced by Colt's Patent Fire Arms Manufacturing Company (Colt PFA Mfg. Co.) of Hartford, Connecticut, although in some cases the actual weapon may be marked differently. It is also the case that Colt has produced vast numbers of models, together with many varieties within those models, and the

company's system of naming and dating is frequently bewildering, even to experts. Colt himself was responsible for developing the first practical revolver, for the first major application of modern machine tool manufacturing, and also for promoting his products tirelessly.

Historical events like the Mexican and Civil Wars were important to Colt's business, bringing government orders for his revolvers. Sadly he did not even see out the Civil War, dying in 1862 at the age of 48. His wife Elizabeth attributed his early death to exhaustion from chronic overwork organizing the company's war production. He died a rich man but ironically many of the greatest Colts, such as the .45 caliber 1873 "Peacemaker" and the M1911 A, weren't created until years after his death. However, the legendary company that he created had a life of its own and is still in business to this day. Colt's guns inspired an old saying: "God created man, Sam Colt made them equal."

Colt Dragoon 1st Model

The Colt Walker revolver was designed for use by the Army's US Mounted Rifles (USMR), which were also known by the European name of "Dragoons." The Walker was a six-shot, .44 caliber weapon with a nine-inch barrel and an overall length of 15.5 inches. It weighed no less

than 4 pounds 9 ounces. This, plus problems of unreliability, led to the development of the Colt Dragoon, or Model 1848, of which some 20,000 were produced for government service between 1848 and 1860.

Type: Single-action percussion revolver
Origin: Colt PFA Mfg Co., Hartford, Connecticut
Caliber: .44
Barrel Length: 7in

Colt Dragoon 3rd Model

Building on the success of the Dragoon, Colt introduced a Second Model Dragoon. This was followed by the most successful version of the Dragoon, the Third Model, which was the main production version. Over 10,000 of these were completed between 1851 and 1860. They can be identified by their round trigger guards, whereas the guards on the earlier two versions were square-backed. Some late-production Third Model Dragoons (such as the one shown here) had a slightly longer, eight-inch barrel.

Type: Single-action percussion revolver
Origin: Colt PFA Mfg Co., Hartford, Connecticut
Caliber: .44
Barrel Length: 8in

Colt Model 1848 Baby Dragoon

Even though Samuel Colt was busy producing weapons for the military, he still managed to find the time to design and produce lighter weapons for the civilian market. One of the first of these was the Model 1848, also known as the "Baby Dragoon." This was a five-round, .31 caliber weapon, of which some 15,500 were produced between 1848 and 1850. These were made with three-inch, four-inch, five-inch or, as seen here, six-inch barrels.

Type: Percussion revolver
Origin: Colt PFA Mfg Co.,
　　　　Hartford, Connecticut
Caliber: .31
Barrel Length: 6in

Colt Model 1849 Pocket Revolver

Successor to the Baby Dragoon, the Model 1849 Pocket Revolver was produced in vast numbers, with some 325,000 being completed from 1850 through to 1873. They were made with three-inch, four-inch, five-inch or six-inch barrels and with five-or six-shot cylinders.

There were many more minor variations, as is inevitable over such a long production run. Obviously the advent of the Civil War increased sales of the weapon and soldiers on both sides purchased these guns privately.

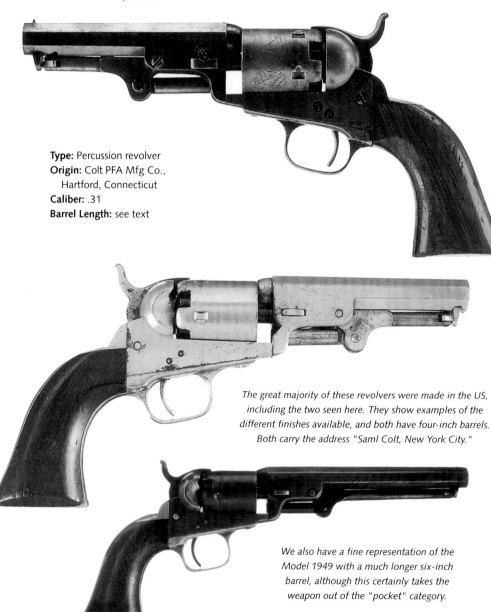

Type: Percussion revolver
Origin: Colt PFA Mfg Co., Hartford, Connecticut
Caliber: .31
Barrel Length: see text

The great majority of these revolvers were made in the US, including the two seen here. They show examples of the different finishes available, and both have four-inch barrels. Both carry the address "Saml Colt, New York City."

We also have a fine representation of the Model 1949 with a much longer six-inch barrel, although this certainly takes the weapon out of the "pocket" category.

74

Colt Model 1849 Wells Fargo

Colt made great efforts to sell its products on the civil market and was very happy to meet requests for special versions for other companies. Nothing is more evocative of the Wild West than a stage-coach driver, under attack from robbers, pulling out his revolver in a final attempt to protect his coach and passengers. It is not surprising that Wells Fargo turned to Colt to meet their requirements for a small, easily-handled weapon as a back-up to a rifle or carbine.

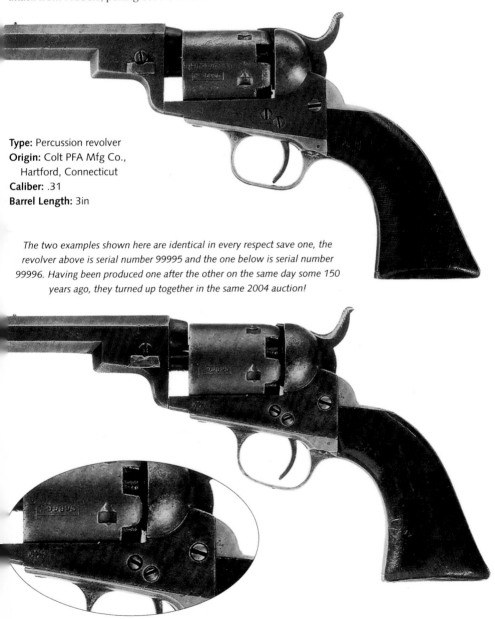

Type: Percussion revolver
Origin: Colt PFA Mfg Co.,
  Hartford, Connecticut
Caliber: .31
Barrel Length: 3in

The two examples shown here are identical in every respect save one, the revolver above is serial number 99995 and the one below is serial number 99996. Having been produced one after the other on the same day some 150 years ago, they turned up together in the same 2004 auction!

Colt Model 1849 Cartridge Conversion

Many thousands of the Colt Pocket Revolvers were also produced as cartridge revolvers, either as new builds or as factory conversions. This is typical of the type, being a Model 1849 frame with a new round barrel (with no ejector) and a rebated cylinder chambered for .38 centerfire.

This one is in excellent condition, with the original nickel plating still present and the stagecoach holdup scene engraving on the cylinder clearly visible. Some 6,000 of these guns were made from 1873 until 1880.

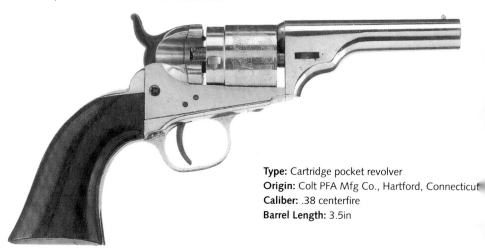

Type: Cartridge pocket revolver
Origin: Colt PFA Mfg Co., Hartford, Connecticut
Caliber: .38 centerfire
Barrel Length: 3.5in

Colt Model 1851 Navy

The Colt Model 1851 Navy revolver was one of the most popular handguns ever made, with some 215,000 manufactured in various Colt factories in 1850 through 1873. It has a 7.5 inch octagonal barrel and a smooth sided cylinder that houses six .36 caliber rounds. In most cases,

the cylinder was decorated with a scene involving a naval battle. It was this decoration that gave the type its "'Navy" designation, and the term ended up being used to describe any military revolver in .36 caliber.

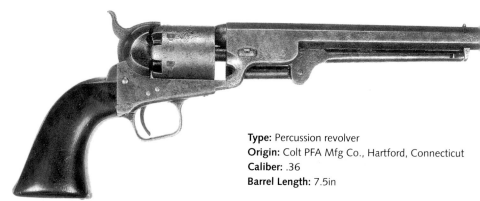

Type: Percussion revolver
Origin: Colt PFA Mfg Co., Hartford, Connecticut
Caliber: .36
Barrel Length: 7.5in

Colt Model 1855 Root Revolver

This design was developed by a Colt employee, Elijah Root, and was the company's first-ever solid-frame design. It had a top-strap across the cylinder joining the barrel and frame. It was fitted with a side-mounted hammer, a stud-trigger without guard, and a single-action lock. It was produced in .28 and .31 calibers, but both versions have a three-and-a-half-inch barrel. It is very popular with gun collectors, who know it simply as "the Root." Specialists have identified no less than twelve minor variations in the actual production weapons.

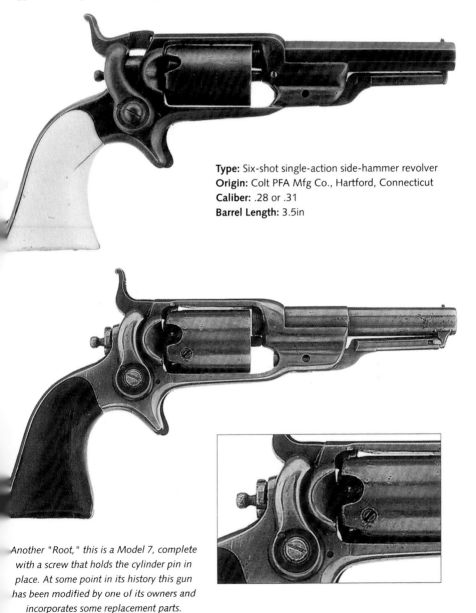

Type: Six-shot single-action side-hammer revolver
Origin: Colt PFA Mfg Co., Hartford, Connecticut
Caliber: .28 or .31
Barrel Length: 3.5in

Another "Root," this is a Model 7, complete with a screw that holds the cylinder pin in place. At some point in its history this gun has been modified by one of its owners and incorporates some replacement parts.

Colt Model 1860 Army

The production figures for the Colt Model 1860 are self-explanatory. The total produced between 1860 and 1873 was 200,500 units, of which the US Government accepted no less than 127,156. Designed as the successor to the Third Model Dragoon, the weapon became one of the most widely used of all handguns during the Civil War, and was equally popular with the Union and Confederate armies. It was a percussion revolver, with rammer loading from the front of the cylinder. Any reasonably experienced shooter ensured that he had a stock of paper cartridges close at hand for rapid reloading. The weapon weighed 2.74 pounds and was fitted with either a seven-and-a-half or eight-inch barrel.

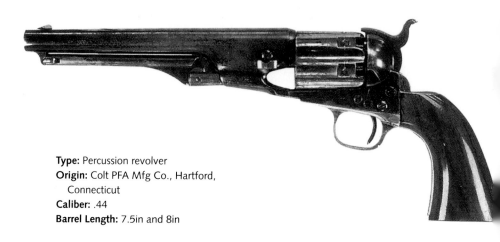

Type: Percussion revolver
Origin: Colt PFA Mfg Co., Hartford, Connecticut
Caliber: .44
Barrel Length: 7.5in and 8in

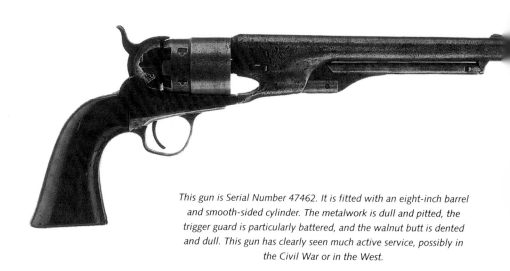

This gun is Serial Number 47462. It is fitted with an eight-inch barrel and smooth-sided cylinder. The metalwork is dull and pitted, the trigger guard is particularly battered, and the walnut butt is dented and dull. This gun has clearly seen much active service, possibly in the Civil War or in the West.

Colt Model 1861 Navy

Although some 39,000 were made, there were remarkably few variations in the Model 1861 Navy revolver. It had a 7.5 inch round rather then octagonal barrel and a smooth-sided cylinder housing six shots. The left front side of the frame was marked: "COLTS/PATENT" in two lines. The caliber marking "36 CAL" is stamped on the left rear side of the trigger guard. Approximately 100 of the first guns made had fluted cylinders with no cylinder scene. Another 100, made between the serial ranges of 11,000 and 14,000 were cut for a shoulder stock. The lower portion of the recoil shield was milled away on those guns. A fourth stud, or screw, for the stock was added to the frame. With the exception of the first fifty or so of this model, all revolvers have a capping groove. With the exception of London marked specimens fitted with iron grip straps, a brass trigger guard and back strap were standard on the 1861 Model Colt Navy.

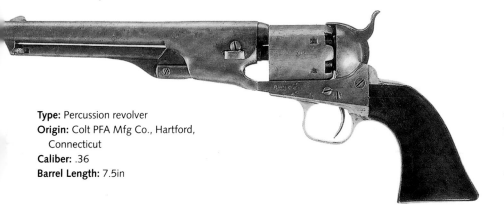

Type: Percussion revolver
Origin: Colt PFA Mfg Co., Hartford, Connecticut
Caliber: .36
Barrel Length: 7.5in

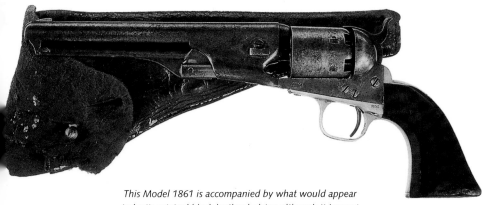

This Model 1861 is accompanied by what would appear to be its original black leather holster, although it has not stood the test of time as well as the gun.

Colt Model 1861 Navy Conversion

When Rollin White's patent expired, most manufacturers began converting their well-proven designs to fire cartridge ammunition. Colt produced about 2,000 new-build Model 1861s, assembled from existing parts but with a new cylinder and barrel assembly. They also modified a large batch for the US Navy and existing weapons from individual purchases. The weapon shown here has the rammer replaced with an ejection rod for removing empty cases from the cylinder. It is marked as belonging to a Lt. Robert I. Netts from Celina, Ohio.

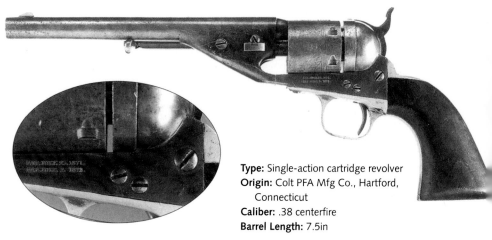

Type: Single-action cartridge revolver
Origin: Colt PFA Mfg Co., Hartford, Connecticut
Caliber: .38 centerfire
Barrel Length: 7.5in

Colt Model 1862 Pocket Navy

Colt manufactured some 19,000 of Pocket Navy revolvers, which were, in essence, a smaller version of the Model 1851 Navy. They were chambered for .36 caliber and with a five-shot, smooth-sided cylinder and decorated with a roll-on engraving of a Western stage-coach holdup. This was an obvious application for the gun in a defensive capacity. The barrels were 4.5, 5.5 or 6.5 inches in length, with the loading-lever attached underneath. The example shown here has a five-and-a-half-inch barrel and is in very good condition.

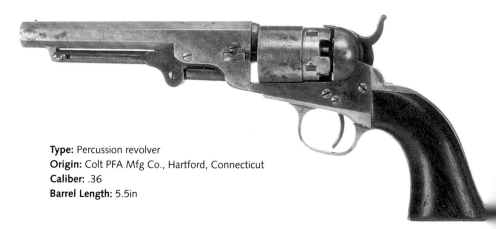

Type: Percussion revolver
Origin: Colt PFA Mfg Co., Hartford, Connecticut
Caliber: .36
Barrel Length: 5.5in

Colt Model 1862 Police

There were some 28,000 of the Model 1862 Police revolver manufactured between 1861 and 1873, but because many of these were later converted to accept the metallic-cased cartridges, unaltered originals have become fairly rare. The gun had a five-round fluted cylinder and barrel lengths were 3.5, 4.5, 5.5 or 6.5 inches. The presentation model shown at top is a standard five-and-a-half-inch inch barrel version apart from the engraved strap, which states that it was "Presented to G.H. Giles by his friends in the N.Y.C.R.R. Machine Shop, Albany, New York." Presumably, the gun was a gift to mark his retirement.

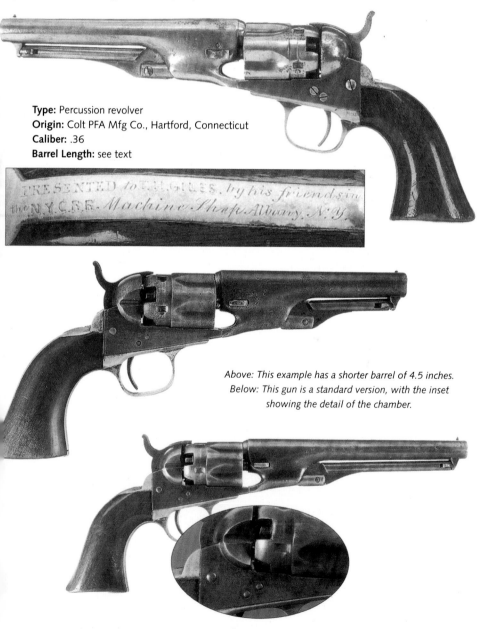

Type: Percussion revolver
Origin: Colt PFA Mfg Co., Hartford, Connecticut
Caliber: .36
Barrel Length: see text

Above: This example has a shorter barrel of 4.5 inches.
Below: This gun is a standard version, with the inset showing the detail of the chamber.

Colt Thuer Conversion

Alexander Thuer patented his process in 1868 and 1870. This involved using a lathe to turn off the base of the cylinder, leaving a hub upon which a disc-shaped "conversion plate" could be placed. This contained the firing pin and ejector button. The cartridges were still loaded from the front of the cylinder. When they had all had been fired, the conversion plate was rotated until the ejector button was aligned with the hammer; the hammer was then used to eject each cartridge case forward and out of the chamber.

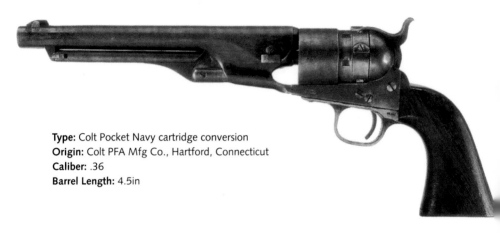

Type: Colt Pocket Navy cartridge conversion
Origin: Colt PFA Mfg Co., Hartford, Connecticut
Caliber: .36
Barrel Length: 4.5in

Colt Richards Conversion

The Thuer conversion was a little too complicated and another inventor, C.B. Richards, came up with simpler solution. This involved removing the old rammer-lever, turning off the rear of the cylinder, and adding a conversion plate. He also added an ejector-rod and a loading gate. This enabled the rimmed cartridges to be loaded and extracted from the rear. The conversion plate also included a backsight, whi● had been lacking in all previous models. We sh● a "Richards Conversion First Type, Model 1860 Army Revolver."

Type: Colt 1860 Army cartridge conversion
Origin: Colt PFA Mfg Co., Hartford,
Connecticut
Caliber: .44
Barrel Length: 8in

Colt House Revolver

In the 1870s, the invention of the metal cartridge case made it possible to develop a new class of self-defense weapon, generally known as the "house" pistol. This was small, easily handled and intended for use against intruders, The first to be developed by Colt was the .41 caliber "House Model Revolver." This was generally known as the "cloverleaf" due to the deep indentations in the four-round cylinder, when seen from the front. The example shown here is the four-round, three-inch barrel version.

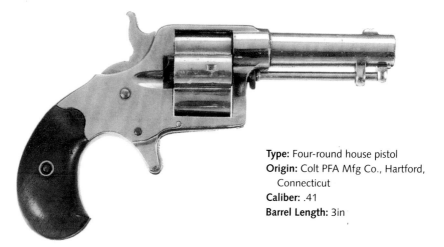

Type: Four-round house pistol
Origin: Colt PFA Mfg Co., Hartford, Connecticut
Caliber: .41
Barrel Length: 3in

Colt Model 1871/2 Open Top Rimfire

The US Army had already decided that its future handguns would have a solid frame and it was clear from military and civil markets that the future lay with the centerfire cartridge. Despite all of this, Colt produced a weapon without a top strap that chambered for the .44 rimfire round. It was not a success but it was Colt's first original design for a metallic round, and it paved the way for the Single-Action Army.

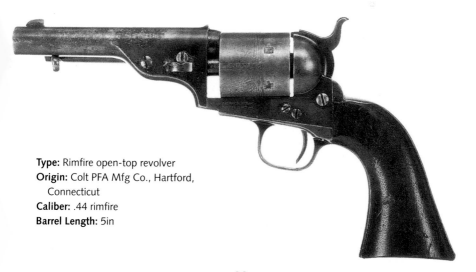

Type: Rimfire open-top revolver
Origin: Colt PFA Mfg Co., Hartford, Connecticut
Caliber: .44 rimfire
Barrel Length: 5in

Colt Model 1873 Single-Action Army Revolver

The Colt Single-Action Army revolver is one of the greatest handguns in history. It was purchased in vast numbers for the US Army, particularly in the American West. Here, it came to symbolize the cowboy era, becoming known as "the Gun That Won the West." There is nothing particularly unusual about the design and construction of the Model 1873, but the inspired combination of simplicity, ruggedness, ease of use, and dependability has made for an enduring and unpretentious classic.

Type: Centerfire, single-action revolver
Origin: Colt PFA Mfg Co., Hartford, Connecticut
Caliber: .45 Colt
Barrel Length: 7.5in

Colt Model 1877 Double-Action "Lightning" and "Thunderer"

Colt was not keen on the idea of double-action revolvers, but when effective systems appeared from other manufacturers they had little choice but to follow suit. The first Colt double-action revolver was the Model 1877 which appeared in two forms, .38 caliber, (known as the Lightning), and .41 caliber, (known as the Thunderer). Both were six-shooters, and both came in a variety of barrel lengths. In appearance, the Model 1877 resembled a slightly scaled down Single-Action Army, except for the butt, which was in the shape of a bird's head.

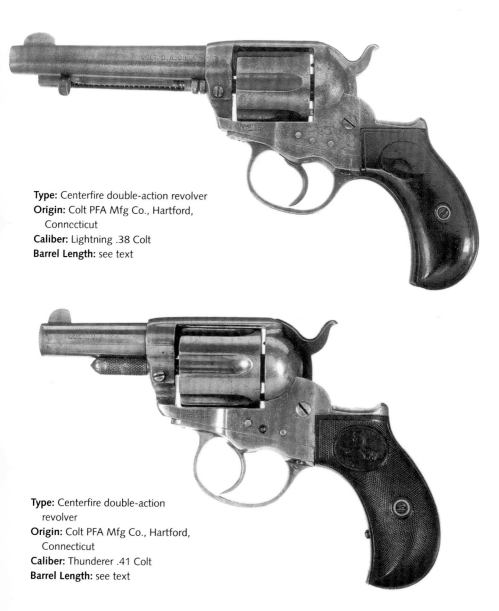

Type: Centerfire double-action revolver
Origin: Colt PFA Mfg Co., Hartford, Connecticut
Caliber: Lightning .38 Colt
Barrel Length: see text

Type: Centerfire double-action revolver
Origin: Colt PFA Mfg Co., Hartford, Connecticut
Caliber: Thunderer .41 Colt
Barrel Length: see text

Colt Model 1878 Frontier

The Colt Model 1878 appeared shortly after the Model 1877 and was another double-action revolver. But it was larger and more robust, with a stronger frame and a removable trigger guard. The fluted cylinder held six cartridges and was not removable, being loaded via narrow gate on the right side of the frame. There were six barrel lengths (3, 3.5, 4, 4.75, 5.5, and 7.5 inches) and a wide variety of chambering from .22 to .476.

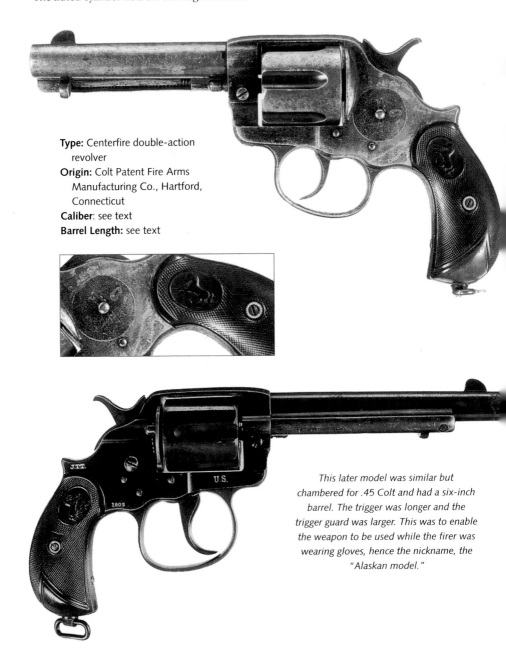

Type: Centerfire double-action revolver

Origin: Colt Patent Fire Arms Manufacturing Co., Hartford, Connecticut

Caliber: see text

Barrel Length: see text

This later model was similar but chambered for .45 Colt and had a six-inch barrel. The trigger was longer and the trigger guard was larger. This was to enable the weapon to be used while the firer was wearing gloves, hence the nickname, the "Alaskan model."

Colt Bisley Flat-Top Revolver

In 1890, a major competitive shooting range was established in England at Bisley in Surrey. The range opened with a widely publicized competition, and Bisely quickly became a byword for national and international shooting. So prestigious was the Bisley revolver competition that Colt designed a weapon specially for it. The Colt Bisley appeared in 1894 and continued in production until 1915, during which time 44,350 were manufactured. It was produced in three barrel lengths, 4.75, 5.5, and 7.5 inch, as well as sixteen different calibers.

Type: Single-action competition revolver
Origin: Colt Patent Fire Arms Manufacturing Co., Hartford, Connecticut
Caliber: see text
Barrel Length: see text

Colt New Series Model

Colt developed this revolver from the new Army and Navy Models of 1892. It was intended specifically for the military market and was first offered to the US Army in 1898. Large numbers were produced, particularly during World War One, when the British and Canadian Armies also took many. The illustration shows a New Service Model chambered for .455 Eley with a six-inch barrel. This particular gun was delivered to the Canadian Army during World War One.

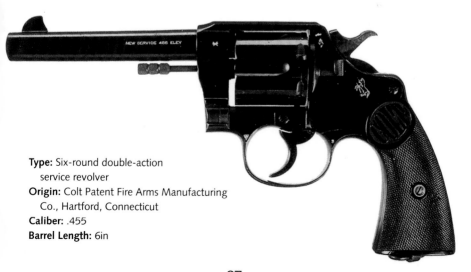

Type: Six-round double-action service revolver
Origin: Colt Patent Fire Arms Manufacturing Co., Hartford, Connecticut
Caliber: .455
Barrel Length: 6in

Cooper Pocket Revolver

James Maslin Cooper was a gunsmith who was in business in Philadelphia from 1850 through 1864 and then at Frankford, Pennsylvania until 1869, when the company ceased to trade. During that time the company's products were limited to a pepperbox and various models of this percussion revolver. There were variants with 4, 5, and 6 inch barrel lengths, but all were chambered for the .31 cartridge. It was unusual for its time in having a double-action mechanism and some 15,000 units were produced.

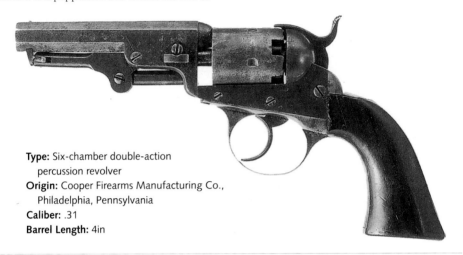

Type: Six-chamber double-action percussion revolver
Origin: Cooper Firearms Manufacturing Co., Philadelphia, Pennsylvania
Caliber: .31
Barrel Length: 4in

Defender (Johnson, Bye) Spur-Trigger Revolver

Iver Johnson and Martin Bye ran a joint business in Worcester from 1871 to 1883, when Johnson bought out Bye and the firm then continued as Iver Johnson Arms & Cycle Works. While Johnson and Bye were together, they produced firearms under various brand names, including one series of revolvers in .22 and .32 caliber under the brand name Defender. A typical example is shown here, in .32 caliber with a barrel length of 2.4 inches. It has a bird's-head butt with ivory grips and, as the name indicates, a spur trigger.

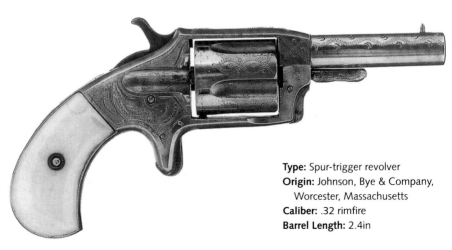

Type: Spur-trigger revolver
Origin: Johnson, Bye & Company, Worcester, Massachusetts
Caliber: .32 rimfire
Barrel Length: 2.4in

Eagle Arms Cup-Primed Revolver

Another Rollin White challenge was mounted by the Plant Manufacturing Company of Norwich, Connecticut, which employed a "cup-primer" cartridge. This had a straight-sided, metal case with a dished base, which was pushed into the chamber from the front. The base of the cartridge was struck by the nose of the hammer through a small hole in the rear-face of the chamber. The Plant revolver was made in .41 and .36 caliber, but the Eagle Arms Company produced the smaller version, seen here, in .31 caliber.

Type: Five-shot double-action cup-primer revolver
Origin: Johnson, Bye & Company, Worcester, Massachusetts
Caliber: .31
Barrel Length: 3.5in

Forehand & Wadsworth Pocket Revolver

When Ethan Allen, the renowned New England gunsmith, died in 1871 his business passed to his two sons-in-law, Sullivan Forehand and Henry Wadsworth. They changed the company's name to reflect the new ownership. Among the first products of the renamed company was a series of pocket revolvers, which featured a solid frame and a five-round fluted cylinder, like the one shown here. Wadsworth's involvement in the company decreased, due to ill health. He sold out to his brother-in-law in 1890, and died in 1892.

Type: Five-shot double-action pocket revolver
Origin: Forehand & Wadsworth, Worcester, Massachusetts
Caliber: .32 S&W
Barrel Length: 3.25in

Hopkins & Allen XL Double-Action

Hopkins & Allen was founded in 1868 and, following a disastrous fire in 1900, was purchased by the Forehand Arms Company. In its heyday Hopkins & Allen produced a large number of low-priced revolvers under a host of brand-names, such as Captain Jack, Mountain Eagle, and others. The weapon seen here was one of the XL-series, which were produced for about twelve years from 1871. These guns were five-shot, solid-frame weapons, made in a variety of calibers.

Hopkins & Allen Hammerless Top-Break Revolver

One of the later Hopkins & Allen products was this hammerless revolver. The barrel hinges forward for reloading and is secured in place by a substantial yoke. This weapon incorporated a "triple action safety" system and was generally considered to be a very good design technically but the gun was unattractive and it failed to revive the company's fortunes.

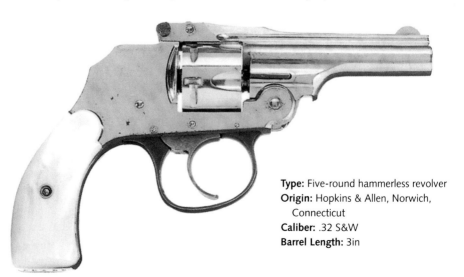

Type: Five-round hammerless revolver
Origin: Hopkins & Allen, Norwich, Connecticut
Caliber: .32 S&W
Barrel Length: 3in

Iver Johnson Hammerless Revolver

An initial inspection of the weapon seen here suggests that this is a standard Iver Johnson Hammerless revolver, a design that was also known as the "Safety Automatic Double-Action Model." This was produced by the company from 1894 until the 1970s, and the grips bear the company's famous "Owl Head" logo. However, the safety mechanism is operated by a second trigger mounted in a slot in the main trigger, a highly unusual modification of the usual Iver Johnson safety arrangement.

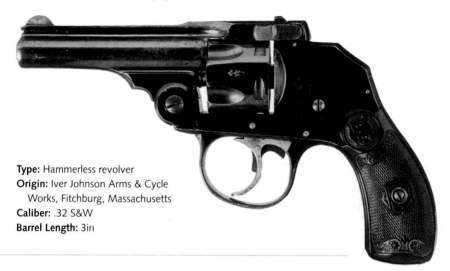

Type: Hammerless revolver
Origin: Iver Johnson Arms & Cycle
   Works, Fitchburg, Massachusetts
Caliber: .32 S&W
Barrel Length: 3in

Manhattan Navy

The Manhattan Firearms Company were one of the many who began manufacturing revolvers when Colt's patent expired in 1857. Their main products were copies of the Model 1851 Navy and Model 1949 pocket series, and were so close to the originals that Colt took legal action to have production stopped. Even so, over 80,000 Manhattan revolvers were made. This is one of the Manhattan "Navy" models, which has features from both the Colt Navy and Pocket revolvers.

Type: Five-shot percussion revolver
Origin: Manhattan Firearms Co.,
   Newark, New Jersey
Caliber: .36
Barrel Length: 5in

Manhattan Tip-Up

Another Manhattan revolver, this time closely resembling a Smith and Wesson Army revolver. Firing a .22 rimfire cartridge, it has fine engraving on both the barrel and cylinder. This is the Second Model; the First had more rounded edges to the frame and fired a shorter cartridge (and so had a shorter cylinder). They were popular and well-made weapons such that over 17,000 were made before a lawsuit stopped production.

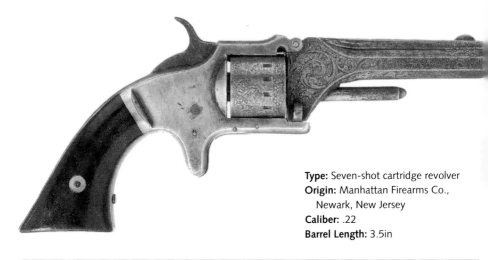

Type: Seven-shot cartridge revolver
Origin: Manhattan Firearms Co.,
Newark, New Jersey
Caliber: .22
Barrel Length: 3.5in

Marlin XXX 1872 Revolver

John Marlin had been an employee of Colt before setting up his own company in New Haven in 1863. He started off making a range of pistols, but began revolver production when Rollin White's patent expired in 1870. A commercial success for Marlin, some 27,000 of this popular little revolver were made from 1872 to 1877. Chambered for a .30in centerfire cartridge, it was made with both octagonal and round barrels. The designation "XXX" is how Marlin referred to his .30 caliber weapons.

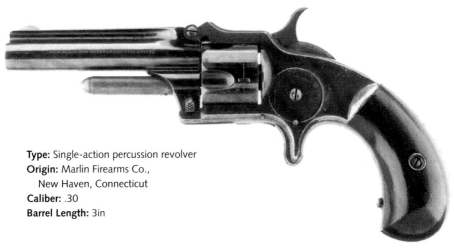

Type: Single-action percussion revolver
Origin: Marlin Firearms Co.,
New Haven, Connecticut
Caliber: .30
Barrel Length: 3in

Massachusetts Arms Co. Dragoon Percussion Pistol

The Massachusetts Army Company operated at Chicopee Falls, Massachusetts from 1849 to 1876, during which time it produced revolvers under licence from other patent-holders. One such was Daniel Leavitt of Cabotsville whose design was produced first by Wesson, Stevens & Miller at Hartford, and subsequently by the Massachusetts Arms Co., and is now commonly known as the "Wesson and Leavitt." This example, made in the early 1850s shows the good finish and neat design.

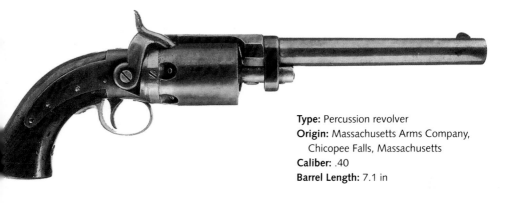

Type: Percussion revolver
Origin: Massachusetts Arms Company, Chicopee Falls, Massachusetts
Caliber: .40
Barrel Length: 7.1 in

Massachusetts Arms Co. Maynard Primed Revolver.

This weapon was made by the Massachusetts Arms Company using Maynard's ignition system that involved a tape in which the primer was laid in small pellets at regular intervals between two narrow strips of paper. The picture shows a .28 caliber weapon with a two-and-a-half-inch barrel and a primer door marked with Maynard's name and his patent number. There is a roll of primers in the box immediately behind the butt and it is still wrapped in its original greaseproof paper.

Merwin Hulbert and Co. Pocket Army

Merwin Hulbert and Co. were New York dealers, promoters and marketers of firearms. They made no weapons themselves but instead contracted with other manufacturers to supply them with guns, usually under their own brand. This 1880s range of neat, compact, centerfire revolvers was made for them by Hopkins and Allen, and came in a number of styles. They all used an unusual loading mechanism, where the barrel and cylinder assembly were twisted sideways, then pulled forwards to allow the cartridge cases to drop out and new rounds to be inserted.

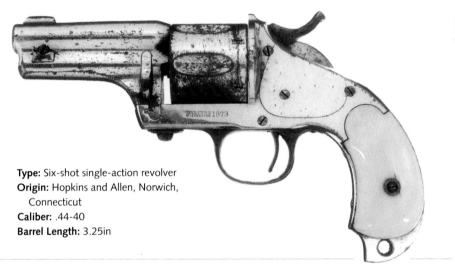

Type: Six-shot single-action revolver
Origin: Hopkins and Allen, Norwich, Connecticut
Caliber: .44-40
Barrel Length: 3.25in

Merwin Hulbert and Co. Pocket Double Action

Hopkins and Allen also made a double-action version of their .44 Merwin Hulbert pocket revolvers, which came in a number of styles. All used an unusual loading mechanism, where the barrel and cylinder assembly were twisted sideways and then pulled forwards to allow the cartridge cases to drop out, and new rounds to inserted. This one has a top strap and ivory gri

Type: Six-shot double-action revolver
Origin: Hopkins and Allen, Norwich, Connecticut
Caliber: .44
Barrel Length: 3.5in

Metropolitan Navy Percussion

When the Colt factory was damaged by fire in 1864, the Metropolitan Arms Company began to manufacture copies of Colt weapons. The demands of the Civil War were still very much in effect and guns were needed. This "Navy" model is almost indistinguishable from the Colt original of the time, even down to the faint remnants of the naval battle scene engraved on the cylinder. It also has a brass trigger guard with walnut grips.

Type: Six-shot single-action revolver
Origin: Metropolitan Arms Co., New York
Caliber: .36
Barrel Length: 7.5in

Nepperhan Revolver

The Nepperhan Fire Arms Company made about 5,000 of these .31 Colt Pocket revolver copies in the early 1860s, during the Civil War. These revolvers are similar to the Bacon and Manhattan Pocket models, all of which featured removable sideplates on the frames. They were all serial numbered, from "1" upwards. The barrel markings as follows, "NEPPERHAN/FIRE ARMS CO./YONKERS, N.Y." The gun has two-piece walnut grips and a blued and casehardened finish.

Type: Five-shot single-action revolver
Origin: Nepperhan Fire Arms Co., Yonkers, New York
Caliber: .31
Barrel Length: 4.25in

Pettengill Army Model

Although this revolver was designed and named after Charles Pettengill, it was actually manufactured by Rogers, Spencer and Co. Pettengill designed the self-cocking firing mechanism, with the hammer completely enclosed within the frame. The firer just pulled the trigger to index the cartridge, raise then drop the hammer. There was no provision for single-action fire, and the heavy trigger force made it difficult to shoot accurately. The Pettengill was the subject of a 5,000-unit order from the US Ordnance Department in 1861, but the gun had to be modified when the first batch was rejected as unsuitable. Eventually only 2,000 of the modified weapons were delivered.

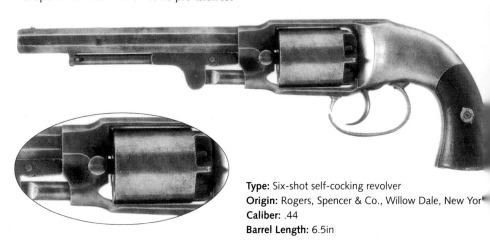

Type: Six-shot self-cocking revolver
Origin: Rogers, Spencer & Co., Willow Dale, New Yor'
Caliber: .44
Barrel Length: 6.5in

Pond Separate Chamber Revolver

Lucius Pond designed this pocket revolver to get round the Rollin White Patent. His single-action, solid-frame revolver featured a cylinder with a solid rear wall and six small ports to enable the nose of the hammer to strike the rear of the cartridge. Forward of this wall were six chambers, each accommodating a removable sleeve, into which the cartridge was inserted an then pushed back by the ejector rod. It was a complicated system and its defects are well illustrated by the example seen here, which is missing four of the removable sleeves. The remaining two are rusted in place.

Type: Six-round separate chamber revolver
Origin: Lucius W. Pond, Worcester,
  Massachusetts
Caliber: .32 rimfire
Barrel Length: 5in

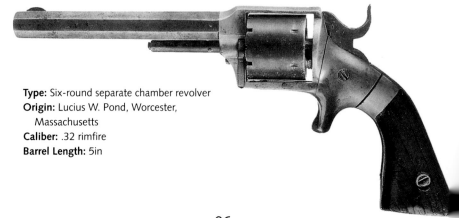

Remington-Beals 1st Model Pocket Revolver

The Remington Armory became a magnet for many skilled engineers and designers, and one such was Fordyce Beals. After an earlier stint at Remington, he went to the Whitneyville Armory in 1854, but was enticed back to Remington after only two years. Back at Remington, he helped the company enter the civilian market with its first ever pistol, this 1st Model Remington-Beals, which was patented in June 1856. It was a small, reliable and effective single-action, five-shot percussion arm.

Type: Five-shot single-action revolver
Origin: Remington Armory, Ilion,
  New York
Caliber: .31
Barrel Length: 3in

Remington-Beals 2nd Model Pocket Revolver

Beal's second model, a .31caliber single-action percussion pocket revolver for Remington, had some minor improvements over the first. The main difference was that it now had a spur trigger rather than the trigger and guard of the first model. The butt had also been reshaped and squared off, with a large brass screw securing it. The grips were now either checkered rubber or, as shown in this case, walnut.

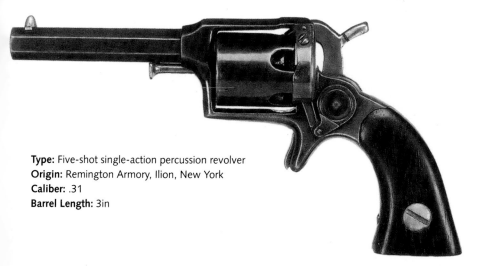

Type: Five-shot single-action percussion revolver
Origin: Remington Armory, Ilion, New York
Caliber: .31
Barrel Length: 3in

Remington-Beals 3rd Model Pocket Revolver

Fordyce Beals continued to develop his pocket rvolver line with this third model. Around 1,000 were made between 1859 and 1860. Larger than the previous two models, the gun had a four-inch barrel. It kept the spur trigger and squared butt of the 2nd Model. The main distinguishing feature is the solid frame extension under the barrel and the attached pivoting rammer. The lever must be lowered before the center pin can be removed. It has hard rubber checkered grips and a blued finish.

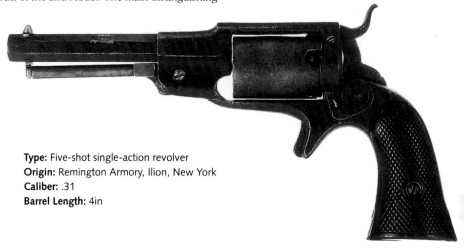

Type: Five-shot single-action revolver
Origin: Remington Armory, Ilion, New York
Caliber: .31
Barrel Length: 4in

Remington-Beals Army Revolver

When Col. Ripley, the Chief of Ordnance examined the Remington-Beals Navy prototypes he immediately placed a large order, but for revolvers in .44 Army caliber. This revolver has similar appearance to the original .36 version but is slightly larger and has a longer barrel. The fir deliveries were made in August 1862. They wer the first of a long line of Remington large calibe percussion revolvers.

Type: Six-shot single-action revolver
Origin: Remington Armory, Ilion, New York
Caliber: .44
Barrel Length: 8in

Remington-Beals Navy Revolver

By the end of the 1850s Remington was producing a range of pocket revolvers, pistols and rifles, but had no weapons suitable for military use. In 1858, Fordyce Beals took the principles of his 3rd Model, and developed an entirely new arm in .36 caliber. It had a large solid frame, complete with integral top strap, octagonal barrel and single-action lock. A large hinged ram sat beneath the barrel. This turned out to be a reliable and effective weapon, and was ordered by the US Government as they rearmed in preparation for the Civil War.

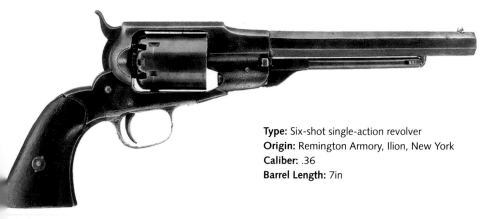

Type: Six-shot single-action revolver
Origin: Remington Armory, Ilion, New York
Caliber: .36
Barrel Length: 7in

Remington Conversion Revolvers

When Rollin White's patent finally expired in 1869, other manufacturers could now legally produce bored-through cylinders without getting permission from Smith and Wesson, and paying them a fee for the privilege. But as there were hundreds of thousands of percussion revolvers still in existence, most armament companies had schemes to convert them to use cartridge ammunition. The conversion usually consisted of replacing the cylinder, but some weapons would need a loading aperture cut into the frame behind the cylinder (or the addition of a loading gate) and sometimes had their loading rams removed.

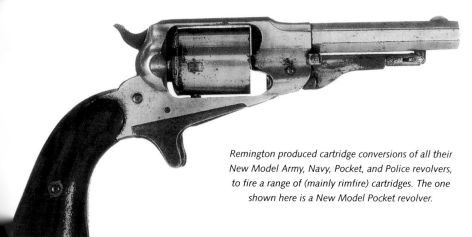

Remington produced cartridge conversions of all their New Model Army, Navy, Pocket, and Police revolvers, to fire a range of (mainly rimfire) cartridges. The one shown here is a New Model Pocket revolver.

Remington Model 1861 Army Revolver

The Model 1861 is also known as the "Old Model Army." It had a distinctive outline, with an integral top strap, large gap in front of the lower edge of the cylinder, and a long sloping web on the loading ram under the barrel. This form set the pattern for all subsequent Remington military percussion revolvers. Solid, reliable, an popular, thousands were made and used durin the Civil War and afterwards on the Western Frontier.

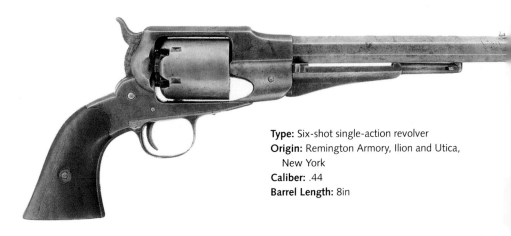

Type: Six-shot single-action revolver
Origin: Remington Armory, Ilion and Utica, New York
Caliber: .44
Barrel Length: 8in

Remington Model 1861 Navy Revolver

As with the Remington-Beals designs, a version of the Model 1861 was also produced in .36 caliber. Also referred to as the "Old Model Navy," it followed the same design as its slightly larger brethren. Total production is estimated as 7000. Just as popular as the Army model, the majorit of those produced saw hard wartime service. The gun has walnut grips and a blued finish wi a casehardened high spur hammer.

Type: Six-shot single-action revolver
Origin: Remington Armory, Ilion and Utica, New York
Caliber: .36
Barrel Length: 7.42in

Remington New Model Army Revolver

Wartime experience showed up some weaknesses in Remington's Model 1861, especially concerning the cylinder fixing system. Remington modified the design by improving the fixing pin and adding safety notches around the rear edge of the cylinder. The end result was one of the finest percussion revolvers ever, and the only one to really challenge Colt's dominance of the military market. Over 120,000 were delivered during the Civil War, and at its peak, production reached over 1,000 a week.

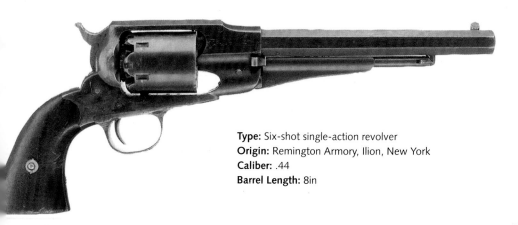

Type: Six-shot single-action revolver
Origin: Remington Armory, Ilion, New York
Caliber: .44
Barrel Length: 8in

Remington New Model Police Revolver

Again taking the New Model design as a basis, this was a much smaller weapon manufactured from around 1865 and intended to compete with the smaller Colt Police and Pocket revolvers. Only single-action, it was made in a range of barrel lengths from 3 to 6 inches. The one shown has a three-inch barrel, and is a compact, concealable, reliable weapon that still packs a hefty punch. It proved to be popular and over 17,000 examples were sold.

Type: Five-shot single-action revolver
Origin: Remington Armory, Ilion, New York
Caliber: .36
Barrel Length: 3in

Remington New Model Pocket Revolver

After the Civil War, Remington brought out this popular series of pocket revolvers to replace the Remington-Beals pocket models. The revolver had a small frame and unguarded spur trigger, but still had the typical Remington outline. Early production was percussion type, but later models were made to fire a rimfire cartridge. Some 26,000 were made in 3, 3.5, 4, and 4.5 inch barrel lengths. Many earlier percussion models were converted to fire cartridges.

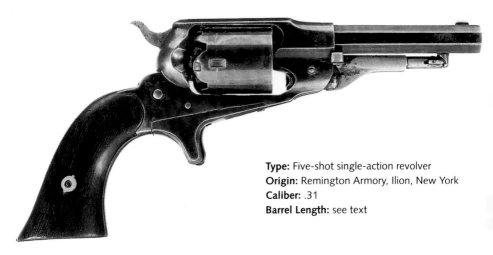

Type: Five-shot single-action revolver
Origin: Remington Armory, Ilion, New York
Caliber: .31
Barrel Length: see text

Remington Iroquois Revolver

Remington produced some 10,000 of this scaled-down new Model No 4 from around 1878. The cylinder held 7 rimfire cartridges of .22 caliber, and the whole package made a light, handy personal defence weapon to compete with the Colt New Line .22 models. Iroquois revolvers were made with both plain (shown here) and fluted cylinders (which are scarce.) The markings are Remington ,Ilion,N.Y. on the side of the barrel but there is no serial number.

Type: Seven-shot single-action cartridge revolver
Origin: Remington Armory, Ilion, New York.
Caliber: .22
Barrel Length: 2.25in

Remington-Kittredge Conversion Revolver

As the Civil War came to an end, it was clear that the metallic cartridge had superseded the percussion mechanism.. As far as revolvers were concerned, Rollin White's 1855 patent had prevented manufacturers from legally using a bored-through cylinder until 1869. Smith and Wesson had bought the rights to the patent from White, and had an almost exclusive market until then. Remington signed an agreement with Smith and Wesson, which allowed them to convert some 4,500 New Model Army large-caliber percussion revolvers to fire .46 rimfire cartridges. They were sold via the Kittredge Company of Cincinnati, Ohio.

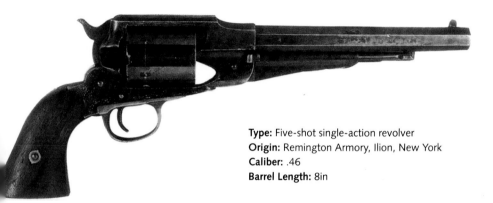

Type: Five-shot single-action revolver
Origin: Remington Armory, Ilion, New York
Caliber: .46
Barrel Length: 8in

Remington No. 1 New Model Revolver (Smoot's Patent)

William Smoot was a US Army Ordnance officer who left the Army and joined Remington as a gun designer. In 1873 Smoot designed this small five-shot spur trigger cartridge revolver which used unusual manufacturing techniques, in that the barrel and frame were forged from a single piece of steel. The butt was of the "bird-beak" style and was fitted with walnut grips. Under the barrel is an ejector rod for pushing spent cartridge cases rearwards out of the cylinder. About 3,000 examples of this model were made.

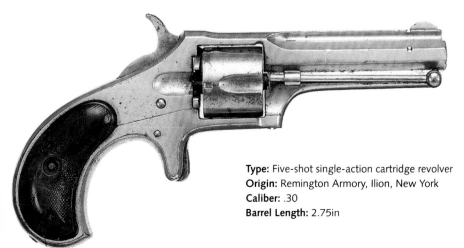

Type: Five-shot single-action cartridge revolver
Origin: Remington Armory, Ilion, New York
Caliber: .30
Barrel Length: 2.75in

Remington No 2. New Model Revolver (Smoot's Patent)

Smoot's second design for Remington was almost identical to the first, and used the same one-piece construction for the frame and barrel. The majority of the 3,000 or so made fired a .32 rimfire cartridge, although some retained the .30 cartridge of the No. 1 New Model. One distinguishing mark is the use of a stepped ejector rod in the .32 version of the gun.

Type: Five-shot single-action cartridge revolver
Origin: Remington Armory, Ilion, New York
Caliber: .30 and .32
Barrel Length: 2.75in

Remington No 3. New Model Revolver (Smoot's Patent)

For the third in this line of pocket revolvers, Smoot and Remington decided to increase their firepower by modifying the basic design for .38 cartridges. Two different types were produced, one which used .38 short rimfire, the other the more powerful .38 centerfire. The more powerful cartridge found favor with the market, and a respectable 25,000 or so revolvers were sold. This revolver also reverted to a more traditional separate frame with longer screw-in barrel, but kept the spur trigger. Early production had a "bird-beak" style butt, but later weapons switched to the "saw handle."

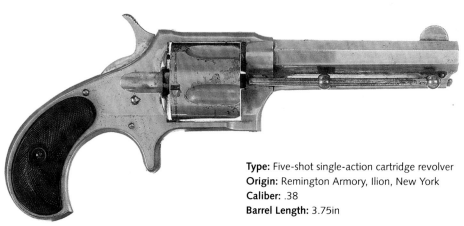

Type: Five-shot single-action cartridge revolver
Origin: Remington Armory, Ilion, New York
Caliber: .38
Barrel Length: 3.75in

Remington No 4. New Model Revolver (Smoot's Patent)

Smoot continued the line of New Model revolvers with this shorter, simpler design with its separate frame and barrel. The "bird-beak" butt and lack of ejector rod are recognition features. The No. 4 was made for .38 short rimfire or centerfire, or .41 short rimfire or centerfire. Again, it proved to be a popular combination of small size and firepower, and over 23,000 were made. The nickel-plating on this gun has survived remarkably well.

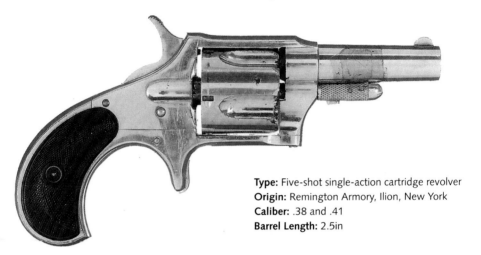

Type: Five-shot single-action cartridge revolver
Origin: Remington Armory, Ilion, New York
Caliber: .38 and .41
Barrel Length: 2.5in

Remington Model 1875 Army Revolver

A heavy Army caliber single-action cartridge revolver, this weapon was launched in 1875 to compete with highly-successful Colt Model 1873. Originally made for Remington's own .44 caliber centerfire cartridge, they were later produced in .44-40 and .45 long Colt calibers. An effective, reliable weapon, the Model 1875 never seriously challenged the Colt's supremacy. No large military contracts were awarded, although a few hundred were purchased by the Interior Department for use in policing the Western reservations.

Type: Six-shot single-action cartridge revolver
Origin: Remington Armory, Ilion, New York
Caliber: .44 and .45
Barrel Length: 7.5in (plus some 5in)

Remington Model 1888 Army Revolver

Scant records of this weapon exist, and there is some dispute that it really was a genuine Remington factory design. However, it appears that these shorter, large caliber revolvers were made in small numbers (less than 1,000) for New York dealers Hartley and Graham, perhaps from parts and sub-assemblies already available at the factory. Notice the absence of the normal Remington triangular web under the barrel. This was probably an attempt to make the gun look more like the Colt.

Type: Six-shot single-action cartridge revolver
Origin: Remington Armory, Ilion, New York
Caliber: .44-40
Barrel Length: 5.5in

Remington-Rider Double-Action Revolver

Remington formed another design partnership, this time with Joseph Rider of Newark, Ohio. Rider chose Remington to manufacture his double-action design, which he had patented in 1859. It had an unusual "mushroom-style" cylinder with the percussion nipples set in towards the chambers and angled outwards to meet the hammer. The trigger guard was also rather large, with a distinctive straight trigger. Many such weapons were later converted to fire metallic cartridges, and have a claim to be the first American double-action cartridge revolver.

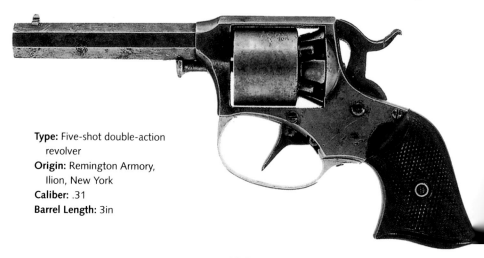

Type: Five-shot double-action
revolver
Origin: Remington Armory,
Ilion, New York
Caliber: .31
Barrel Length: 3in

Rogers & Spencer Army Revolver

The partnership of Rogers and Spencer was established in about 1861 and produced a number of firearms, including this Army contract six-round percussion revolver. The gun is serial numbered 1, and marked "Rogers & Spencer/Utica, N.Y." on the top strap over the cylinder. The order placed by the ordnance department in November 1864 was for 5,000 units, but it is believed that only about 2,000 had been delivered by the time the Civil War ended and the contract was terminated.

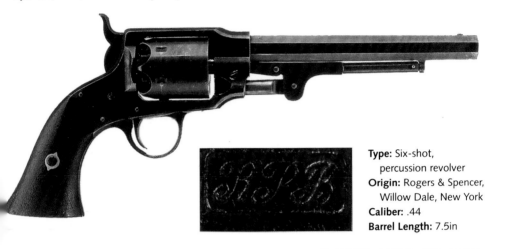

Type: Six-shot, percussion revolver
Origin: Rogers & Spencer, Willow Dale, New York
Caliber: .44
Barrel Length: 7.5in

Savage Navy Revolver

Edward Savage and Henry S. North started to cooperate in the early 1850s, their only known design being the "Figure-8 Revolver," and some 400 were produced between 1856 and 1859. Edward Savage then formed the Savage Revolving Firearms Company in 1860 and received two known major government contracts, the first of which was for some 25,000 Model 1861 Springfield muskets. The second contract was for the revolver seen here, which was marked as being designed to North's patents of 1856, 1859, and 1860. Some 20,000 were produced, of which 11,284 went to the Navy.

Type: Figure-8 revolver
Origin: Savage Revolving Firearms Co., Middletown, Connecticut
Caliber: .36
Barrel Length: 7.1 in

Otis Smith Model 1883 Spur-Trigger Revolver

Otis Smith appears to have established his gun making business in 1872 or 1873 and his company produced a number of undistinguished revolver designs before going out of business in 1898. The Model 1883, seen here, was chambered for .32 rimfire and has a barrel length of 2.9 inches. The protruding rod below the barrel is not a cylinder arbor pin but is a patented device for releasing the cylinder for reloading. This was one of the last revolvers to be manufactured with a spur trigger.

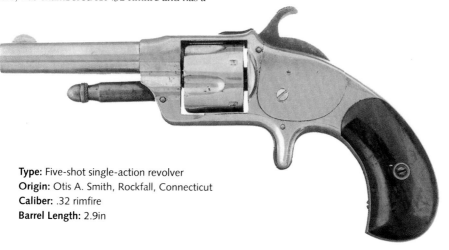

Type: Five-shot single-action revolver
Origin: Otis A. Smith, Rockfall, Connecticut
Caliber: .32 rimfire
Barrel Length: 2.9in

Smith & Wesson Model 1 2nd Issue

The Smith & Wesson Model 1 went through various "types" and "issues" before the Model 1- appeared in 1865. In 1868, this was followed by the Model 1- 2nd Issue (seen here) whereupon the 1865 became the Model 1- 1st Issue or "Old Model." The 1868 weapon then became the Model 1- 2nd Issue or "New Model." It was made with two barrel lengths, 2.5 and 3.5 inches, and had a bird's head grip and a five-round fluted cylinder. About 100,700 units were completed between 1868 and 1875.

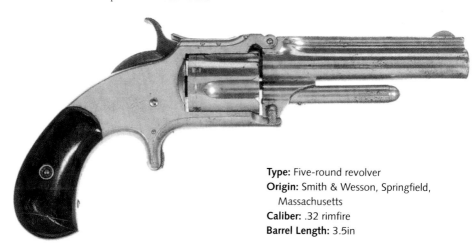

Type: Five-round revolver
Origin: Smith & Wesson, Springfield, Massachusetts
Caliber: .32 rimfire
Barrel Length: 3.5in

Smith & Wesson Model 2 Army Revolver (1861)

Smith and Wesson had the good fortune that the Model 2 became available just as the Civil War broke out. Important to its success was that it fired self-contained .32 rimfire cartridges which were not effected by climate or humidity, and it was light enough to be carried as a back- up to a rifle. It was the very latest design and became an immediate success with Union troops, resulting in a huge backlog of orders for the company. The Model 2 was available with 4, 5, or 6 inch barrels.

Type: Six-round, service revolver
Origin: Smith & Wesson, Springfield,
Massachusetts
Caliber: .32 rimfire
Barrel Length: 5in

Smith & Wesson 0.38 Single-Action 2nd Model

The .38 Single-Action 1st Model, sometimes known as the "Baby Russian" was produced between 1876 and 1867, during which time some 25,000 examples were completed. The 2nd Model, seen here, looked identical to the 1st Model but had a better extractor mechanism and was available in six barrel lengths: 3.25, 4, 5, 6, 8, and 10 inches. Over 108,000 were made. The example shown here is in typical nickel-plated finish, with a ribbed barrel, five-round fluted cylinder and unguarded spur trigger.

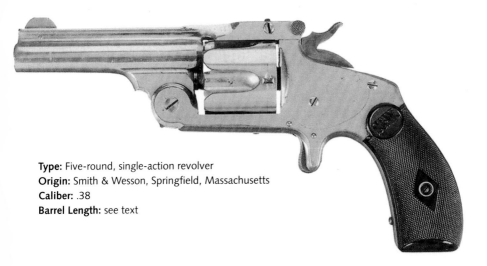

Type: Five-round, single-action revolver
Origin: Smith & Wesson, Springfield, Massachusetts
Caliber: .38
Barrel Length: see text

Smith & Wesson Model 3 Schofield

The Model 3 was a major success for the company and there were many variations, one of the most interesting being the "Schofield model." Major George Schofield of the US Cavalry liked the Model 3 Smith & Wesson but he patented a number of improvements, designed to make it easier to use on horseback and, in particular, to reload while holding the reins. In essence, Schofield's improvements included a modified barrel catch, improved extraction and a barrel reduced to seven inches.

Type: Six-round, hinged-frame, single-action revolver
Origin: Smith & Wesson, Springfield, Massachusetts
Caliber: .45 S&W
Barrel Length: 7in

Smith & Wesson Model 3 "Russian"

The Model 3 series was one of the most successful revolvers Smith and Wesson produced, and included a bewildering array of sub-types and variations to the basic design. Some of the most popular Model 3s were known as the "Russians." In 1871, the Russian Government selected the Model 3 to re-equip their army. Once it had bee modified to take the Russian .44 necked cartrid some 130,000 revolvers were delivered over the next eight years.

Type: Six-round, hinged-frame, single-action revolver
Origin: Smith & Wesson, Springfield, Massachusetts
Caliber: .44 Russian
Barrel Length: 6in

Smith & Wesson .38 Safety Hammerless "New Departure"

The .38 Safety Hammerless revolver remained in continuous production from 1886 to 1940. Its hammer was completely enclosed within the frame, and which could only be fired by a long pull on the trigger. Known today as "double-action only," at that time, the gun was introduced as "The New Departure." The design originated when Daniel B. Wesson read a press report that a child had been killed when it cocked and fired a conventional revolver and he determined to produce a design in which this was impossible.

Type: Five-round, hinged-frame double-action revolver
Origin: Smith & Wesson, Springfield, Massachusetts
Caliber: .38 S&W Special
Barrel Length: 3.25in

Spiller & Burr Revolver

The Spiller & Burr revolver was based on the Whitney 1858 Navy revolver but due to shortages of materials in the South, its creator James H. Burton had to adapt the design. He used iron instead of steel for the cylinder, and brass instead of iron for the lock-frame. This example shows the strong resemblance to the Whitney, but the gun has a poorer standard of finish, although there is no reason to think it did not work as well. Some of the surviving examples are marked with the name "Spiller & Burr" and others with "C.S." (Confederate States).

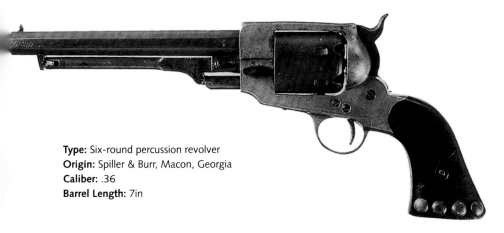

Type: Six-round percussion revolver
Origin: Spiller & Burr, Macon, Georgia
Caliber: .36
Barrel Length: 7in

Springfield Arms Revolver

The Springfield Arms Company was in business from 1851 to 1869, when it was taken over by the Savage Arms Corporation. The general manager, James Warner, patented a number of designs, but ran foul of Smith & Wesson who sued him for infringing their patents and won, as a result of which Springfield Arms had to hand over 1,500 weapons. The gun seen here is a Springfield-Warner Navy Model of 1851, with a smooth-sided cylinder, .36 caliber barrel, and walnut grips.

Type: Six-round percussion revolver
Origin: Springfield Arms Company, Springfield, Massachusetts
Caliber: .36
Barrel Length: 6in

Starr Model 1858 Army Revolver

The Starr Arms Company had its offices on Broadway, New York, and its factories at Binghampton, Morrisania, and Yonkers. The company manufactured weapons designed by Ebenezer (Eben) T. Starr and also guns designed by its president, H. H. Wolcott. The company produced a number of derringers and pepperpots designed by Starr and also some very effective revolvers. These were six-round, smooth-sided cylinder weapons. The first Army revolver made by Starr was the Model 1858 Double-Action, which had a six-inch barrel and a six-round, smooth-sided cylinder.

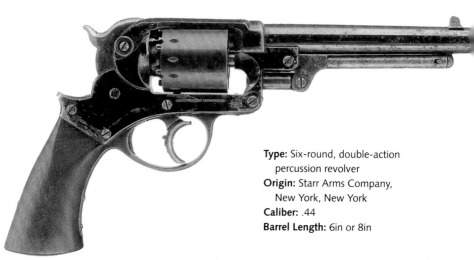

Type: Six-round, double-action
    percussion revolver
Origin: Starr Arms Company,
    New York, New York
Caliber: .44
Barrel Length: 6in or 8in

Starr Model 1863 Army Revolver

The Model 1863 was generally similar, but with a single-action and an eight-inch round barrel. The company made some 23,000 Model 1858s, while some 32,000 Model 1863s were produced between 1863 and 1865, under government contract. The Starr Single-Action was designed as an improved and was a less costly follow-up to the Model 1858. Next to Colts and Remingtons, the Starr was the most numerous revolving handgun bought by the US Government in the Civil War period.

Type: Six-round single-action percussion revolver
Origin: Starr Arms Company, New York, New York
Caliber: .44
Barrel Length: 6in or 8in

Starr Model 1858 Navy Revolver

The Starr Model 1858 Navy was a double-action percussion revolver with a six-inch barrel, similar to the Model 1858 Army but in .36 caliber. Unusually for American revolvers of the time, the mechanism was double-action only, such that the hammer could not be cocked by hand to allow a more accurate single-action option. Some 3,000 were made between 1858 and 1860.

Type: Six-round double-action percussion revolver
Origin: Starr Arms Company, New York, New York
Caliber: .36
Barrel Length: 6in

Starr Model 1858 Navy Revolver (Modified)

A sample batch of the Model 1858 Navy was actually supplied to the US Navy, but the guns were rejected and returned to the maker. Many were then sold to a gun dealer, who sold them to a Belgian factory where they were converted to centerfire, to take the French 11 x 17.8mm cartridge. Complete with a five-round cylinder, they were then sold to the French Army, which used them in the Franco-Prussian War. The example seen here is an 11mm conversion.

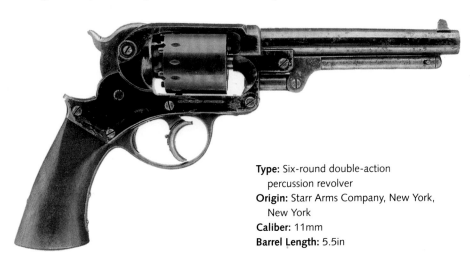

Type: Six-round double-action percussion revolver
Origin: Starr Arms Company, New York, New York
Caliber: 11mm
Barrel Length: 5.5in

Walch Pocket Revolver

Revolver designers have sought to Increase the number of rounds available to the firer by Increasing the diameter of the cylinder, but John Walch found a different way of doing this, by Increasing the length. In this system, the cylinder has five chambers, each of which accommodates two rounds, one behind the other. There are ten nipples and in each cylinder a channel leads from the right nipple to the front load, while the left nipple fires directly into the rear of the chamber. Each separate pull of the trigger fires one round.

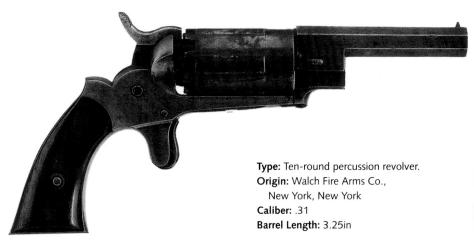

Type: Ten-round percussion revolver.
Origin: Walch Fire Arms Co., New York, New York
Caliber: .31
Barrel Length: 3.25in

Warner Pocket Revolver

James Warner, General Manager of the Springfield Arms Company (see page 112) also produced revolvers under his own name. This neat rimfire cartridge revolver was an attempt to get back into the pocket revolver business in the late 1850s. Although Colt's patent had expired, Warner's bored-through cylinder cartridge revolvers then ran up against the Rollin White/Smith & Wesson patent and as a result, production was halted after only 1,000 had been made.

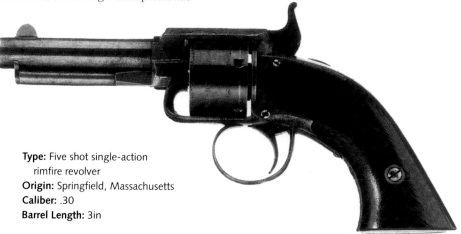

Type: Five shot single-action rimfire revolver
Origin: Springfield, Massachusetts
Caliber: .30
Barrel Length: 3in

Whitney Navy Percussion Revolver

The Whitney Company's first experience of manufacturing handguns was in 1847 when they made revolvers for Samuel Colt. Whitney went on to develop weapons to their own design, and by the late 1850s, they were making a series of military caliber weapons to compete with the Colt Navy. Unlike the Colts, the Whitney revolvers had a solid frames with an integral top strap above the cylinder. This made for a stronger, more robust design. The gun shown here is known as the Second Model, and has an octagonal barrel, brass trigger guard, and loading ram under the barrel. The Whitney Navy proved popular in the Civil War, and over 33,000 were made.

Type: Six-shot single-action percussion revolver
Origin: Whitneyville Armory, New Haven, Connecticut
Caliber: .36
Barrel Length: 7.5in

115

Modern Pistols

Bersa Model 383A

The Argentinean firm of Ramos Mejia produced this small semi-automatic pistol in three different versions. The Model 323 was a single-action .32 ACP caliber, while the Models 383 and 383A (shown here) were .380 ACP caliber, single- and double-action, respectively. All had a barrel length of 3.5in, with fixed sights, and a seven-round, detachable box magazine. The grips are sculpted walnut .The gun is available in blued finish and nickel.

Type: Double-action semi-automatic
Origin: Fabrica Ramos Mejia, Argentina
Caliber: .380 ACP
Barrel Length: 3.5in

HAFDASA Army Model 1927

HAFDASA (Hispano-Argentina Fabricas de Automoviles SA) was commissioned in the 1930s to manufacture a version of the .45in Colt M1911A1 for the Argentine Army. The decision was taken modify the original Browning design to facilitate and economize production. The main changes were the elimination of the grip safety, a backstrap that was integral to the frame and a pivoting trigger with a side-mounted sear bar and disconnector. Consequently, while the completed HAFDASA design bore a strong external similarity to the Colt M1911A1, only the barrel and magazine are interchangeable with the Colt pistol.

Type: Semi-automatic pistol
Origin: HAFDASA, Argentina
Caliber: .45 ACP
Barrel Length: 5in

Ballester-Molina Semi-Automatic Pistol

Ballester-Molina took over production of this pistol from HAFDASA (see the previous entry) and made a few minor changes to the design. These Included a marginally longer slide and a butt sized for a slightly smaller hand. The only visual distinction between the HAFDASA and Ballester-Molina weapons is that the former has the standard Colt regular finger grips on the slide, whereas those on the latter are irregularly spaced.

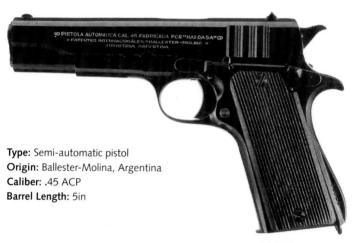

Type: Semi-automatic pistol
Origin: Ballester-Molina, Argentina
Caliber: .45 ACP
Barrel Length: 5in

Glock Model 17

The Glock 17 was the first pistol designed and manufactured by the Austrian company Glock. It is a locked breech, short recoil 9 mm Parabellum semi-automatic pistol with a standard magazine capacity of seventeen rounds of ammunition. The designation "17" is derived from the gun being Glock's seventeenth patent, rather than its magazine capacity. The Glock 17A (shown here) is a variant produced for the Australian market, to conform to local laws. The only differences are that the 17A has a barrel length of 4.6 inches, so that it visibly protrudes from the frame. It also has a ten-round magazine.

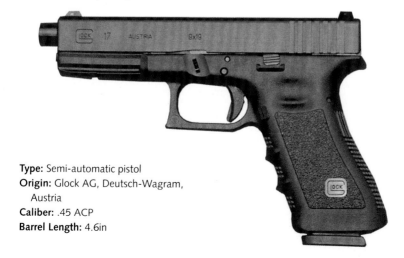

Type: Semi-automatic pistol
Origin: Glock AG, Deutsch-Wagram, Austria
Caliber: .45 ACP
Barrel Length: 4.6in

Glock Model 21

This pistol gained some notoriety as a "plastic" pistol, undetectable by security screening devices. Actually, this is not true, as some forty percent of the weapon is made from plastic materials, but there remains enough metal in the critical parts, such as the slide and barrel, so that any X-Ray or magnetic screening device will detect the gun. The Models 20 and 21 are identical in design except that the former is chambered for the 10mm Auto round and the latter for the .45in ACP round. The Model 21 shown here has a 13-round magazine and weighs approximately 25.25 ounces.

Type: Semi-automatic pistol
Origin: Glock AC, Deutsch-Wagram, Austria
Caliber: .45 ACP
Barrel Length: 4.6in

Glock Model 22

In 1990 Glock introduced the Model 22, which is virtually identical to the Model 17, but is chambered for the 0.40 S&W round. It is very slightly larger with an overall length of 7.4 inches, a height (with sights) of 5.16 inches, and a width of 1.18 inches. The barrel length is 4.49 inches. The weight, empty and without a magazine, is 22.36 ounces. The gun has a fifteen-round magazine and the Glock "Safe-Action" trigger system.

Type: Semi-automatic pistol
Origin: Glock AC, Deutsch-Wagram, Austria
Caliber: .40 S&W
Barrel Length: 4.49in

Glock Model 34

The Glock 34 is known as the "Tactical/Practical" and its numerical designation is the 9mm Model 34. The gun is chambered for the 9 x 19mm round and is midway in size between the four-and-a-half-inch barrel of the G17 and G22, and Glock's six-inch barrel target guns, the G17L and the G24. Barrel length on the Model 34 is 5.3 inches, and it has an overall length of 8.15 inches. Its weight is a feathery 23 ounces. The magazine holds seventeen rounds, but in some areas, you are limited to ten according to local laws.

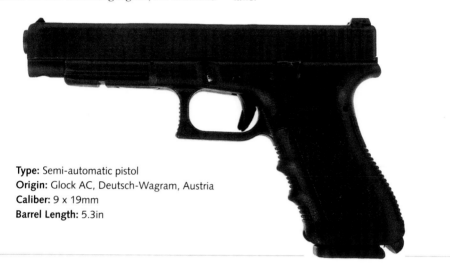

Type: Semi-automatic pistol
Origin: Glock AC, Deutsch-Wagram, Austria
Caliber: 9 x 19mm
Barrel Length: 5.3in

Glock Model 35

The new Glock Model 35 represents a change of direction for the company, which had been downsizing its guns for some time. It was felt that there was a need for a slightly longer version of the Model 22 (.40 S&W), which was not filled by the previous long barreled Glock Model 24 (.40S&W). The Model 35 has a 5.32-inch barrel (utilizing the frame of the standard Model 22 pistol) that gives the gun the muzzle feel of a Colt M1911. Legal magazine capacity is ten rounds.

Type: Semi-automatic pistol
Origin: Glock AC, Deutsch-Wagram, Austria
Caliber: .40 S&W
Barrel Length: 5.3in

Mannlicher Model 1905

This was the last of the Mannlicher series of automatic pistol designs, and was a short barrel weapon, chambered to fire the 7.63mm Mannlicher cartridge.A rather ungainly looking weapon, it was essentially an improved Model 1901, several thousand being manufactured at the Osterreichische Waffenfabrik Gesellschaft at Steyr in Austria. These were made mostly for the civilian market, with a small number being produced for the Argentine government. All production had ceased by 1910.

Type: Semi-automatic pistol
Origin: Mannlicher, Austria-Hungary
Caliber: 7.63mm Mannlicher
Barrel Length: 4.62in

Owa Automatic Pistol

The Osterreichische Werke Anstalt manufactured this small automatic pistol in some numbers in the early 1920s. This is always abbreviated to OWA, as seen on the butt of the weapon in the picture. The weapon operated on a unique, patented system, with a separate slide and breechblock. Its hammer is mounted in the frame, and rises through the slotted rear portio of the block to hit the firing pin, forcing it forward to fire the round. The weapon was 4.7i long, (unloaded) it weighed 14.5 ounces, and it had a six-round magazine.

Type: Semi-automatic pistol
Origin: Osterreichische Werke Anstalt, Austria
Caliber: 6.35mm Auto
Barrel Length: 1.97in

Roth-Steyr M1907

This pistol entered service with the Austro-Hungarian army in 1907. This was the first time that a major power had adopted a self-loading pistol. Unusually in a pistol, the Roth-Steyr fires from a locked bolt, and when fired the bolt and barrel recoil together within the hollow receiver. The barrel actually rotates through ninety degrees before unlocking and beginning the extraction/reloading cycle. The ten-shot magazine is fixed, and has to be reloaded through the open breech using a charger clip.

Type: Semi-automatic pistol
Origin: Osterreichische Waffenfabrik, Steyr, Austria
Caliber: 8 x 18.5mm Roth
Barrel Length: 5in

Steyr M1912

The M 1907 was issued mainly to the Austrian cavalry, but the rest of the army was given the later M 1912. The barrel still rotated, but the receiver was now a moving slide, closer in concept to today's automatics. The magazine was still an integral fixed box, holding up to eight of the powerful 9mm cartridge.

Type: Semi-automatic pistol
Origin: Osterreichische Waffenfabrik, Steyr, Austria
Caliber: 9 x 23mm Steyr
Barrel Length: 5in

Steyr M1917

This was a late version of the Steyr M1911, and the gun is marked "08." This means that it has been converted to use the Model 1908 cartridge. The German military designation of this is the 9x19, or the 9mm Luger. The marking was applied to prevent confusion with unaltered guns that would take the original 9mm Steyr (a longer cartridge.) The gun loads through the top using a "stripper" clip. Following the Anschluss (the annexation of Austria by Germany in 1938), many weapons like this one were taken over by the Germans.

Type: Semi-automatic pistol
Origin: Osterreichische
   Waffenfabrik, Steyr, Austria
Caliber: 9mm Luger
Barrel Length: 5in

Fabrique Nationale, Belgium

The American gun designer, John Moses Browning (1855-1926), is widely considered to have been the greatest ever gun designer and during his life, he was responsible for some eighty designs, together with well over a hundred patents. Browning's designs have covered a whole range of small arms, from semi-automatic pistols through single-shot rifles, repeater rifles, and machine guns.

John M. Browning was born in Ogden, Utah, in 1855, into a world of gunsmithing. His father was a gunsmith who was already well known for a number of innovations in the field. As a young boy, John spent hours in his father's shop and allegedly knew the name of every part of a gun before he could read. It's hardly surprising that at age twenty-three, he was filing his first patent for the "J. M. Browning Single-Shot Rifle." He inherited his father's small gun making workshop in Ogden, Utah. With funds of less than a thousand dollars, he turned it into a thriving gun making company with seven employees. One of Browning's guns was chanced upon by a representative of Winchester, who admired the design so much that the Winchester managing director made the six-day journey to Utah to conclude several lucrative commercial deals. Browning's designs for Colt, and the manufactu of many familiar Colt guns, also helped boost hi company's reputation as a premier gun maker. I the late 1890s, Browning went to Europe to find partner to manufacture his new design for a ser automatic shotgun. He found this in Fabrique Nationale, located in Herstal, Belgium. FN was a young company that had been established in 1889 by a group of Belgian businessmen in orde to manufacture Mauser rifles for the Belgian Army. The Browning/FN relationship proved to be a very effective business deal, and was highl satisfactory for both parties.

Some years later Browning established a new relationship with Colt and it was subsequently agreed that Colt would market Browning designs in the Western hemisphere, while FN marketed them in the East. The US-based Browning Company also continued, but existed almost entirely to market FN products in the United States. For ease of reference, all FN and Browning designs are listed here under "Belgium."

Browning Baby

This gun was named the "Browning Baby," and was introduced in 1932. It was chambered for the .25ACP round and had the frame extended forwards to give a very square appearance. The grip safety, which had featured on the Model 1906, was deleted, being replaced by a button just behind the trigger guard. Early models had the word "Baby" on the grip plates but this was omitted as production continued. The example shown here is a standard model with the word "Browning" on the grips.

Type: Vest-pocket
 semi-automatic pistol
Origin: Fabrique Nationale,
 Herstal, Belgium
Caliber: .25ACP
Barrel Length: 2in

Browning Capitan

The Browning Capitan model, introduced in 1993, is a derivative of the basic J. M. Browning design of the 1920s, which was finished and brought into production by FN after his death in 1927. The gun features added adjustable tangent rear sights and other minor modifications. It has a polished blued finish and walnut grips. Unlike the rest of the GP 35 Model range, the Capitan is not available chambered for the .40 S&W cartridge.

Type: Semi-automatic pistol
Origin: Fabrique Nationale,
 Herstal, Belgium
Caliber: 9mm
Barrel Length: 4.75in

Buck Mark Pistols

Browning added this .22 rimfire pistol to their range to echo the Challenger/Huntsman ethos of the 1950s. It was a lightweight .22, chambered for the Long Rifle Cartridge, and designed to appeal to outdoorsmen. The action is a straight blow-back design, with a single-action trigger, and an aircraft grade aluminum frame for lightness. It has a Pro-target adjustable rear sight. Ultra-Grip RXT provides the latest in hand grip technology with ergonomic grooving putting the shooters hand in the same place on the grip for every shot.

Above: The Camper model is a rugged matt blued pistol with a tapered bull barrel.

Type: Semi-automatic pistol
Origin: Fabrique Nationale, Herstal, Belgium
Caliber: .22 rimfire
Barrel Length: 5.5in

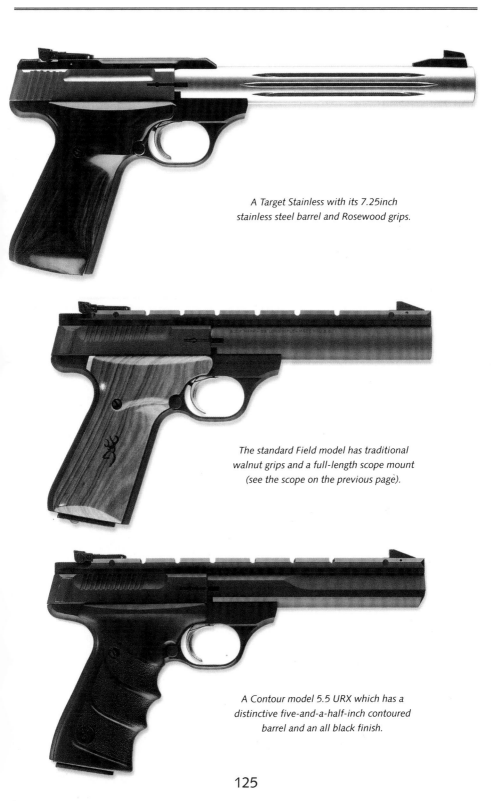

A Target Stainless with its 7.25inch stainless steel barrel and Rosewood grips.

The standard Field model has traditional walnut grips and a full-length scope mount (see the scope on the previous page).

A Contour model 5.5 URX which has a distinctive five-and-a-half-inch contoured barrel and an all black finish.

Browning Hi-Power

John Browning worked on this design from 1914 until his death in 1926, which is a logical development of the M1911 Colt. After his death, FN continued to work on the project. An FN employee, Dieudonne Saive, completed the final design work. The gun entered production in 1935. The gun was coded GP 35, derived from its first production year, and its original FN title, "Grand Puissance." Roughly translated, this means "high power." Since then, the gun has been adopted by many armed forces, and has also sold well on the civilian market.

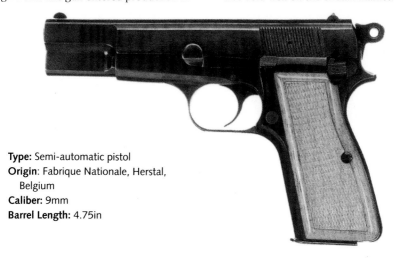

Type: Semi-automatic pistol
Origin: Fabrique Nationale, Herstal, Belgium
Caliber: 9mm
Barrel Length: 4.75in

Browning FN Model 1910

John M. Browning designed this blowback-operated, semi-automatic pistol in 1909 and 1910. It was immediately accepted for testing and manufacture by Fabrique Nationale, as a replacement for the Model 1900. The Model 1910 differed from his earlier designs by having the recoil spring wrapped around the barrel, which was chambered for either of two rounds which Browning himself had designed: the .32 ACP (7 x 17 mm) and .38 AGP (9 x 17 mm). It was in production from 1910 to 1954, during which time over 500,000 units were manufactured.

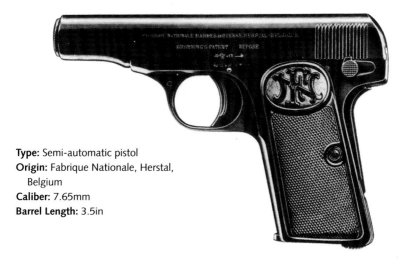

Type: Semi-automatic pistol
Origin: Fabrique Nationale, Herstal, Belgium
Caliber: 7.65mm
Barrel Length: 3.5in

Browning Model 10/71

Based on the Browning Model 1910, the Model 1910/22, had a longer barrel and an eight-round magazine. This proved a very durable design and was adopted by many armed forces, including the German army during World War Two, which designated it the Pistole 626(b). The design continued in production after the war, and was relaunched in the 1970s when a number were produced as the Model 1910/71, as seen here, with a four-and-a-half-inch barrel. It has both fore and backsights, and fires the .380 round.

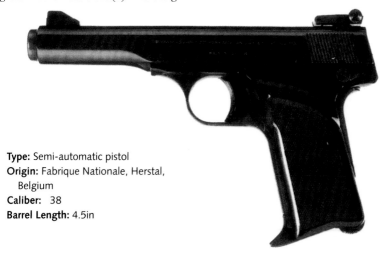

Type: Semi-automatic pistol
Origin: Fabrique Nationale, Herstal, Belgium
Caliber: 38
Barrel Length: 4.5in

Browning Pistole Model 640(b)

When the Germans overran Belgium in 1940, they took over the FN plant and continued production of the GP 35 model range for the German Wehrmacht under the designation Pistole Modelle 640(b) and carrying the factory code "CH." These guns were generally roughly finished, partly because the workforce was working against its will but also due to the pressing need for guns during wartime. Following the German defeat the weapon was marketed as the "High Power," a translation of the original factory designation "Grand Puissance."

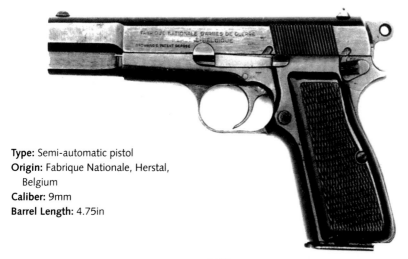

Type: Semi-automatic pistol
Origin: Fabrique Nationale, Herstal, Belgium
Caliber: 9mm
Barrel Length: 4.75in

Browning FN Model 49

This stunning looking modern gun is a relative of the original J.M. Browning designs. Introduced in 2000, the Model 49 is built for police (with sixteen rounds) or civil use (with ten rounds) and is available chambered for either .40 S&W or 9mm Parabellum ammunition. The frame is made of polymer and the slide is made of steel. This can be either black-coated or stainless (as seen here). Sights are fixed and marked with white dots.

Type: Police/civilian semi-automatic pistol
Origin: FN Herstal, Belgium
Caliber: 9mm
Barrel Length: 4.25in

Browning/Fabrique National FNP-9

Features of the new FNP USG polymer framed autoloading pistol, include a stainless steel (or black oxide coated) slide, a polymer frame, tactical rail, ambidextrous controls, and changeable back strap inserts to change the grip feel and size. The pistol comes in a wide choice of calibers: .45ACP, .40 S&W, .357 SIG and (as seen here) 9x19 Parabellum. The frame rails are replaceable allowing the pistol to be rebuilt after extensive use. The USG comes in a unique dark earth toned or black polymer frame.

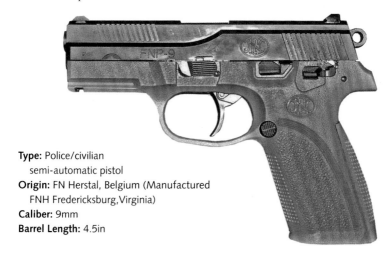

Type: Police/civilian
semi-automatic pistol
Origin: FN Herstal, Belgium (Manufactured
FNH Fredericksburg, Virginia)
Caliber: 9mm
Barrel Length: 4.5in

Robar Jieffeco (2)

The patent for this design was owned by a Belgian firm named Janssen et Fils Compagnie, which was then abbreviated for the US market, to "Jieffeco." The original pistol, the Jieffeco (1), was marketed prior to World War One, and was available in 7.65mm and 6.35mm versions. After the war, production was restarted and marketed in the US by the Davis-Warner Arms Corporation of New York City. This new weapon, chambered for the 0.25in round, was known as the Jieffeco (2).

Type: Semi-automatic pistol
Origin: Robar et Cie, Liege, Belgium
Caliber: .25in
Barrel Length: 3.5in

Robar Liegoise Melior

The Melior pistol was essentially a variant of the Jieffeco (2), chambered for the, .380in round for the US market. It has a seven-round magazine. The external design of this gun is very reminiscent of the Browning Model 1910, except for the positioning of the safety catch which is located on the frame behind the trigger instead of at top rear of the grips on the Browning. The circular Melior logo is cast into the black rubber grips.

Type: Semi-automatic pistol
Origin: Robar et Cie, Liege, Belgium
Caliber: .380in
Barrel Length: 3.5in

Pieper Bayard Model 1908

Chevalier de Bayard was a French knight and his name was taken as a trademark for a series of pistols produced by the Belgian firm of Henry Pieper, based on the patents of a M. Clarus. The Clarus action involved a unique hammer and sear system, and it was claimed that it was these features that made it possible for such a small pistol (4.92 inches in length, with a weight of 1(ounces) to fire such a large round. This picture shows the Model 1908, the first in the line.

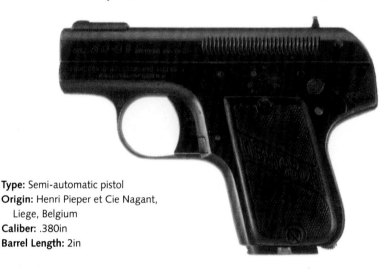

Type: Semi-automatic pistol
Origin: Henri Pieper et Cie Nagant, Liege, Belgium
Caliber: .380in
Barrel Length: 2in

Pieper Bayard Model 1912

A further model in the Bayard series, the Model 1912 was chambered for 6.35mm and ammunition and was marginally smaller (with a length of 4.5 inches) and lighter (weighing 12 ounces) than its predecessors. It remained in production until 1914, when production ceased due to the German invasion, but restarted in 1919. On all pistols bearing this name, there is an engraving of a medieval knight (the Chevalie de Bayard) on the left side of the weapon and the word "Bayard" on a diagonal strip on the hard rubber grips.

Type: Semi-automatic pistol
Origin: Anciens Etablissements Pieper, Herstal, Liege, Belgium
Caliber: 6.35mm Auto
Barrel Length: 2.2in

(Pieper) Bergmann Bayard Model 1910

The German company, Bergmann, won an order for their Mars pistol from the Spanish Army, which was to have been manufactured by another German company, Schilling, which was based at Suhl. When the latter withdrew, Bergmann negotiated a production deal with Pieper of Belgium who then fulfilled the Spanish contract with a slightly modified weapon. This is now designated the Bergmann-Bayard Model 1908. Shortly afterwards, Pieper won another pistol contract from the Danish Army; these weapons, although virtually identical to the Model 1908, were designated the Model 1910.

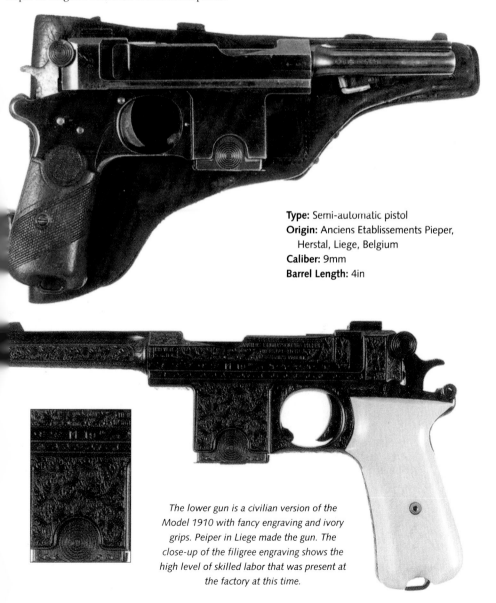

Type: Semi-automatic pistol
Origin: Anciens Etablissements Pieper, Herstal, Liege, Belgium
Caliber: 9mm
Barrel Length: 4in

The lower gun is a civilian version of the Model 1910 with fancy engraving and ivory grips. Peiper in Liege made the gun. The close-up of the filigree engraving shows the high level of skilled labor that was present at the factory at this time.

131

Taurus Model PT-99AF

Taurus is a Brazilian arms manufacturer that has been in business since 1889. The PT-99 was based on the earlier PT092 and weighs 34 ounces. It has a fifteen-round magazine.

It has a fully adjustable, three-dot rear sight and is chambered for the 9mm round. It has walnut grips and a matt black finish to the frame.

Type: Semi-automatic pistol
Origin: Taurus International, Porta Alegre, Brazil
Caliber: 9mm
Barrel Length: 5in

Taurus Model PT-111

The neat and business-like PT-111 was introduced in 1997. It operates on a double-action only system and has a 3.5in barrel firing 9mm rounds. It has a polymer frame, with a ter round magazine housed in the butt. It weighs about sixteen ounces.

Type: Semi-automatic pistol
Origin: Taurus International, Porta Allegre, Brazil
Caliber: 9mm
Barrel Length: 3.3in

Taurus Model PT-908

The Taurus PT-908 is a semi-automatic, double-action only weapon, chambered for the 9mm Parabellum cartridge; eight rounds are carried in the magazine. It is fitted with a fixed foresight and a 3-dot rear sight, which can be adjusted for drift.

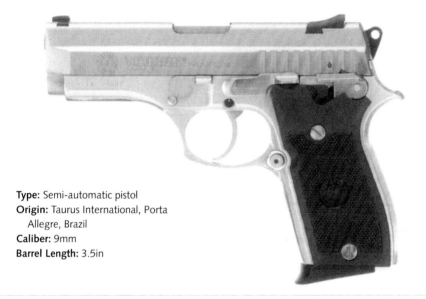

Type: Semi-automatic pistol
Origin: Taurus International, Porta Allegre, Brazil
Caliber: 9mm
Barrel Length: 3.5in

Norinco Type 51 (TT1933)

The Russian weapon designer, Fedor Tokarev, was working at the Tula Arsenal in the USSR when he designed his famous pistol, which was chambered for the 7.63mm Mauser cartridge. This was adopted by the Red Army under the designation Tula Tokarev Model 1933 (TT1933) and was immediately placed into large volume production. The TT1933 was also manufactured in Hungary (Model 1948) and in the People's Republic of China (as seen here) as the Type 51.

Type: Semi-automatic pistol
Origin: Norinco, China
Caliber: 7.62mm
Barrel Length: 3.5in

133

Norinco Type 54

As described in the previous entry, the Tokarev TT1933 was produced in Hungary. In the late 1950s the Hungarian government arsenal at Fegyvergyan, Budapest, developed an improved version for the Egyptian police, designated the Tokagypt 58. This had various modifications including a positive safety and wrap-around stocks. It was chambered for the 9mm Luger cartridge. This was a distinct improvement, which was immediately adopted by the People's Republic of China, who placed it in production as the Type 54, superseding their earlier Type 51

Type: Semi-automatic pistol
Origin: Norinco, China
Caliber: 7.62mm
Barrel Length: 4.5in

NorInco Type 59

This is a copy of the Soviet Pistolet Makarov (PM), which is chambered for the standard Makarov 9mm cartridge, which is known in China as the Type 59 round. The Type 59 is six-and-a-half inches long and has an empty weight of 23 ounces. The detachable box magazine carries a maximum of eight rounds.

Type: Semi-automatic pistol
Origin: Norinco, China
Caliber: 9mm Makarov
Barrel Length: 3.75in

Norlnco 1911 A1 (NP29)

Norinco's 1911 series handguns have a reputation for durability and reliability, comparing quite favorably with similar offerings from domestic manufacturers, which cost considerably more. Colt no longer make a 9mm "Government Model" so the Norinco 1911 becomes a good option. The gun is popular with custom gunsmiths who recognize the potential of its rugged forged ordinance steel. After-market accessories are available for the 1911 Norinco, and with a little fitting these can make a basic, reliable gun into a match grade pistol. Shown here is the 1911A1 (NP29) 9mm.

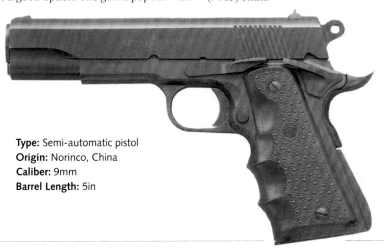

Type: Semi-automatic pistol
Origin: Norinco, China
Caliber: 9mm
Barrel Length: 5in

Ceska Zbrojovka CZ 1924

This gun was based on a design by Josef Nickl, a Mauser engineer. In the 1920s, he helped the Czech weapons industry to set up for the licensed production of Mauser rifles. Nickl's CZ Model 1922 was a simple blowback weapon firing 9mm Short cartridges, and the later Model 1924 shown here is a further development of the design. It uses a conventional barrel and slide blowback system, unusual in that the barrel unlocks from the slide by rotating slightly. The hammer is partially shrouded, although it remains just visible.

Type: Semi-automatic pistol
Origin: Ceska Zbrojovka, Strakonitz, Czechoslovakia
Caliber: 9mm
Barrel Length: 3.5in

Ceska Zbrojovka CZ 1927

Frantisek Myska developed Nickl's Model 1922/24 design further to create this Model 1927. He remodeled it for the less powerful 7.65 x 17mm cartridge, allowing him to dispense with the barrel/slide locking mechanism. Instead, the pistol relied on the inertia of the slide to hold the breech shut until the gas pressure had dropped to a safe level. It was a successful design, and even remained in production for the Wehrmacht after the Germans occupied Czechoslovakia. The last Model 1927 was made in 1951.

Type: Semi-automatic pistol
Origin: Ceska Zbrojovka, Strakonitz, Czechoslovakia
Caliber: 7.65mm
Barrel Length: 3.9in

Ceska Zbrojovka CZ 1938/39

First entering service in 1938, this pistol was designed to be simple to use and quick to get into action. As such, it had no safety device and didn't need any cocking operation. Once a round was chambered, the mechanism was double-action only, the user simply pulling the trigger to fire. Unfortunately, the heavy trigger made accurate shooting difficult. Another unusual feature is that access to the mechanism and barrel is by hinging the whole barrel and sliding upward around a pivot under the muzzle.

Type: Semi-automatic pistol
Origin: Ceska Zbrojovka, Strakonitz, Czechoslovakia
Caliber: 9mm
Barrel Length: 4.65in

Dusek "Duo" Pistol

The Dusek factory manufactured weapons from the mid-1920s until 1948, when the newly-installed Communist government transferred its facilities to the state-owned Ceska Zbrojovka (CZ) factory. The "Duo" was marketed from 1926 onwards and was quite successful, being sold all over the world; it remained in production until 1949. Chambered for the 6.35mm cartridge and with a blowback operation, its design was based on that of the 1906-pattern Browning.

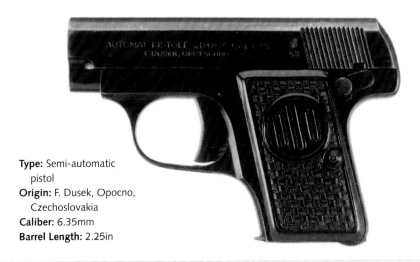

Type: Semi-automatic
  pistol
Origin: F. Dusek, Opocno,
  Czechoslovakia
Caliber: 6.35mm
Barrel Length: 2.25in

MAB Model A

MAB was established in 1921 and produced a number of successful pistols until it was forced to close in the mid-1980s. The Model A, shown here, was the first to be produced. It was chambered for the 6.35mm cartridge and, like so many automatics of that period, was based on the 1906 Browning. The weapon pictured here has grips bearing the logo of the US importer, WAC. The logo for models not intended for the US market was the parent company's "MAB."

Type: Semi-automatic pistol
Origin: Manufacture d'Armes de
  Bayonne (MAB), France
Caliber: .25 ACP
Barrel Length: 2in

MAB Model D 1933

This is another MAB pistol based on the Browning Model 1910. This gun was first issued as the Model C, in 1933, and used a simple unlocked blowback operating cycle. The butt and grip were soon redesigned the brand name MAB cast into the hard rubber grips and the pistol renamed Model D. In this form, it turned out to be a successful compact pistol, and remained in production until 1988.

Type: Semi-automatic pistol
Origin: Manufacture d'Armes de Bayonne (MAB), France
Caliber: 7.65mm
Barrel Length: 3.2in

MAPF Mikros

MAPF was established in 1923 to manufacture automatic pistols. Up until 1939, it concentrated on the French military and police market, although numbers were also sold on the civilian market. The weapons were given model names rather than numbers and the Mikros was manufactured between 1934 and 1939. The design was based closely on that of the Walther Model 9 and most were chambered for the 6.35mm cartridge like this example, although some were chambered for the more powerful 7.35mm round.

Type: Semi-automatic pistol
Origin: Manufacture d'Armes de Pyrenees Francaises, Hendaye (MAPF), France
Caliber: 6.35mm
Barrel Length: 2in

Borchardt Pistol

Hugo Borchardt designed this complex weapon in 1893 using similar principles to those devised by Maxim in his machine gun using a toggle system to eject and reload. The pistol was large and rather clumsy to use, and was normally seen with the combined wooden stock/holster as seen here. It was also expensive and complex to make. However, it was one of the first reasonable successful semi-automatic pistols, and the design concepts were developed further to make the outstanding Luger series.

Type: Semi-automatic pistol/carbine
Origin: Hugo Borchardt and Loewe & Cie, Berlin
Caliber: 7.65mm
Barrel Length: 6.5in

BSW Prototype

This pistol was one of a number of designs submitted to the German army in the late 1930s as a replacement for the Luger. It was designed and made by the Berlin-Suhler Waffen und Fahrrad Fabrik (Berlin/Suhl Weapons and Bicycle Factory; BSW). There was stiff competition at the time and although the weapon had a neat appearance and was well made, it was not outstanding, was too complicated for service use and never got beyond the prototype stage.

Type: Semi-automatic pistol
Origin: Berlin-Suhler Waffen und
Fahrrad Fabrik (BSW), Berlin
Caliber: 9mm
Barrel Length: 5in

Dreyse 6.35mm Model 1907

The German company Rheinmetall purchased the assets of the failing gunsmith Dreyse Waffenfabrik in 1901 but continued to produce weapons under the original name for some years. One of these was the 6.35mm Model 1907. The overall design of the weapon was similar to that of the 1906 Browning (but without the grip safety.) Note that the weapon shown here has the word "Dreyse" on the side, with the Rheinmetall logo at the head of the grip.

Type: Semi-automatic pistol
Origin: Rheinmetall, Sommerda,
    Germany
Caliber: 6.35mm
Barrel Length: 2in

The Luger

The Selbstladepistole Parabellum (self-loading pistol, Parabellum) is one of the most famous firearms of the twentieth century and will always be known, quite simply, by its designer's name as "the Luger." An Austrian, Georg Johann Luger was born in Steinach-am-Brenner in 1849 and was educated in Padua, Italy and Vienna, Austria. After compulsory military service he worked as a foreign sales representative for the German armaments firm, Loewe, selling the Mannlicher series of rifles and later the Borchardt self-loading pistol. The latter was criticized by potential customers as being too large and heavy, as well as poorly balanced.

Georg Luger set to work to put these drawbacks right, greatly simplifying the mechanism, improving the balance and Increasing the angle of the grip. Although not fitted in the earliest models, a grip safety was added in 1904, but was deleted in 1908 and replaced by a lever type safety. He also developed a new cartridge, the 7.65 Parabellum (known in the US as the .30 Luger) which was 2mm shorter than that employed in the original Borchardt.

Some potential customers criticized this round for lack of stopping power, so Georg produced a new round, the 9 x 19mm Parabellum, in which form the pistol was accepted by the German Navy as the "P.O.S." Despite its fame and high reputation, the Luger had its drawbacks. It was mechanically complicated, making it expensive to manufacture and to buy, and contributing to a lack of reliability in service. On the other hand it was very powerful and accurate. In the end there were much simpler, more reliable, and cheaper designs available.

DWM Luger Model 1900 Swiss

The Swiss were the first to adopt the Luger as the sidearm for issue to their military units. After a series of test trials from 1898 to 1900, the Swiss accepted a small initial quantity of pistols drawn from the earliest DWM commercial production. Serial numbers on these pistols extend into the 800 range. The Model 1900 Swiss Lugers were issued with unique holsters of Swiss manufacture. The magazines for these early pistols were fabricated with polished metal inserts pressed into the wooden bases and are prized collectibles in themselves.

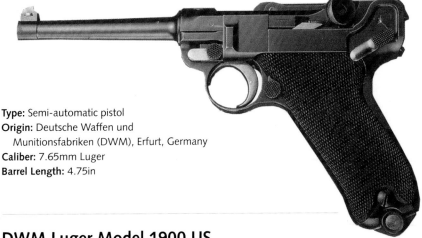

Type: Semi-automatic pistol
Origin: Deutsche Waffen und
   Munitionsfabriken (DWM), Erfurt, Germany
Caliber: 7.65mm Luger
Barrel Length: 4.75in

DWM Luger Model 1900 US

This exceptionally clear picture shows one of the 1,000 Model 1900 Lugers sent for trial by the US army. An American eagle device is stamped above the chamber and a grip safety Incorporated. These weapons were issued to the US Cavalry for field trials, but no order was ever placed. This particular weapon obviously remained in service after the trials, as it comes complete with a Model 1910 Officer's Garrison Belt, an unusual left-handed leather, russet-colored holster and a pouch for four magazines.

DWM Commerical Model 1900

The first Lugers were produced in 1899 and1900 in a successful bid to win a contract for the Swiss Army. Although DWM clearly saw the military market as potentially the most profitable, a number of weapons were produced for the civil market. These included the Model 1900

Commercial. This beautifully preserved specimen has the serial number 4907 and has the DWM crest on the toggle and the word "Germany" below the serial number. There is no crest above the chamber.

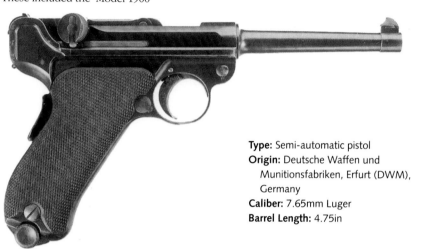

Type: Semi-automatic pistol
Origin: Deutsche Waffen und Munitionsfabriken, Erfurt (DWM), Germany
Caliber: 7.65mm Luger
Barrel Length: 4.75in

DWM Model 1902 Commercial "American Eagle"

As explained in the introduction, Georg Luger designed a new cartridge for his pistol, the 9mmm Parabellum round. This was introduced from about 1902 onwards. This model was intended for the US civil market and had an

American eagle engraved above the chamber. The barrel was some 0.75in shorter than on other Lugers, leading to the nickname, which is occasionally applied of "the Fat Barrel Luger."

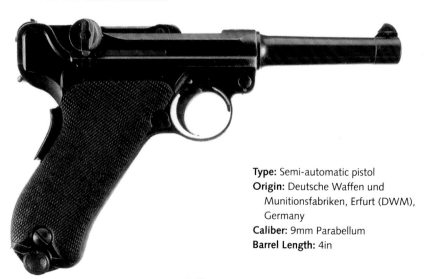

Type: Semi-automatic pistol
Origin: Deutsche Waffen und Munitionsfabriken, Erfurt (DWM), Germany
Caliber: 9mm Parabellum
Barrel Length: 4in

DWM Model 1906 Navy 1st Issue

DWM won its first domestic contract in 1904 when the Reichsmarineamt (Imperial naval office) ordered some 1,500 Navy Model 1904. This was known in German as the Pistole Marine-Model 1904, System Borchardt-Luger. This was followed by a further order for some 12,000 of the Navy Model 1906, which incorporated changes to the spring and the safety lever, as well as a two position rear sight, which could be set to either 100m and (rather optimistically) also to 200m.

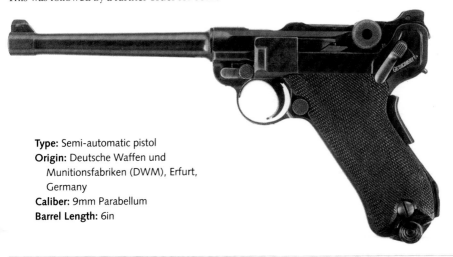

Type: Semi-automatic pistol
Origin: Deutsche Waffen und
  Munitionsfabriken (DWM), Erfurt,
  Germany
Caliber: 9mm Parabellum
Barrel Length: 6in

DWM Parabellum M1908

The M 1908 took the best aspects of the Model 1906, and was adopted by the army to become one of the best-known pistols of all time. It was known as the "9mm Selbstladepistole 1908" which was initially shortened to "Pistole 1908" and finally to simply "P.08." Many other countries bought the Luger, and it served with distinction during World War One. The Luger was put back into production as soon as possible after the war, and was to serve once more in large quantities during World War Two.

Type: Semi-automatic pistol
Origin: Deutsche Waffen und
  Munitionsfabriken (DWM), Erfurt,
  Germany
Caliber: 9mm Parabellum
Barrel Length: 4in

DWM Long Model 1908 Artillery

The German army subsequently adopted a further version of the Luger for its field gun and machine gun crews with a lengthened (8in) barrel and a nine-position, tangent-leaf backsight located at the rear of the barrel. It also had a lug on the heel of the butt for a detachable shoulder stock. This was designated "Die Lange Pistole 1908" (long pistol 1908) but has always been known as the "Artillery Model" and the weapon shown here has its year of manufacture (1917) stamped on the chamber top.

Type: Semi-automatic pistol
Origin: Deutsche Waffen und
Munitionsfabriken (DWM),
Erfurt, Germany
Caliber: 9mm Parabellum
Barrel Length: 8in

DWM Long Model 1918 Reissued to Weimar Navy

This is a Lange Pistole 1908 but with a 1918 date of manufacture stamped on the chamber. This year of manufacture is, in itself, unusual, but it is also rare that it should have survived the Allied occupation, since they had taken a major dislike to this weapon and destroyed a great number. Finally, the weapon has stamps to show that it was reissued to the Reichsmarine, the name given to the reconstituted navy formed in 1921 that became the Kriegsmarine under Hitler.

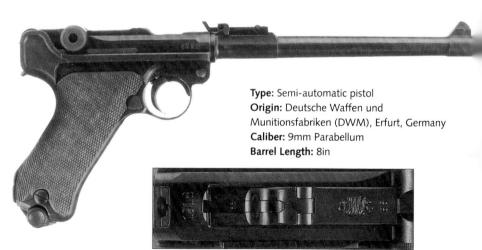

Type: Semi-automatic pistol
Origin: Deutsche Waffen und
Munitionsfabriken (DWM), Erfurt, Germany
Caliber: 9mm Parabellum
Barrel Length: 8in

DWM Model 1920 Carbine

The first carbine version of the Luger was produced in 1902, but the version shown here is the Model 1920, produced by Simson & Co. of Suhl, Germany, in the immediate aftermath of World War One. These carbines were built on P.08 weapons, but with a much longer barrel, ramped foresight, tangent backsight and other changes. This particular weapon has an American eagle over the chamber indicating that it was made for export. Note the grip safety.

Type: Semi-automatic carbine
Origin: Simson & Co., Suhl, Germany
Caliber: 9mm Parabellum
Barrel Length: 11.75in

Krieghoff P.08

As the pace of rearmament increased, following Hitler's access to power there was, naturally, a lot of money to be made. Thus, the Krieghoff Company acquired production machinery from Simson & Co. and manufactured some 15,000 pistols at a very cheap price to gain access to further contracts. Of this batch, 1,300 failed the Luftwaffe acceptance procedures. This is one of those guns, as attested by the five-pointed rejection star stamped on the body. These rejects were then sold on the civilian market.

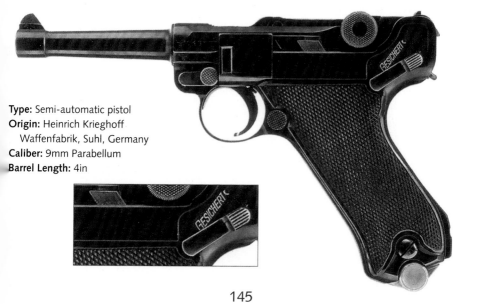

Type: Semi-automatic pistol
Origin: Heinrich Krieghoff
 Waffenfabrik, Suhl, Germany
Caliber: 9mm Parabellum
Barrel Length: 4in

Mauser "byf 41" (Luger P.08)

Weapons factories in Germany were allocated production codes, which had to be stamped on their weapons; in Mauser's case this was "byf" which was followed by the last two digits of the calendar year. Thus, Mauser produced this byf 41 Luger in 1941. This particular weapon belonged to the adjutant to General Maximilian Fretter-Pico who in March/April 1945 was the Commanding-General of Military District IX. Fretter-Pico's adjutant was captured by troops of the US Army's 1st Infantry Division and this gun was confiscated.

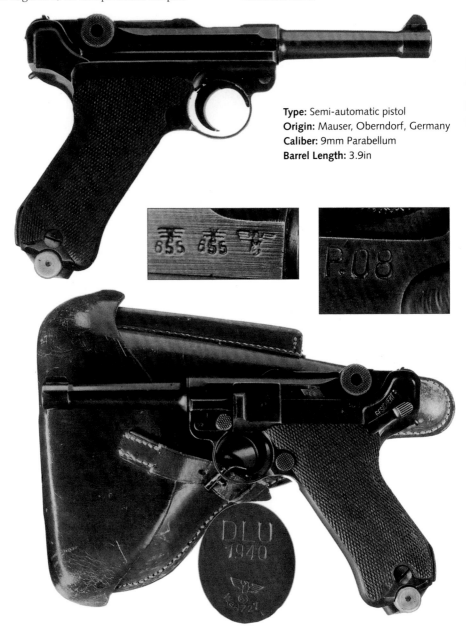

Type: Semi-automatic pistol
Origin: Mauser, Oberndorf, Germany
Caliber: 9mm Parabellum
Barrel Length: 3.9in

Haenel-Schmeisser SAP

The famous Hugo Schmeisser arrived at Haenel as chief engineer, in 1921 with his design for a 6.35mm pocket automatic pistol. The resulting weapon was small (4.7 inches long), light (only 13.4 ounces) and neat. This gun was produced from 1922 to 1930, when it was superseded by the Model 2 (seen here), which was both shorter (at 3.9 inches) and lighter (at ll.8 ounces). The grips on the Model 1 bore the monogram "HS," while on the Model 2 they bore the designer's name, "Schmeisser."

Type: Semi-automatic pistol
Origin: C. G. Haenel Waffen und
    Fahrradfabrik, Suhl, Germany
Caliber: 6.35mm Auto
Barrel Length: 2.05in

Heckler & Koch USP

The USP or Universal Self-loading Pistol is a clever amalgam of old and new.
The use of new materials such as the molded polymer frame and anticorrosion nitrided surface coating works successfully alongside the linkless locked breech action system of J.M.Browning's GP 35. H&K have successfully employed the strong points of their previous pistols including the MK23, which was tested in extreme combat situations to produce the USP range. The standard model is available in .40 S&W, 9mm Parabellum and .45ACP. The Compact model shown here is also available in .357 SIG.

Type: Semi-automatic pistol
Origin: Heckler & Koch, Oberndorf,Germany
Caliber: see text
Barrel Length: 3.58in

Heckler & Koch USP Custom Sport

The USP Custom Sport is a further variant of the USP series with only subtle differences from the standard Model. Identical to the USP in most respects, the Custom Sport has a match grade barrel; extended floor plate on the magazine, match trigger and adjustable sights. The modified Browning locking buffer system reduces recoil considerably making this an accurate target weapon. We show a 9mm type but the gun is also chambered for .40S&W and .45ACP.

Type: Semi-automatic pistol
Origin: Heckler & Koch, Oberndorf,
Germany
Caliber: 9mm x 19
Barrel Length: 4.4in

Mauser "Broomhandle" Pistols

Gebrüder Mauser (Mauser brothers) set up business in Oberndorf in 1872, becoming Waffenfabrik Mauser AG in 1884, and the company quickly became famous due to its outstanding rifle designs. Their early handgun designs, the Model 1877 and 1878 revolvers, were, however, less successful, as was the Model 1886 (C/86) repeater pistol. However, the staff of the company included the three Feederle brothers, who produced a design for an automatic pistol, firing the 7.65mm Borchardt round, which was designated the Mauser C/96. It was initially rejected by the German army and achieved its first successes in the civilian market, proving to be the first in a very long line of outstanding pistols. The design remained in production until 1939 and was affectionately nicknamed "the broomhandle" from the shape of the butt.

There were numerous minor changes over the forty-three years the weapon remained in production, although the basic features remained constant. The barrel length was altered, as was the rifling and the mode of operation of the safety catch. The great majority of versions had a fixed six- or ten-round magazine, but the C/06-04 had a detachable 20- round box. Similarly, most had recesses milled into the sides, but some produced in the early 1900s had flat (or slab) sides. Finally, the shape of the hammer changed over the years. Approximately one million of all versions of the Model 1896 were produced. The unique shape of the C/96 makes it instantly recognisable. It had considerable range and stopping power and was very reliable, but was both heavy and bulky, while reloading was time consuming. It should be noted that many cheap copies of the "broomhandle" pistol were produced in various countries over the years, particularly in Spain, and some of these have since been refurbished and passed off as expensive Mauser factory originals.

Mauser Model 1896 (C/96)

The Model 1896 (C/96) was the first in the line of "broomhandle" weapons. It operated on a short-recoil, blowback system. Our picture shows a professionally refurbished Model 1896 with a small hole hammer- one of the minor differences in design that differentiate these weapons. This early gun also lacks the two recesses machined on the top of the frame above the magazine housing. These small details are important to collectors of these guns.

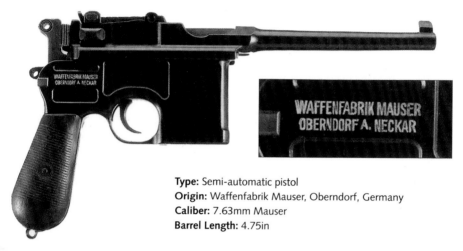

Type: Semi-automatic pistol
Origin: Waffenfabrik Mauser, Oberndorf, Germany
Caliber: 7.63mm Mauser
Barrel Length: 4.75in

Variations On The Broomhandle Theme

A number of models appeared with smooth sides, as here, but although the recesses were unnecessary from an engineering point of view they were visually preferable and were normally retained. This Model 1896 also has the large hole hammer making it subtly different from the previous entry. The unique shape of the C/96 makes it instantly recognisable. It had considerable range and stopping power and was very reliable, but was both heavy and bulky, while reloading was time-consuming.

Type: Semi-automatic pistol
Origin: Waffenfabrik Mauser,
   Oberndorf, Germany
Caliber: 7.63mm Mauser
Barrel Length: 4.75in

During World War One, some 150,000 Model 1896s were produced chambered for the 9mm Parabellum round. Other than in caliber, these were identical to the 7.63mm version, so a large figure "9" was cut into the butt and painted red. This particular weapon is one of that series, but has been reworked in the early 1920s for police use by having the barrel shortened and the rear sight removed.

This model is a cutaway version of a Model 1896 which would have been used for training purposes. Note the close-up showing clearly how the action works.

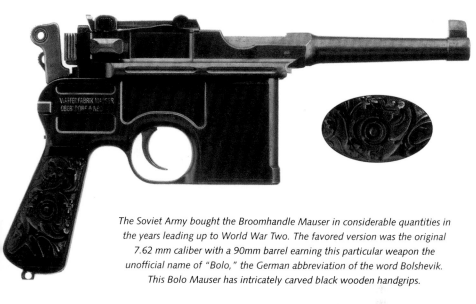

The Soviet Army bought the Broomhandle Mauser in considerable quantities in the years leading up to World War Two. The favored version was the original 7.62 mm caliber with a 90mm barrel earning this particular weapon the unofficial name of "Bolo," the German abbreviation of the word Bolshevik. This Bolo Mauser has intricately carved black wooden handgrips.

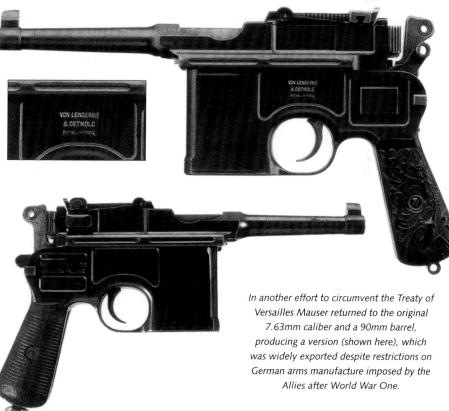

In another effort to circumvent the Treaty of Versailles Mauser returned to the original 7.63mm caliber and a 90mm barrel, producing a version (shown here), which was widely exported despite restrictions on German arms manufacture imposed by the Allies after World War One.

Mauser Model 1914

In 1914, Mauser introduced a new version of the Model 1910, slightly enlarged and chambered for the 7.65mm Auto round. The unusual shape of the slide, as shown in the picture below, led to it being referred to as "the hunchback" model. The German army ordered a large number of these pistol in 1915 and production continued well into the 1930s. We show two examples, one which comes with its own holster plus a close-up of a trigger.

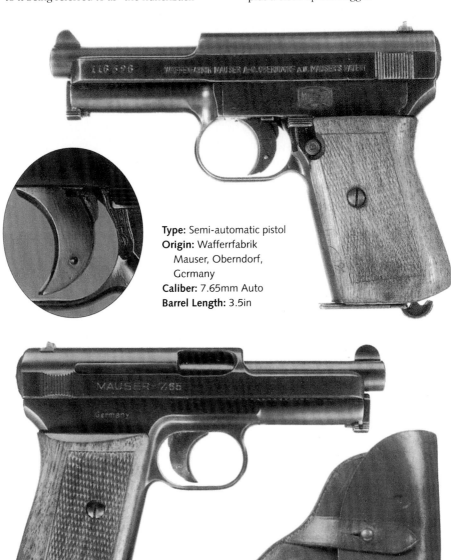

Type: Semi-automatic pistol
Origin: Wafferrfabrik Mauser, Oberndorf, Germany
Caliber: 7.65mm Auto
Barrel Length: 3.5in

Mauser Model 1910

Mauser introduced a totally new blowback pistol in 1909, chambered for the increasingly popular 9mm Parabellum round, but the weapon was not particularly successful. As a result, in the following year the company introduced a modified version chambered for the 6.35mm Auto (Browning) round, which proved much more popular, with some 60,000 being sold between 1910 and the outbreak of war in 1914. The weapon shown here bears a Portuguese marking and is in its original cardboard box.

Type: Semi-automatic
  pistol
Origin: Waffenfabrik
  Mauser, Oberndorf,
  Germany
Caliber: 6.35mm Auto
Barrel Length: 3in

Mauser Model 1934

With increasing aggression building inside Germany and a more martial state developing the demand for handguns grew in the 1930s. The Mauser Model 34 was essentially a tidied-up version of the M1914 to cater for that market, the most noticeable changes being a somewhat more fully shaped grip and a polished nickel finish. This gun bears the motif of the Reich's eagle holding a Swastika on the side of the frame above the right hand grip.

Type: Semi-automatic pistol
Origin: Waffenfabrik Mauser,
  Oberndorf, Germany
Caliber: 7.65mm Auto
Barrel Length: 3.4in

Mauser "byf 42" (Walther P.38)

The enormous wartime expansion of the German armed forces was accompanied by a massive demand for weapons. One consequence was that Mauser undertook production of the Walther P.38, with the first weapons leaving the factory in mid-1942. This is one of those, as proved by the marking "byf 42" the Mauser production code accompanied by the last two digits of the calendar year. The mark can be seen to the right of the "P38" on the body of the weapon.

Type: Semi-automatic pistol
Origin: Waffenfabrik Mauser,
   Oberndorf, Germany
Caliber: 9mm Parabellum
Barrel Length: 5in

Mauser "byf 44" (Walther P.38)

Produced in 1944, this P.38 can only be distinguished from a Walther-built version by the code "byf 44" stamped onto the body. This being the factory code for Mauser. The gun has a brown finish rather than the more usual black.

This particular weapon appears to have been initially issued to the police, but it was in military use when captured by Gerard P. Finn of Springfield, Virginia during the Battle of the Bulge in the Ardennes, Belgium in late 1944.

Type: Semi-automatic pistol
Origin: Waffenfabrik Mauser,
   Oberndorf, Germany
Caliber: 9mm Parabellum
Barrel Length: 5in

Mauser WTP

The Westentaschenpistole (waistcoat pocket pistol or WTP) was designed following the end of World War One and entered production in 1921. It was a blowback design, carried six 6.35mm rounds, weighed 10.6 ounces and was a mere 4.0 in long. The Model 2, with improvements appeared in 1938. The easiest way to tell the difference is by looking at the grips. The Model 1 (shown here) has wrap around grips that don't go all the way up to the slide, and the Model 2 has separate grips on each side and go up to the slide.

Type: Semi-automatic pistol
Origin: Waffenfabrik Mauser, Oberndorf, Germany
Caliber: 6.35mm Auto
Barrel Length: 2.4in

Mauser 9mm Nickl Experimental

Josef Nickl, an Austrian, worked in the production department of the Mauser factory from about 1912 to 1921, when he moved to Czechoslovakia. Apart from being a production engineer, he was also interested in design, and small number of pistols of his design was produced between 1916 and 1917. This weapon was designed around the 9mm Kurz (Luger) round and featured a rotating barrel and a locked-breech mechanism on a Mauser Model 1912/14 frame. The gun was later produced in Czechoslovakia as the VZ22.

Type: Semi-automatic pistol
Origin: Waffenfabrik Mauser,
Oberndorf, Germany
Caliber: 9mm Parabellum
Barrel Length: 3.44in

Mauser HSc

Faced in the 1930s with increasing competition in 7.65mm caliber weapons from the Walther PP and PPK, Mauser developed a new weapon designated the Seblstspannerpistole mit Hahn (self-cocking pistol with hammer). When however, it appeared that this might infringe some Walther patents, the design was completely recast to produce the Hahnlos, Selbstladung Pistole Modellee a (hammerless, self-loading pistol, model a, or HSa). Initial trials led to modifications, resulting in the HSb, but yet further modifications were found necessary and the HSc finally entered production in 1940. Some 250,000 had been produced by May 1945.

Type: Semi-automatic pistol
Origin: Waffenfabrik Mauser,
  Oberndorf, Germany
Caliber: 7.65mm Auto
Barrel Length: 3.4in

Menz Model II

Menz introduced a new small, blowback pistol in 1920, named, appropriately, the Lilliput. It was chambered for the unusual caliber of 4.25mm and although it proved a popular weapon Menz offered a 6.25mm Auto version in 1925, followed by a few in 7.65mm Auto. This more powerful round may have proved too much for the design, as the company then marketed a new, slightly larger version of the weapon chambered for the 6.35mm Auto, designated the Model II (seen here), with the caliber carefully marked in red on the grip.

Type: Semi-automatic pistol
Origin: Waffenfabrik August Menz
  Suhl, Germany
Caliber: 7.65mm auto
Barrel Length: 2in

Mauser Prototype 0.45 Self-Loading Pistol

The completion details of this pistol are beyond doubt, as it is clearly stamped with the company's name "WAFFENFABRIK MAUSER A.G. OBERNDORF a.N" and "KONSTRUKTIONSDATUM 17:2:1915." Meaning that the date of manufacture is February 17, 1915. Other than that, however, its history is somewhat obscure. It is known that Mauser produced a small number of prototype .45in caliber pistols in the years prior to World War One with the aim of breaking into the American market, at least one of which was tested (and rejected) by the US army.

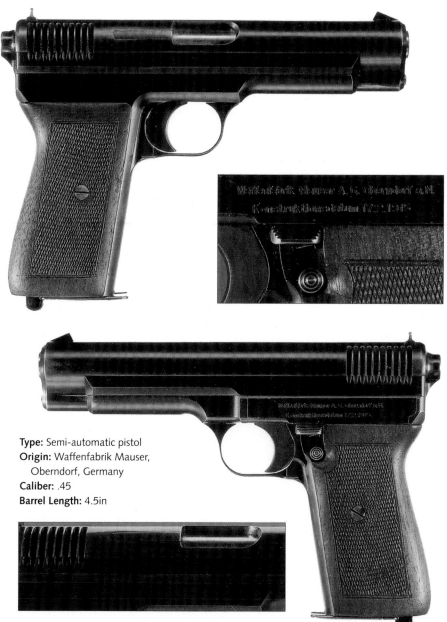

Type: Semi-automatic pistol
Origin: Waffenfabrik Mauser, Oberndorf, Germany
Caliber: .45
Barrel Length: 4.5in

Ortgies Semi-Automatic Pocket Pistol

Heinrich Ortgies returned to his native Germany in 1918 armed only with a patent for a new design of semi-automatic, blowback-operated pistol. Despite the depressed conditions in post-war Germany, he managed to put this into production and enjoyed such success that he was bought out by Deutsche Werke in 1921. The Ortgies pistol weighed some 22.6 ounces and had an eight-round box magazine housed in the butt. As produced by Ortgies, the pistol was available or in 7.65mm caliber, but Deutsche Werke introdu further models in 6.35mm and 9mm Short.

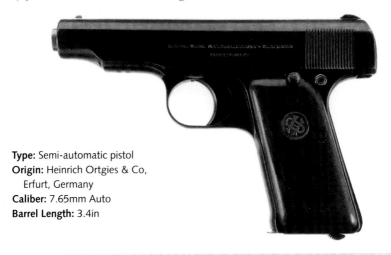

Type: Semi-automatic pistol
Origin: Heinrich Ortgies & Co,
    Erfurt, Germany
Caliber: 7.65mm Auto
Barrel Length: 3.4in

Rheinmetall Prototype 9mm

The Rheinische Metalwaren und Maschinenfabrik (Rhine Metalware and Machine Factory, or Rheinmetall) made several attempts in the 1920s and 1930s to develop a 9mm pistol for the rapidly expanding German armed forces. The first was an adaptation of the Dreyse 7.65mm described in the previous entry, but rechambered for 9mm, while the second was the totally new design shown here. This examplⅇ is finished to a very high standard but has no serial number or proof marks, suggesting that it was a prototype. No order was ever received.

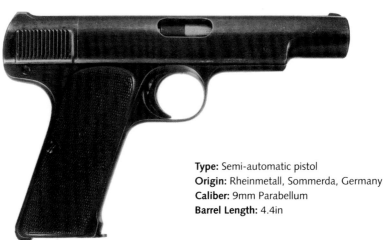

Type: Semi-automatic pistol
Origin: Rheinmetall, Sommerda, Germany
Caliber: 9mm Parabellum
Barrel Length: 4.4in

Sauer Model 1930

The Sauer company produced firearms from 1751, but only became involved in pistols in 1900, producing various models under license. This led to their own design, the Sauer Model 1913, a 7.65mm weapon of which some 100,000 were manufactured. The company then developed the Model 1930, which was essentially a product-improved Model 1913, with detailed modifications resulting from some twenty years' service. This is the Behorden-Modelle (official model), developed for the police market. Production of all versions of the Model 1930 ended in 1937. This picture shows a duralumin-framed version of the weapon.

Type: Semi-automatic pistol
Origin: J. P. Sauer & Sohn,
   Erfurt and Eckenforde,
   Germany
Caliber: 7.65mm auto
Barrel Length: 5in

Sauer Model 38-H

Sauer had major success in the late 1930s with the Model 38 and the later Model 38-H. Both Model 38 and 38-H were excellent handguns, being well made, reliable and accurate. There were five variations in the design, partly resulting from improvements, but also due to the war, as increasing shortages of time and materiel meant that the standard of finish became lower. The gun shown is a standard Model 38-H in blue finish, with black plastic grips.

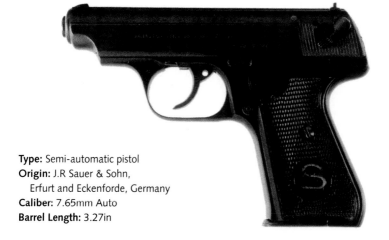

Type: Semi-automatic pistol
Origin: J.R Sauer & Sohn,
   Erfurt and Eckenforde, Germany
Caliber: 7.65mm Auto
Barrel Length: 3.27in

Walther Waffenfabrik

Carl Walther founded his Waffenfabrik in Zella-Mehlis in Thuringia in 1886 and for many years concentrated on designing and producing sporting guns. By the start of the twentieth century he was being assisted by his three sons and in 1907 the eldest, Fritz, designed their first handgun, a 6.35mm blowback, subsequently designated the Model 1. It was the improved Model 2 that made the company's name and the numbered series then continued until the Model 9, which was introduced in 1921. Thereafter, the models were given names rather than numbers, such as the most famous of the company's products, the PP (Polizei Pistole) and the PPK.

In 1931 when the model PP was the main production weapon, Walther introduced a pocket version. The gun was the same as the PP except that the barrel had been shortened. The internal mechanism was the same, however the parts that were affected by size were of course different. The most significant change was in the frame. The total length of the PPK is 155 mm. The magazine holds one less cartridge. The barrel has six clockwise riflings. The firm then came up with the model designation PPK or "Polizei Pistole Kriminal." The name symbolized that it was to be used for covert undercover police work, designed specifically for police use. This gun found fame as fictional Secret Agent James Bond's issued weapon.

The PPK was highly praised because of its compactness and reliability as well as the unique signal pin indicating that the gun was either loaded or unloaded. It protrudes from the rear of the slide when the chamber is loaded. This was followed by the Pistole 1938 (P.38), which was produced in vast numbers between 1939 and 1945. The company's original base having been swallowed up in Communist East Germany, Walther established itself anew in Ulm in West Germany and a hundred and twenty years after its foundation it is still in business.

Walther Model 1

This tiny pistol had an overall length of 4.5 inches and weighed 13 ounces with a magazine. It was put on the market in 1910 and was produced in two versions. In the first, the slide release catch was in front of the trigger-guard (as seen here) and in the second, introduced in 1912, it was moved to the right side of the frame.

Type: Semi-automatic pistol
Origin: Carl Walther, Zella-Mehlis, Germany
Caliber: 6.35mm
Barrel Length: 2in

Walther Model 3

The Model 1 was followed by the Model 2, which was a simplified version of the first design, with a full-length slide. The Model 3, seen here, followed this in 1913. It was enlarged to accommodate the 7.65mm cartridge. One surprising, and unwelcome, characteristic was that the ejection port was on the left side of the weapon, which meant that, for a right-handed firer, the empty cartridge case flew across the firer's face.

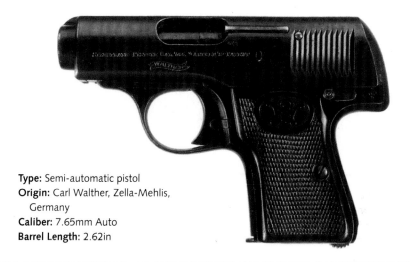

Type: Semi-automatic pistol
Origin: Carl Walther, Zella-Mehlis,
    Germany
Caliber: 7.65mm Auto
Barrel Length: 2.62in

Walther Model 4

Models 1 through 3 had a six-round magazine, but in the Model 4 this was increased to eight, necessitating a slightly longer butt. In addition, the barrel was lengthened, as was the slide, although the left-side ejection slot was retained. This model was ordered in large numbers which were delivered between 1915 and 1918, with production continuing, albeit at a slower pace until1923.

Type: Semi-automatic pistol
Origin: Carl Walther, Zella-Mehlis,
    Germany
Caliber: 7.65mm auto
Barrel Length: 3.35in

Walther Model 5

The Model 5 was not a successor to the Model 4, but a product-improved Model 2, firing the same 6.35mm round. It had six, as opposed to two, rifling grooves, and a fixed-notch rear sight, and was manufactured to higher tolerances. The actual weapon shown here is heavily engraved in an oak leaf pattern, with the name "H. PAULI" appearing on the left side.

Type: Semi-automatic pistol
Origin: Carl Walther, Zella-Mehlis, Germany
Caliber: 6.35mm Auto
Barrel Length: 2in

Walther Model 6

This seems to have been the Walther factory's first attempt at a military pistol and was, in effect, an enlarged Model 4, chambered for the 9mm Parabellum round, and with the ejection slot moved to the right side. In the event, the 9mm round proved to be rather too powerful for the gun and the design was not accepted by the German armed forces. Some 1,000 were produced between 1916 and 1917.

Type: Semi-automatic pistol
Origin: Carl Walther, Zella-Mehlis, Germany
Caliber: 9mm Parabellum
Barrel Length: 4.7in

Walther Model 7

The Walther Model 7 is a smaller version of the Model 6. It was manufactured for only a twelve-month period during 1917 and 1918. This pistol is chambered in 6.35 caliber and was popular with German officers during World War One. They had to buy them at their own expense because it was not an official military procurement. It is also a blowback single-action design with a concealed hammer. This pistol ejects cartridges to the right and features the bottom magazine release.

Type: Semi-automatic pistol
Origin: Carl Walther, Zella-Mehlis, Germany
Caliber: 6.35mm Auto
Barrel Length: 3in

Walther Model 8

The Model 8 was Walther's first post-war pistol and its popularity can be gauged by the fact that some 250,000 were sold. Production began in 1920 and ended in 1943. It had a longer butt to house an eight-round magazine and an unusual feature was that the trigger guard served also as the stripping catch. Although the vast majority of those produced were in the conventional dull black finish, there were, as usual, some presentation models, such as the example seen here, with its elaborate engravings and ivory grips.

Type: Semi-automatic pistol
Origin: Carl Walther, Zella-Mehlis, Germany
Caliber: 6.35mm auto
Barrel Length: 2.5in

Walther Model 9

The Model 9, was a small blowback pocket pistol chambered for the 6.35mm auto cartridge. Essentially, it was an updated version of the Walther Model 1. As in the Model 1, the top of the slide is cut away to expose the full length of the barrel. The Model 9 had a cocking indicator pin that protrudes from the rear of the slide when the gun is cocked. The Model 9 was approximately four inches long and weighed 9.5 ounces. The magazine capacity was six rounds.

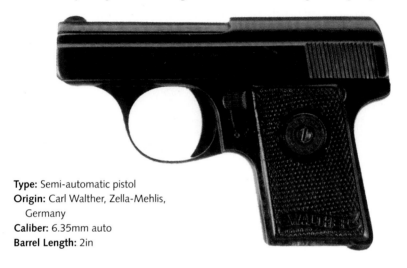

Type: Semi-automatic pistol
Origin: Carl Walther, Zella-Mehlis,
    Germany
Caliber: 6.35mm auto
Barrel Length: 2in

Walther Model 1925 Sport

The Model 1925 Sport used Model 6 frames left over from the war, combined with a new and longer barrel, chambered for the .22 round. This particular example has serial number "1004" and may have been a prototype. Note the three-position change-lever on the left of the gun, which allows the shooter to select safe, breech open or single shot modes.

Type: Semi-automatic pistol
Origin: Carl Walther, Zella-Mehlis, Germany
Caliber: .22
Barrel Length: 7.5in

Walther Model 1936 Olympia

A German competitor won a silver medal at the 1932 Los Angeles Olympics using the Model 1926 pistol, so the Walther factory produced an improved version for the 1936 Berlin Olympics. There were various barrel lengths and chambering for either .22LF or .22 Short depending upon the competition, weights could be added to improve balance, and all had ten round magazines, except for the Modern Pentathlon weapon which carried six. The Swedish company Hammerli reintroduced the gun in the 1950s.

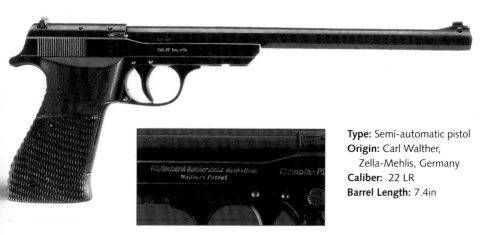

Type: Semi-automatic pistol
Origin: Carl Walther,
    Zella-Mehlis, Germany
Caliber: 22 LR
Barrel Length: 7.4in

Walther Grip Safety Experimental

This experimental model appears to have been part of the development path from the Model 8 which led to the PP. It is slightly larger than the Model 8 and is much the same size as the future Model PP, but its features are quite different. There is no serial number, nor are there any proof marks, indicating that it never left the factory, before being captured in 1945 when advancing US army units overran the Walther factory.

Type: Semi-automatic pistol
Origin: Carl Walther, Zella-Mehlis, Germany
Caliber: 7.65mm
Barrel Length: 3.5in

165

Walther PP

Walther's next pistol design, known as the PP or Polizei Pistole (police pistol) was aimed squarely at police and paramilitary requirements, and turned out to be a spectacular commercial and operational success. From its introduction in 1929, it was taken up by several European police forces, and was also adopted as the standard service pistol by the Luftwaffe. It is a neat, smooth pistol, it included a number of safety features, and was the first truly successful automatic pistol to use a double-action mechanism combined with external hammer.

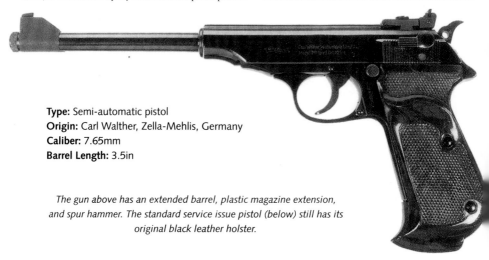

Type: Semi-automatic pistol
Origin: Carl Walther, Zella-Mehlis, Germany
Caliber: 7.65mm
Barrel Length: 3.5in

The gun above has an extended barrel, plastic magazine extension, and spur hammer. The standard service issue pistol (below) still has its original black leather holster.

Most PPs held eight rounds of 7.65mm ammunition, but there were also small numbers made in 6.35mm, .22LR, and 9mm Short. Some pistols also had a plastic extension on the bottom of the magazine to give a slightly better grip.

Walther PPK

In 1931 Walther introduced this smaller version of the PP, known as the PPK, or Polizei Pistole, Kriminal Polizei (police pistol, criminal police). Its overall length was 5.8 inches and it was a compact, yet reasonably powerful weapon, intended for concealed carriage by plain-clothes or undercover police officers. The combination of small size, reasonable firepower and the ability to quickly draw and shoot made the PPK an instant hit, and it was sold to many police forces around the world.

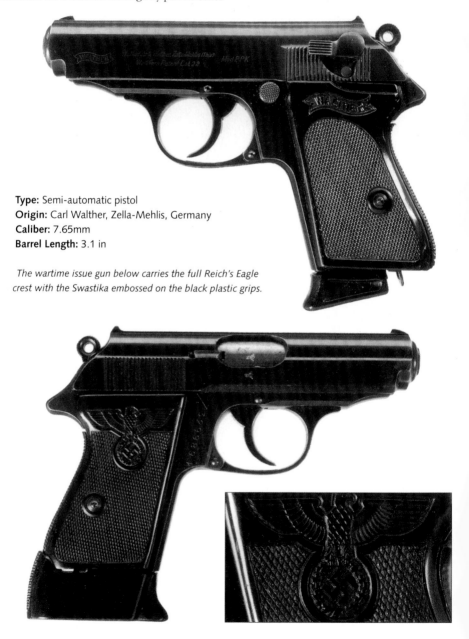

Type: Semi-automatic pistol
Origin: Carl Walther, Zella-Mehlis, Germany
Caliber: 7.65mm
Barrel Length: 3.1 in

The wartime issue gun below carries the full Reich's Eagle crest with the Swastika embossed on the black plastic grips.

*Another wartime issue with black plastic Walther branded grips,
this time stamped with the Reich Eagle on the frame. The top gun
with brown plastic grips has its original brown leather holster.*

Walther PPK Rarities

The top gun has the letters "DRP" (Deutsche Reich Pistol, or German state pistol) stamped on the left side of the frame. It may have been issued to the German Post Office. Shown below is a PPK that was made for the Deutsche Reichsbank (German State Bank or DRB). This came complete with a shoulder/waist holster.

The grips and finger extension on the magazine are made of brown, mottled plastic, while the weapon itself has the normal black satin finish. Quite why employees of the DRB needed such weapons is not clear, but they may have been for self-protection of special investigators.

Type: Semi-automatic pistol
Origin: Carl Walther, Zella-Mehlis, Germany
Caliber: 7.65mm
Barrel Length: 3.1 in

Walther Armee-Pistole (AP)

As always with automatics, military contracts were the key to real success, and in 1936, Walther produced the totally new Armee-Pistole, of which perhaps a hundred were made, that shown here being the forty-eighth in the series. It had a lightweight duralumin frame and the top of the frame was open, enabling the breech end of the barrel to be seen. The weapon had an internal hammer and this was one particular feature that the Germany army singled out for adverse comment.

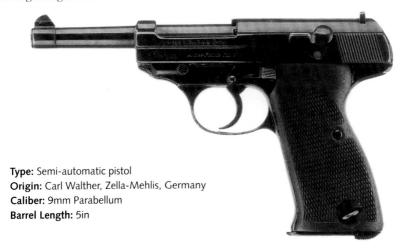

Type: Semi-automatic pistol
Origin: Carl Walther, Zella-Mehlis, Germany
Caliber: 9mm Parabellum
Barrel Length: 5in

Walther Model Heeres-Pistole (HP)

Walther's next effort to win army approval was the Model HP (Heeres-Pistole, or army pistol) of 1937, which sought to correct the problems with the Model AP, being fitted with a revised slide and an external hammer. After careful examination, the German Army requested certain minor modifications, which resulted in the famous P.38. The Model HP was also offered on the civilian market chambered for 7.65mm, 9mm Parabellum, .38 Super Auto, and .45 ACP. However, the model shown here is a military version marked with the German army acceptance stamp.

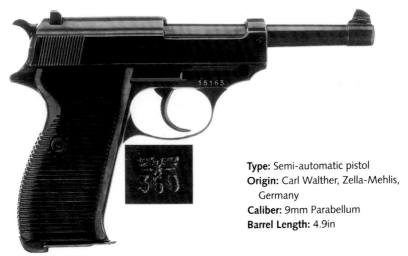

Type: Semi-automatic pistol
Origin: Carl Walther, Zella-Mehlis,
Germany
Caliber: 9mm Parabellum
Barrel Length: 4.9in

Walther P.38

Walther's efforts finally paid off when this pistol was adopted by the German army as a replacement for the Luger P.08. It began entering service from 1938 onwards, although it never fully replaced the Luger during World War Two. The P.38 used a similar double-action mechanism to that employed by the PP, allowing the user to safely carry the pistol with a round in the breech. A safety catch at the back of the slide locked the firing pin before dropping the hammer into an uncocked position.

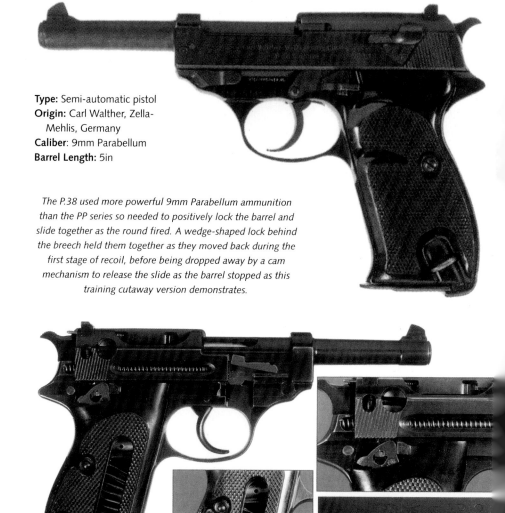

Type: Semi-automatic pistol
Origin: Carl Walther, Zella-
 Mehlis, Germany
Caliber: 9mm Parabellum
Barrel Length: 5in

The P.38 used more powerful 9mm Parabellum ammunition than the PP series so needed to positively lock the barrel and slide together as the round fired. A wedge-shaped lock behind the breech held them together as they moved back during the first stage of recoil, before being dropped away by a cam mechanism to release the slide as the barrel stopped as this training cutaway version demonstrates.

Two views of the P.38 with a different grip pattern to the ones on the previous page, which have black plastic checkered grips. This gun has brown plastic grips with horizontal bars, which are more common. The detail of the markings with the "ac" code shows that this example was made at the Walther factory. The P.38 was also made by Mauser, FN in occupied Belgium, Waffenwerke Brunn and Cseska Zbrovoka in Czechoslovakia.

Walther 9mm Ultra

The German World War Two 9mm Ultra project was an attempt to develop the most powerful cartridge that could be used with a simple blowback mechanism. The most powerful round the unlocked PP series could handle was the 9mm Short while the Parabellum pistols such as the P.38 all needed some sort of locking arrangement. The Ultra round involved using the projectile from the 9mm Parabellum system, but mounted in a shorter straight-sided case. The Genschow Company manufactured the cartridge and Walther designed this pistol to use them.

Type: Semi-automatic pistol
Origin: Carl Walther, Zella-Mehlis, Germany
Caliber: 9 x 18mm Ultra
Barrel Length: 5in

Walther P1

When West Germany entered NATO in 1955 and began to build-up its new army, the latter adopted the P.38 as its standard handgun. A new Walther factory had been established at Ulm and this rapidly tooled-up, with production starting in 1957. The weapon, which incorporated minor changes from the wartime P.38, was re-designated the Pistole 1 (PI) in 1963. The weapon has also been sold on the civil market, chambered for, 7.65mm and 9mm, and (with a revised blowback system) for .22LR rimfire.

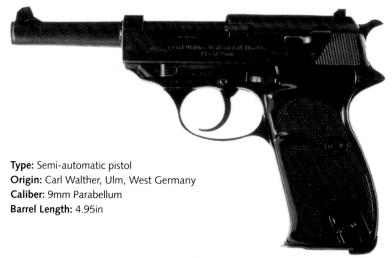

Type: Semi-automatic pistol
Origin: Carl Walther, Ulm, West Germany
Caliber: 9mm Parabellum
Barrel Length: 4.95in

Makarov Pistol

The former German Democratic Republic, or GDR (generally known as "East Germany") was totally under the thumb of the former Soviet Union. The GDR took over the former arms factories at Suhl in Thuringia in the late 1940s and designated them a Volkeigener Betrieb (VEB; or "people-owned factory"), named after an obscure Communist "hero," Ernst Thaelmann. This factory undertook licensed production of various Soviet-designed weapons, one of which was the Makarov pistol, an example of which is shown here.

Type: Semi-automatic pistol
Origin: Ernst Thaelmann VEB,
   Suhl, East Germany
Caliber: 9 x 18mm
Barrel Length: 3.75in

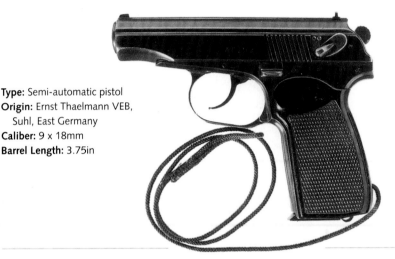

Fegyvergyar Model 29M

The Model 29M (Pisztoly 29 Minta; pistol, model 29) was a revised and updated version of the General Manager of Fegyvergyar, Rudolph Frommer's "Baby" and "Stop" pistols chambered to take the 9mm Short cartridge. It weighed 26 ounces (with a magazine but without ammunition) and was six-and-a-half-inches long. It was immediately accepted as the standard pistol for the Hungarian army and was a success for the company, with some 50,000 being manufactured between 1929 and 1935.

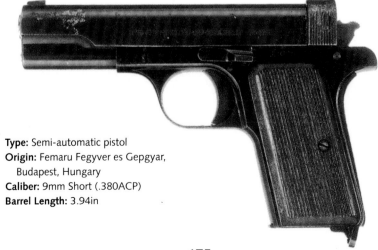

Type: Semi-automatic pistol
Origin: Femaru Fegyver es Gepgyar,
   Budapest, Hungary
Caliber: 9mm Short (.380ACP)
Barrel Length: 3.94in

Fegyvergyar Model 37M

Frommer died in 1936 and his last design appeared a year later as the Model 37M. This was, essentially, a mechanically simpler version of the Model 29M, intended to be easier and cheaper to produce and maintain. This was produced initially for the Hungarian army, but in 1941 the German placed an order for 50,000 (later increased to 90,000) for the Luftwaffe, most of which were issued to aircrew. These weapons were officially designated Pistole M.37 Kaliber 7.65mm.

Type: Semi-automatic pistol
Origin: Femaru Fegyver es Gepgyar, Budapest, Hungary
Caliber: 7.65mm Auto
Barrel Length: 4.3in

The detail shows the factory markings: the FEG code "jhv" and date, along with the usual "waffenamt" German inspector's markings.

Fegyvergyar PJK-9HP

In the post-World War Two era, the Hungarian FEG manufactured the Model PJK-9HP, which was a Browning Hi-Power clone. It was a well-regarded weapon, being made to a high engineering standard.

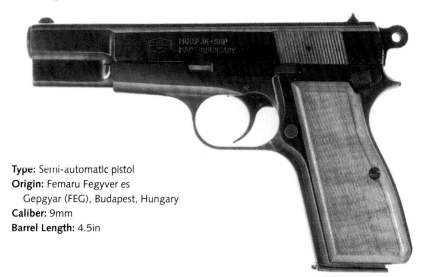

Type: Semi-automatic pistol
Origin: Femaru Fegyver es Gepgyar (FEG), Budapest, Hungary
Caliber: 9mm
Barrel Length: 4.5in

Beretta

Fabbrica D' Armi Pietro Beretta S.p.A., maker of James Bond's trusty .25 caliber Beretta pistol, is one of the oldest manufacturing firms in the world. A single family has controlled the company throughout its history. The home of Fabbrica D'Armi Pietro Beretta S.p.A. is the village of Gardone, in the center of the northern Italian valley known as Val Trompia. Iron ore in the hills of northern Italy made the area an iron-working center from the Middle Ages. Bartolomeo Beretta was born in 1490. The earliest documentary evidence of his forge is a contract from the Doges of Venice, dated October 3, 1526, for 185 "arquebus" barrels. The arquebus was a type of musket so heavy it had to be propped up with supports. Beretta's first product was quite a contrast to the handguns for which it later became known.

The sons and grandsons of Bartolomeo also carried on the business and by 1698, the Berettas were the second largest barrel producer among thirty-three in Gardone, making 2,883 barrels, mostly destined for long arms. Whereas much of the company's previous history had been dominated by military production, in the 1850s Giuseppe Beretta focused the factory on producing fine sporting guns. The company was making at most three hundred guns a year through 1860. Twenty years later, annual production had increased to as many as 8,000 guns a year. Beretta was also marketing, via their catalog, guns made by other manufacturers, including Colt, Remington, Smith & Wesson, and Winchester. Beretta began making military firearms once more after the unification of Italy in 1861. Their first self-loading pistol was the Model 1915, made for the Italian army in World War One. It was a simple unlocked blowback design chambered for 7.65mm or 9mm Short. The Model 1934 is a well-made and reliable arm that served as the standard Italian military pistol through World War Two. In 1985, Beretta won a hotly contested bid to replace the Colt .45 in the US arsenal. However, sporting arms comprise about three-quarters of Beretta's production; most of these are exported.

Beretta Model 1934

This Model 1934 is a direct descendant of the Model 15, chambered for the 9mm Short round, and with an external hammer, which can be manually cocked. It remains an unlocked blowback type, and is a well-made and reliable arm, which served as the standard Italian military pistol through World War Two. A small and compact weapon, many Model 1934s had spur extensions under their magazines to give a slightly longer grip area for users with large hands.

Type: Semi-automatic pistol
Origin: Armi Beretta SpA,
   Brescia, Italy
Caliber: 9mm Short (.380 ACP)
Barrel Length: 3.75in

One feature is that when the magazine is emptied, the magazine follower blocks the slide and holds it open as an indicator to the user. This means that the user has to pull the slide back before releasing the empty magazine, an awkward and time-consuming action, especially if under fire.

Beretta Model 1935

A year after the introduction of the Model 1934, Beretta released a similar pistol but this time it was chambered for the less powerful 7.65mm round, It was taken up by the Italian navy, air force, and police. The gun is identical in appearance to the previous Model.

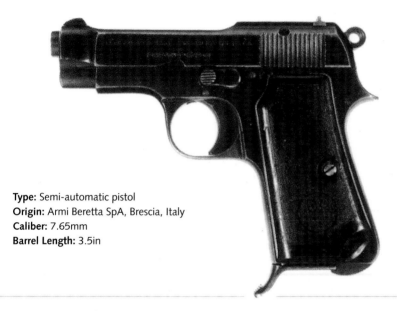

Type: Semi-automatic pistol
Origin: Armi Beretta SpA, Brescia, Italy
Caliber: 7.65mm
Barrel Length: 3.5in

Beretta Model 70

The Model 70 design could be traced back via the Model 948 to the Model 1934, with minor changes to the safety and holding-open device. The styling of the pistol is more rakish with a more angled grip and trigger guard flowed in to the bottom of the barrel. The basic model was chambered for the 7.65mm cartridge, but variants included the Model 70S, which had a magazine safety and was produced in .22LR, 7.65mm Auto (as seen here) and 9mm Short versions.

Type: Semi-automatic pistol
Origin: Armi Beretta SpA, Brescia, Italy
Caliber: 9mm Short (.380 ACP)
Barrel Length: 3.5in

Beretta Model 92/92S

The Model 1951 was the first Beretta pistol to use a breech locking mechanism to handle the 9mm Parabellum cartridge. The Model 92 was introduced in 1976, and was a further development of this pistol, with a larger butt to hold a fifteen-shot magazine. It also used a double-action mechanism, allowing the user to fire without having to cock the hammer first. The Model 92S introduced some further safety features, and had the safety catch moved from the frame to the slide.

Type: Semi-automatic pistol
Origin: Armi Beretta SpA, Brescia, Italy
Caliber: 9mm Parabellum
Barrel Length: 4.3in

By 1980, the US army had accepted that the long-serving Colt M1911A1 had reached the end of its service life, and trials were undertaken to find a replacement. Beretta put the slightly modified Model 92SB forward and it eventually won the trials, seeing off tough competition from a range of homegrown and international products.

Beretta Model 75

The Beretta Jaguar .22 pistol was introduced into the US market in the mid-1950s and was available with two different barrel lengths. The parallel versions for the European market were designated the Models 72 through to 75, the actual designation depending on the length of the barrel. The weapon seen here, the Model 75, had a 4.2-inch barrel.

Type: Semi-automatic pistol
Origin: Armi Beretta SpA, Brescia, Italy
Caliber: .22LR
Barrel Length: 4.2in

Beretta Model 92F

Despite its success in the US armed forces' competition, the US authorities required some minor changes to the Model 92SB before it was put into production. This resulted in the Model 92F, which was designated M9 in US service. Selection of the M9 was not without controversy, as some serving personnel felt that the 9mm Parabellum wasn't sufficiently powerful compared to the well-liked .45 of the Colt. However, the M9 has now seen hard service in large quantities, and has proven to be an effective military pistol in both American and other hands.

Type: Semi-automatic pistol
Origin: Armi Beretta SpA, Brescia, Italy
Caliber: 9mm
Barrel Length: 4.3in

Beretta Model 80

The Beretta Cheetah, also known with its original model name of "Series 80," is a line of compact blowback operated semi-aut014c pistols. They were introduced in 1976 and include models in .32 ACP, .380 ACP, and 9mm Short (Models 84, 85 and 86) and .22 LR (Model 87).There are two distinct 87 models both chambered for .22LR. The standard model (introduced in 1986) is similar to other models, but the 87 Target (shown here), which was introduced in 2000, has a longer barrel and a slide that can accept optical sights. It is single-acion only.

Type: Semi-automatic pistol
Origin: Armi Beretta SpA, Brescia, Italy
Caliber: .22
Barrel Length: 5.9in

Beretta 92 FS

The FS (shown here) is pretty much the state of the art gun due to the modifications that have been made, based on its use in action. It has an enlarged hammer pin that fits into a groove on the underside of the slide. The main purpose of this is to retard the slide from flying off the frame to the rear if it cracks. This was in additon to modifications already made such as making all parts one hundred percent interchangeable, modifying the grip and forward trigger guard for easier aiming, and hard chroming the barrel bore to reduce wear.

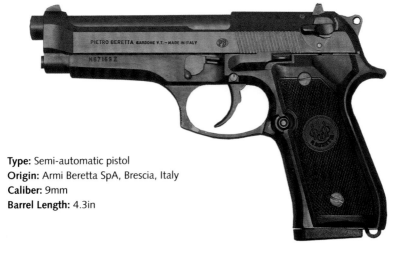

Type: Semi-automatic pistol
Origin: Armi Beretta SpA, Brescia, Italy
Caliber: 9mm
Barrel Length: 4.3in

Bernardelli Baby Pocket Pistol

This was one of a series of small semi-automatic pistols produced by Bernardelli. Bernardelli was another famous Italian gun maker from Gardone in the Val Trompia. Between 1945 and 1968, they produced weapons under the designation "Baby." Versions were produced chambered for 6.35mm (.25 ACP), 7.65mm, and .22in cartridges and the magazine normally held five rounds, although an extended butt version accommodating eight rounds was also produced.

Type: Semi-automatic pistol
Origin: VIncenzo Bernardelli,
Gardone Val Trompia, Italy
Caliber: .25 ACP
Barrel Length: 2in

Nambu 4th Year Pistol 9mm Type A

Colonel Kirijo Nambu designed this pistol, the first Japanese semi-automatic to be produced. Known as the Model 04 it bears a visual resemblance to the P.08 Luger, although there is no design commonality whatsoever. Adopted by the Japanese navy in 1909, the Model 04 was never adopted in quantity by the Japanese army. Commercial sales were few, as were independent sales to military officers. It was a rather cumbersome, fragile, unreliable piece, and within the context of Japanese industry at the time, expensive to make.

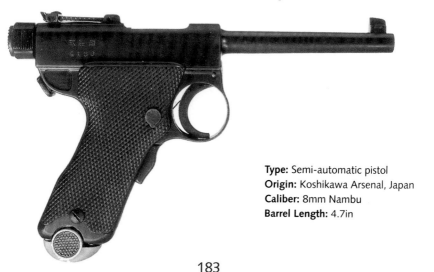

Type: Semi-automatic pistol
Origin: Koshikawa Arsenal, Japan
Caliber: 8mm Nambu
Barrel Length: 4.7in

Nambu 4th Year Pistol 7mm Type B

In an attempt to overcome customer resistance to the larger Model 04, Nambu redesigned it to produce this smaller pistol chambered for his newly developed 7mm cartridge. Also know as the "Baby Nambu," it remained more expensive than contemporary western types, and was still less reliable than most of them. It did not prove any more of a success than the Type A and only a few thousand were made.

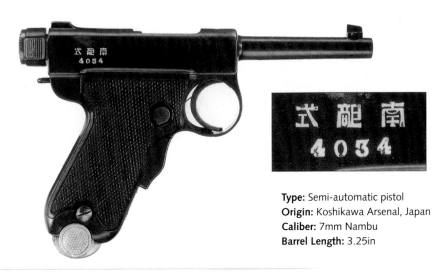

Type: Semi-automatic pistol
Origin: Koshikawa Arsenal, Japan
Caliber: 7mm Nambu
Barrel Length: 3.25in

Nambu 14th Year Pistol

Introduced in 1925, this was an attempt to improve the Model 04 by simplifying the design. The grip safety was removed and replaced by an awkward safety catch. The magazine hold open device was retained, and combined with the strong recoil springs made it very difficult to remove an empty magazine in a hurry. It saw extensive service in Manchuria and in World War Two, and one of the results of combat experience was an early modification to enlarge the trigger guard to enable users to wear winter gloves.

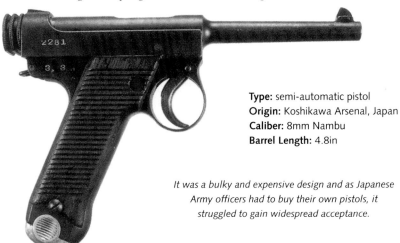

Type: semi-automatic pistol
Origin: Koshikawa Arsenal, Japan
Caliber: 8mm Nambu
Barrel Length: 4.8in

It was a bulky and expensive design and as Japanese Army officers had to buy their own pistols, it struggled to gain widespread acceptance.

Nambu Type 94

In 1926, Nambu designed a cheaper, simpler automatic for military use. The basic design was already flawed, but was made worse by interference from the ordnance department. The final pistol ended up more expensive than its predecessors, and unsafe for its users. It was possible to fire a round before the breech was properly closed, and an exposed sear made all too easy to fire accidentally with an accidental impact. These characteristics were made worse by the poor workmanship and material in late-war production.

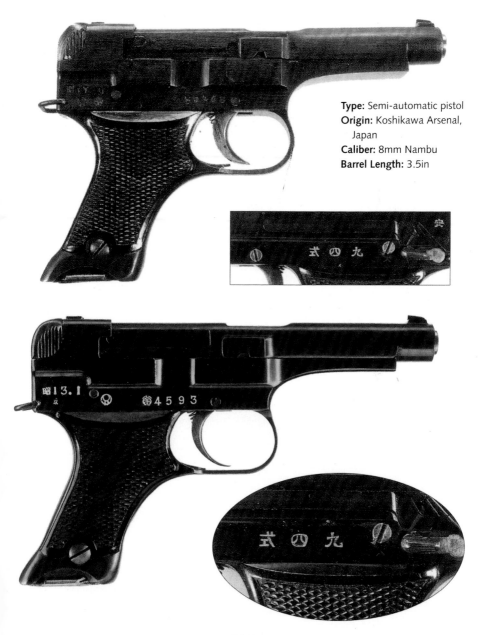

Type: Semi-automatic pistol
Origin: Koshikawa Arsenal, Japan
Caliber: 8mm Nambu
Barrel Length: 3.5in

Obregon 0.45

The Mexican Army used the Colt M1911A1, but in the early 1930s, the government encouraged the development of this weapon. At first sight, it certainly looks like yet another M1911A1 clone. It is, however, a different weapon, which was designed by a Mexican, Alejandro Obregon, for use by his country's armed forces. The "Obregon system" involved a rotating bolt, which moved through some seventeen degrees before unlocking. Only a thousand weapons completed between 1934 and 1938 were then sold on the civil market, making the example shown here very rare.

Type: Semi-automatic pistol
Origin: Fabrica Nacional de Armas
  Mexicanos, Mexico City,
  Mexico.
Caliber: .45 ACP
Barrel Length: 5.0in

Radom Vis-35

This Polish weapon appeared in 1935, and like many, if not most, other automatic pistols, it owed a lot to the designs of John M. Browning. One of the differences was the addition of a grip safety, and a decocking lever on the slide, which allowed the user to safely carry the pistol with a round in the chamber. Manually cocking the hammer was all that was needed to get the pistol ready for action.

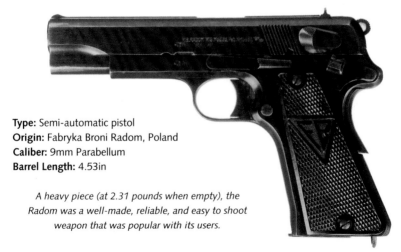

Type: Semi-automatic pistol
Origin: Fabryka Broni Radom, Poland
Caliber: 9mm Parabellum
Barrel Length: 4.53in

A heavy piece (at 2.31 pounds when empty), the Radom was a well-made, reliable, and easy to shoot weapon that was popular with its users.

During the German occupation of Poland, the gun was
made for German forces as the Pistole 35(p), although
these examples have much cruder finish and a
simplified safety system. The Polish eagle engraved on
the slide can identify Polish pistols.

Baikal MP-446 "Viking"

This gun is a 9mm Sporting version of the current Russian service pistol (Yarygin PYa / MP-443 "Grach"), which was added to Russian army arsenal in 2003. The frame is made from a very tough high-strength polymer with steel slide guides, which also accommodates the trigger mechanism. The gun has rear adjustable sights, a ten shot double column billet steel magazine and a chamber-loaded indicator that allows visual or touch control. The exposed hammer firing mechanism allows you to fire single shots in single-action or double-action mode.

Type: Semi-automatic pistol
Origin: Izhevsky Mechanichesky Zavod, Izhevsk, Russia
Caliber: 9mm
Barrel Length: 4.45in

Pistolet Makarov (PM)

The Makorov entered service as the standard military pistol for the Soviet Army and client states in the 1950s. A simple, unpretentious design, it fires a specially-designed 9mm x 18 round from an eight-shot magazine, which as about as powerful a cartridge as can be handled in a simple unlocked blowback pistol. It has a double-action mechanism and a decocking lever allowing the user to carry it safely with a round chambered. Like almost all Russian weapons, the Makarov is a no-nonsense cheap, tough, reliable and easy to use gun.

Type: Semi-automatic pistol
Origin: Soviet State Arsenals
Caliber: 9mm Makarov
Barrel Length: 8.86in

Tula-Tokarev Model 1930 (TT-30)/Model 1933 (TT-33)

Feodor Tokarev developed the Model TT-30 military pistol in 1930, basing it on Browning's design. A simple unlocked blowback weapon, it entered production at the Tula Arsenal in 1930 and soon became the standard sidearm for the Soviet army. Three years later, the TT-33 was introduced, incorporating minor modifications to make the pistol easier to make and to maintain in field conditions. One feature was that the whole hammer and lock mechanism could be removed from the frame as a single unit, giving much easier access for repair.

Type: Semi-automatic pistol
Origin: Tula Arsenal, Russia
Caliber: 7.62 x 25mm Russian
Barrel Length: 8.86in

The TT-33 quickly replaced the earlier TT-30, and served as the Russians' main military pistol throughout the Russo-Finnish War and World War Two.

This cutaway weapon shows the internal construction and mechanism for instructional purposes.

Semi-Automatic Target Pistol

Despite the modern requirement that all firearms must be fully documented, weapons can still be found without any trace as to their origin. Thus, this well-made and carefully designed .22 caliber Russian target pistol bears no evidence as to its manufacture apart from the serial number "K5660C." Both front and rear sights are adjustable. The grips have a "Walther" look to them.

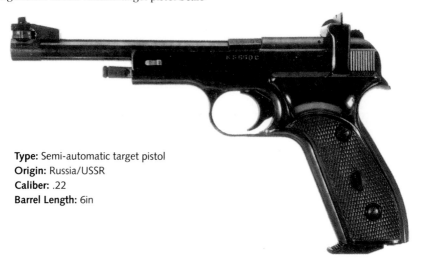

Type: Semi-automatic target pistol
Origin: Russia/USSR
Caliber: .22
Barrel Length: 6in

Pretoria Arms Factory (PAF) Junior

This little blowback automatic was produced in South Africa in the 1950s. It was chambered for the 6.35mm Auto cartridge and weighed, with an empty magazine, just 13.4 ounces. The detachable box magazine held six rounds. It is believed that some 10,000 were manufactured, and all bear the factory logo four times: one the grip and on the slide, and either side. It is an ideal pocket arm for self-defense in a tight corner.

Type: Semi-automatic pistol
Origin: Pretoria Arms Factory (PAF),
    Pretoria, Republic of South Africa
Caliber: 6.35m
Barrel Length: 2in

Arizmendi Walman

This weapon was produced in Spain, primarily for the US market, and early production models were marked "American Automatic Pistol Walman Patent" although the word "American" was later dropped. The pistols were available in 6.35mm or 7.65mm, the example shown here being of the latter caliber. The Walman was in production throughout most of the 1920s, but the company went out of business in 1936.

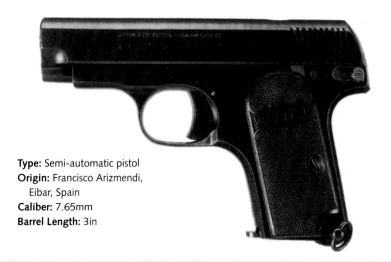

Type: Semi-automatic pistol
Origin: Francisco Arizmendi,
    Eibar, Spain
Caliber: 7.65mm
Barrel Length: 3in

Astra-Unceta Model 300

Curiously, the Astra 300 seems to have followed the Astra 400 into production. Both were the result of improving the Campo-Giro Model 1913-16 "tubular" design in which an annular recoil spring surrounded the barrel and was retained by a muzzle bush. The Model 300 was manufactured in 7.65mm Browning and 9mm Short calibers, with the latter being procured by the Spanish navy in the 1920s. It remained in production throughout the 1930s and some 85,000 were purchased for use by the German army and navy during World War Two.

Type: Semi-automatic pistol
Origin: Astra-Unceta SA, Guernica, Spain
Caliber: 7.65mm
Barrel Length: 3.5in

Astra-Unceta Model 600/43

The Model 600 was manufactured in 1943 to 1944 for the German armed forces, which took delivery of some 10,500 examples. Following this, approximately 50,000 more examples were produced for the commercial market. It was descended from the Campo-Giro design and was chambered (as here) for the 9mm Parabellum round, although some may also have been chambered for the 7.65mm Parabellum round.

Type: Semi-automatic pistol
Origin: Astra-Unceta SA,
  Guernica Spain
Caliber: 9mm Parabellum
Barrel Length: 5.5in

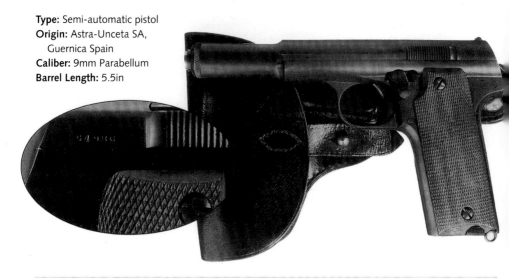

Astra-Unceta Cub

The Astra 200 had a production run lasting from 1920 to 1966 and was particularly successful in the United States where it was generally known as the "Firecat." This was succeeded by the Astra 2000, which was chambered for either 6.35mm or .22 (as seen here). It was first sold in the United States as the "Colt Junior" and, later, as the "Cub."

Type: Semi-automatic pistol
Origin: Astra-Unceta SA, Guernica Spain
Caliber: .22
Barrel Length: 2in

Bernedo 6.35mm

During World War One, the Bernedo Company was involved in the manufacture of Ruby pistols, but once the war finished, they produced this pocket blowback pistol. Cheap and simple, it carried six rounds in the magazine. The majority of those made were sold in the United States as an inexpensive self-defense arm.

Type: Semi-automatic pistol
Origin: Vincente Bernedo y Cia, Eibar, Spain
Caliber: 6.35mm
Barrel Length: 2in

Campo Giro Model 1913-16

Venancio Lopez de Caballos y Aguirre, Count of Campo Giro, a lieutenant colonel in the Spanish Army, developed an automatic pistol. This was entered for army trials in 1904. The design was constantly refined over the following decade. Markings on this weapon identify it as the Model 1913-16. The Spanish army acquired 13,000 units between 1916 and 1919, and a further 500 to 600 were sold on the commercial market. When complaints of frame failures were made, the weapon was modified and returned to the market as the "Astra 400."

Type: Semi-automatic pistol
Origin: Lieutenant Colonel, the Count of Campo Giro, Spain
Caliber: 9mm Bergmann
Barrel Length: 6.4in

Echeverria (Star) Model B

Star is the brand name used by the firm of Echeverria, who have been making military self-loading pistols since 1908. This Star Model B was introduced in 1928 and as can be seen by the gun's appearance, is based on the Colt M1911A1. However, it had no grip safety and fires 9mm Largo rather than .45 ACP ammunition. Robust and simple, it was an effective enough pistol and remained in Spanish military service until the 1980s.

Type: Semi-automatic pistol
Origin: Star Bonnifacio Echeverria,
 Eibar, Spain
Caliber: 9 x 23mm Largo
Barrel Length: 5in

Llama-Gabilondo Model Omni

The Model Omni was marketed in three versions in the early 1980s. The Omni I was chambered for .45ACP with a seven-round magazine; the Omni II, for 9mm Parabellum, and a nine-round magazine; and Omni III, chambered for 9mm. This version had an extended butt housing a thirteen-round magazine. Llama-Gabilondo went into liquidation in 1992 and was resurrected as Fabrinor S.A.L., cooperative of former employees who carried on operating the company.

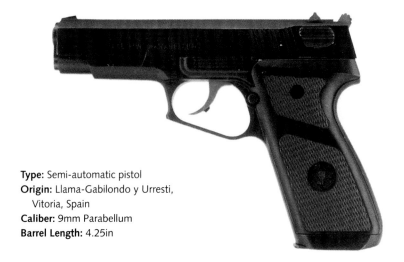

Type: Semi-automatic pistol
Origin: Llama-Gabilondo y Urresti,
 Vitoria, Spain
Caliber: 9mm Parabellum
Barrel Length: 4.25in

Husqvarna Model 1907

The Husqvarna Model 1907 was a licensed copy of the FN Browning Model 1903, which was made in Sweden for the Swedish Army. This was identical with the original in every respect except for the markings, which bore the legend "HUSQVARNA VAPENSFABRIK AKTIEBOLAG" and the Swedish royal arms at the top of the black, hard rubber grips. As made for the Swedish army they were 9mm caliber, but when replaced in Swedish service many were converted to .38 and exported to the United States, as was this specimen.

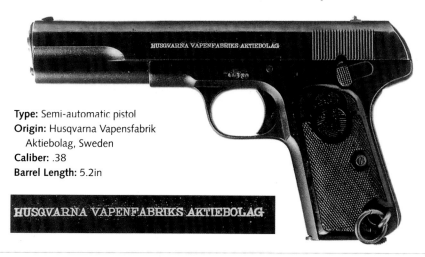

Type: Semi-automatic pistol
Origin: Husqvarna Vapensfabrik
  Aktiebolag, Sweden
Caliber: .38
Barrel Length: 5.2in

SIG/SIG-Sauer P-226

The P-226 was developed to enter the 1980 US army competition to replace the Colt M1911A1. In the event, the SIG lost out to the Beretta 92 mainly on price. This hasn't stopped the P-226 selling successfully to police forces and military users around the world, and it is a fine example of modern high-quality weapon engineering. Chambered for the 9mm Parabellum cartridge, it carries fifteen rounds in the butt. Using a double- action mechanism with a decocking lever and mechanical safety devices, it can be safely carried with a round chambered, and the user can simply pull the trigger to fire the first shot.

Type: Semi-automatic pistol
Origin: SIG / J.P. Sauer & Sohn,
  Switzerland and Germany
Caliber: 9mm Parabellum
Barrel Length: 4.4in

SIG/SIG-Sauer P-228/P-229

The P-228 is based on the earlier P-225 police model, but carries thirteen rounds instead of the eight of the earlier model. The P-229 is the same weapon chambered for larger .40 S&W or .357 SIG rounds. The only difference is a change of barrel. A wide range of agencies, including the FBI and United States Drug Enforcement Agency, has adopted both these weapons, and the P-226 series.

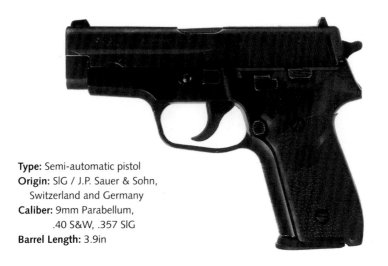

Type: Semi-automatic pistol
Origin: SIG / J.P. Sauer & Sohn,
    Switzerland and Germany
Caliber: 9mm Parabellum,
    .40 S&W, .357 SIG
Barrel Length: 3.9in

SIG/SIG-SAUER P-239

SIG modified the P-220 series to make a weapon with a narrower grip, intended for users with smaller hands, and especially female users. It packs the same punch as the other pistols though, albeit with a single stack magazine carrying only 8 rounds. The P-239 is also popular as a concealable weapon for plain clothes and undercover law-enforcement officers. While most use the 9mm Parabellum round, it is also available in .40 S&W and .357 SIG.

Type: Semi-automatic pistol
Origin: SIG / J.P. Sauer & Sohn,
    Switzerland and Germany
Caliber: 9mm Parabellum, .40 S&W,
    .357 SIG
Barrel Length: 3.6in

Webley No. 1 Mk1 .455 Pistol

At the dawn of the twentieth century, gun makers were waking up to the fact that the automatic pistol had a military future. Webley and Scott experimented with a couple of designs, including the Webley-Mars, followed by the Model of 1904. Revolvers were proven, and Webley faced an uphill struggle to get any new design taken seriously by the British services. Eventually they developed this pistol, chambered for a massively powerful .455 cartridge, similar to the one used in service revolvers. The angular butt held seven rounds, while a grip safety protruded from the back.

Type: Semi-automatic pistol
Origin: Webley & Scott, Birmingham, England
Caliber: .455
Barrel Length: 5in

AMT Auto Mag Baby

This weapon was originally designed in the 1960s around the .44 Auto Magnum cartridge (hence the name) and marketed by Sanford Arms. This company became the Auto-Mag Corp in October 1970 but went out of business in 1972, when the rights were purchased by the TDE Corporation. Production then restarted, with TDE doing the manufacturing while Hi Standard were responsible for marketing. This arrangement ended in 1977, but production restarted only to end again in 1980. Finally, AMT produced about 100 Model Cs chambered for the .22 Winchester round, of which the first two were presented to Clint Eastwood.

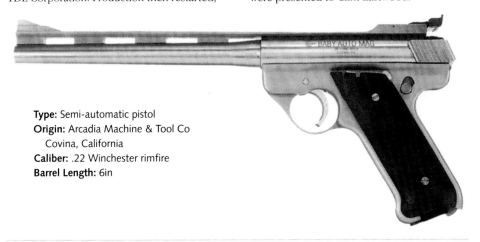

Type: Semi-automatic pistol
Origin: Arcadia Machine & Tool Co
    Covina, California
Caliber: .22 Winchester rimfire
Barrel Length: 6in

AMT Back-Up

The AMT Back-Up, as its name implies, is a very small weapon designed to be used as a last resort when other weapons have failed or are otherwise unavailable. It was originally produced in.22LR caliber, but has since appeared in .38 ACP (as in this example) and, in a slightly modified 9mm form. It is made mainly from stainless steel and weighs eighteen ounces. It is fitted with both grip and manual safeties, and the magazine holds five rounds.

Type: Semi-automatic pistol
Origin: Arcadia Machine & Tool Co.,
    Covina, California
Caliber: 38 ACP
Barrel Length: 2.52in

AMT Model 1911A1 Hardliner

The first weapon produced by AMT was the ever popular M1911A1 with various company-designed customized features, but they then went on to produce a new version made from stainless steel and designated the "Hardballer." This features a matt-finished slide, longer grips, an adjustable trigger, and a greatly extended manual safety lever. There is also a special version with a two-inch longer barrel and slide, designed to achieve higher muzzle velocity from the same .45 ACP round.

Type: Semi-automatic pistol
Origin: Arcadia Machine & Tool Co,
Covina, California
Caliber: .45 ACP
Barrel Length: 5in

Colt Model 1900

At the end of the nineteenth century Colt was the first among US weapons companies to appreciate the importance of the automatic pistol. As in all aspects of the weapons industry, the crucial factor was to gain a military contract and with this aim in view, Colt set about developing a reliable and effective pistol for the US army and navy. The first fruit of this was the M1898 and this was quickly developed into the M1900, chambered for the .38 ACP cartridge, and which had exceptionally functional lines as shown in this example.

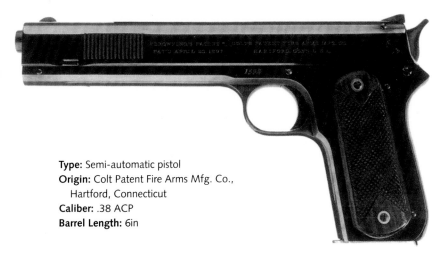

Type: Semi-automatic pistol
Origin: Colt Patent Fire Arms Mfg. Co.,
Hartford, Connecticut
Caliber: .38 ACP
Barrel Length: 6in

Colt Model 1902 Sporting Pistol

The Model 1902 Sporting pistol was essentially a Model 1900 for the civil market, which incorporated a number of minor modifications, including a revised firing pin and hammer, and moulded rubber grips. There was a parallel Military Model 1902, which was marginally larger than the Sporting model and incorporated a number of other refinements, including a larger magazine holding eight rounds. Most people therefore bought the Military Model 1902 which was sold on the civil market remaining in production until 1928, whereas the Sporting Model was phased out of production in 1908.

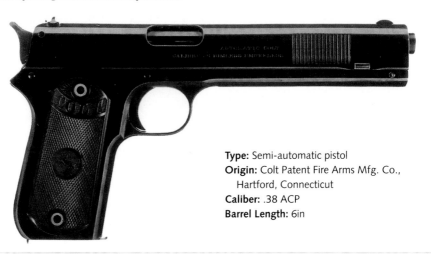

Type: Semi-automatic pistol
Origin: Colt Patent Fire Arms Mfg. Co.,
   Hartford, Connecticut
Caliber: .38 ACP
Barrel Length: 6in

Colt Model 1903 Pocket Pistol

Introduced in 1903, this light, compact yet effective pistol was the first Colt automatic with a concealed hammer. Based on Browning's design it carried eight rounds of .32 ammunition in the butt magazine, and operated using a simple unlocked blowback method. A grip safety also s in the rear of the grip. A neat, well-balanced arr it was one the most popular Colt pistols ever. Many thousands were made for both military ar civilian use, and it was sold around the world.

Type: Semi-automatic pistol
Origin: Colt Patent Fire Arms Mfg. Co.,
   Hartford, Connecticut
Caliber: .32 ACP
Barrel Length: 3.75in

Colt Model 1903 General Officer's

General officers need a personal weapon which is unobtrusive and does not interfere with their work, but which is available and effective, if required, and the Model 1903 Hammerless was one of the first to be issued to meet this requirement. The example shown here was the personal weapon of Brigadier-General Steve A. Chappius, US army, issued to him in 1965. During World War Two the general commanded the 502nd Regiment when it smashed the German attack during the epic Battle of Bastogne, as commemorated by the plaque in the picture.

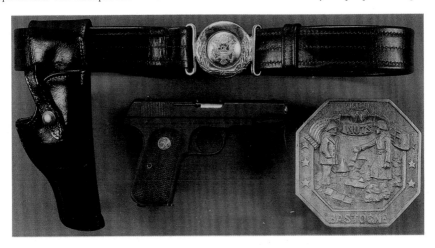

Colt Model 1908 Hammerless .38 Pocket Pistol

The Colt Model 1908 .38 pistol was virtually identical with the .32, but chambered for the more powerful .38 ACP cartridge. The particular weapon seen here was issued to Brigadier-General George C. McDonald of the US Army Air Force, who, during World War Two, was an intelligence staff officer at the headquarters of General Carl Spaatz in England. General McDonald flew with the Wright brothers, was a personal friend of Charles Lindbergh, and was involved in the great bomber offensive against Germany between 1943 and 1945. He was truly an aviation pioneer.

Colt Model 1908 Hammerless .25 Pocket Pistol

In 1908, Colt produced this diminutive pistol. It is only four-and-a-half inches long and weighs 14 ounces. It carries six rounds of .25 ammunition. It was originally a Browning design and was produced by FN in Belgium until Colt bought the rights. A simple blowback design, it still had a grip safety, although most shooters can only get one finger on the trigger and one more on the grip. Intended as a concealable personal defense weapon, it also found use with military covert operations forces.

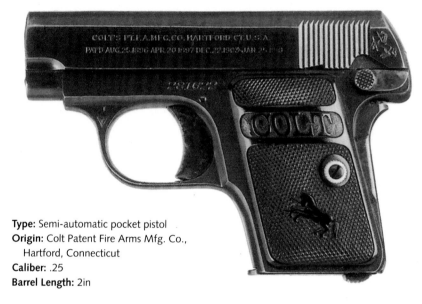

Type: Semi-automatic pocket pistol
Origin: Colt Patent Fire Arms Mfg. Co., Hartford, Connecticut
Caliber: .25
Barrel Length: 2in

Colt Model 1911

One of the classic all-time greats, this superbly effective pistol was another developed from Browning's design but intended from the start to be a service pistol. Built to chamber Colt's new .45 ACP (Automatic Colt Pistol) cartridge, a lethal round with more than enough stopping power, it carried seven shots in the magazine. Such a powerful round demands the barrel and slide be locked when firing, and lugs on the barrel upper surface are designed to do just that.

Type: Semi-automatic pistol
Origin: Colt Patent Fire Arms Mfg. Co.,
   Hartford, Connecticut
Caliber: .45 ACP
Barrel Length: 5in

Colt M1911A1

Effective as the Model 1911 was, combat experience indicated that some minor improvements could still be made. The hammer shape was changed slightly, the butt safety enlarged, some internal changes made and two chamfered cutouts added to the frame, just behind the trigger. The ensuing Model 1911A1 entered service in 1926, and ended up even more successful than the earlier version. It gave sterling service through World War Two, then Korea, Vietnam, and anywhere else the American fighting man was sent.

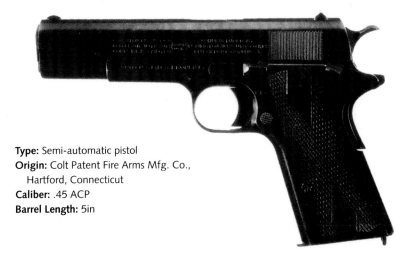

Type: Semi-automatic pistol
Origin: Colt Patent Fire Arms Mfg. Co.,
   Hartford, Connecticut
Caliber: .45 ACP
Barrel Length: 5in

Colt M1911 "Tansley Loaded-Weapon Indicator"

One of the perceived shortcomings of automatic pistols in the early days was that it was impossible to tell by visual inspection whether or not there was a round in the chamber, and various methods were devised to overcome this. One method, invented by a man named Tansley, was trialed on the very early Model 1911, seen here. The indicator consisted of a long extractor, which extended under the rear sight and almost to the back end of the frame. When a cartridge was chambered the front end of the extractor was raised and this could be clearly seen.

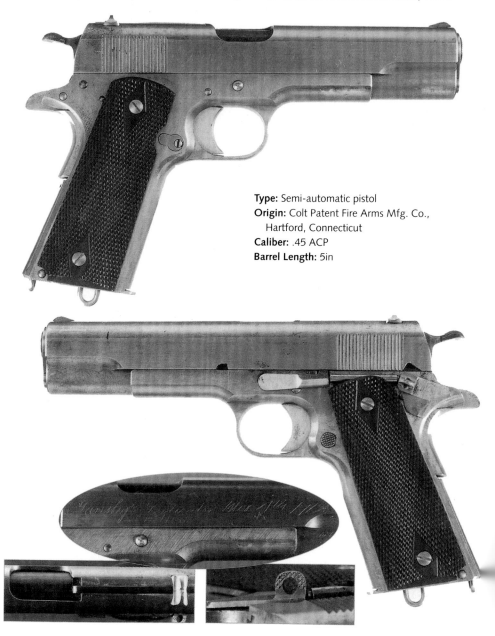

Type: Semi-automatic pistol
Origin: Colt Patent Fire Arms Mfg. Co.,
Hartford, Connecticut
Caliber: .45 ACP
Barrel Length: 5in

Colt-Browning M1911 Commemorative Issues

The production of commemorative "special issue" firearms has become popular among collectors, with elaborately engraved weapons mounted in display cases and supported by authenticating documents. The weapons shown here are all Model 1911s. Colt issued the gun at the bottom of the page in 1967 to commemorate the 50th anniversary of US entry into World War One commemorating the Battle of Belleau Wood. The gun at the top was produced by Auto-Ordnance commemorating E. A Doyle's service in Korea.

World War I Commemorative   Colt .45 Automatic Pistol

THE BATTLE OF BELLEAU WOOD
"... it was, indeed, the one battle that halted the German offensive, began the ebb tide of German fortunes ... and saved Paris from occupation...."

Colt Lightweight Commander

The Colt submission for the M1911A1 replacement was the Commander, which had a frame fabricated from a lightweight aluminum alloy. None of the participants in the competition obtained a military order, but Colt placed the Commander in production for civil use, chambered for .45 ACP, 9mm Parabellum, .38 Super and 7.65mm. In 1970 a new model with a steel frame was introduced as the Combat Commander whereupon the aluminum-framed version was redesignated the Lightweight Commander, one of which is seen here.

Type: Semi-automatic pistol
Origin: Colt Patent Fire Arms Mfg. Co, Hartford, Connecticut
Caliber: 9mm Parabellum
Barrel Length: 4.25in

Colt Government Model National Match

Master Engraver Alvin A. White did this exceptional engraving on a Colt Government Model M1911A1 National Match pistol, chambered for .45 ACP. Inlaid gold wire outlines all the edges on the gun, including the trigger guard, the back and front straps, and virtually all the flat surfaces are engraved. The grips are of ivory, one having a carved buffalo's head, with the eyes being picked out by diamonds.

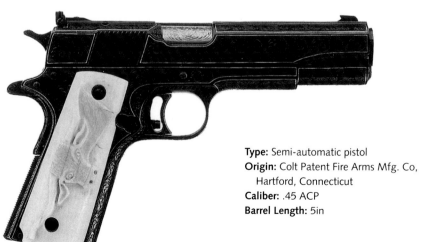

Type: Semi-automatic pistol
Origin: Colt Patent Fire Arms Mfg. Co, Hartford, Connecticut
Caliber: .45 ACP
Barrel Length: 5in

Colt Combat Commander

The Colt Combat Commander, introduced in 1971, was the steel-framed version of the aluminum-framed Commander/Lightweight Commander, which resulted in an increase in weight to thirty-six ounces. We show one chambered for .45 ACP with a 4.25 inch barrel, a seven round magazine, and satin nickel finish. The gun is complete with its leather service holster.

Type: Semi-automatic pistol
Origin: Colt Patent Fire Arms Mfg. Co.,
　　Hartford, Connecticut
Caliber: .45 ACP, 9mm Parabellum
Barrel Length: 4.25in

Colt Delta Elite

The 10mm Auto Pistol cartridge was designed in the 1970s and placed in limited production by Norma of Sweden, but leading weapons manufacturers steered clear of it until Colt produced the Delta Elite, which entered the market in 1987. In essence, this weapon is an M1911A1 re-engineered for the larger caliber round and most of those produced had a large red triangle on the black neoprene butt plate to indicate the different ammunition used. The example seen here, however, has Pachmayr grips without the Delta logo.

Type: Semi-automatic pistol
Origin: Colt Patent Fire Arms Mfg. Co.,
　　Hartford, Connecticut
Caliber: 10mm Auto Pistol
Barrel Length: 5in

Colt Mk IV Series 70 Government

In the course of its long career, which is by no means over yet, the Model 1911A1 has been given a whole series of modifications in an effort by Colt to keep it "modern." The Model 1911A1 was replaced in production in 1971 by the Mark IV Series 70 Government Model which had a marginally heavier slide and a few other, very detailed, modifications. The example shown here has a bright satin finish and is chambered for .45 caliber cartridges.

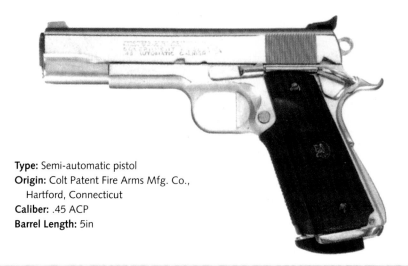

Type: Semi-automatic pistol
Origin: Colt Patent Fire Arms Mfg. Co.,
    Hartford, Connecticut
Caliber: .45 ACP
Barrel Length: 5in

Colt Pre-Woodsman SAP

Colt produced .22 pistols from 1915 onwards in four, essentially similar designs. The original was the .22 Target Model, intended, as the name implies, for target shooters, but when Colt realised that it was also very popular with hunters, they redesignated it, from 1927 onwards, as "The Woodsman." As a consequence, those produced before this date have become known as the "Pre-Woodsman." Seen here is an original "Pre-Woodsman" version, which, in this particular case, was manufactured in 1927.

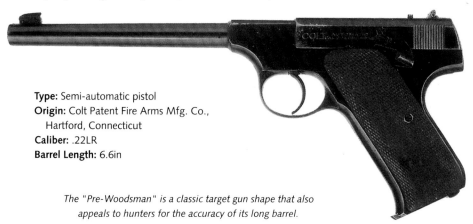

Type: Semi-automatic pistol
Origin: Colt Patent Fire Arms Mfg. Co.,
    Hartford, Connecticut
Caliber: .22LR
Barrel Length: 6.6in

The "Pre-Woodsman" is a classic target gun shape that also
appeals to hunters for the accuracy of its long barrel.

Colt Huntsman Semi-Automatic Pistol

In the early 1950s Colt introduced the Series 2 Woodsman and accompanied the new range with an economy model named the Challenger. This had fixed sights and various parts were either simplified or omitted; for example, there was no lanyard ring. When the Series 3 was introduced in 1955, the very similar Huntsman, seen here, replaced the Challenger, which could be obtained with either a four-and-a-half-inch or six-inch barrel.

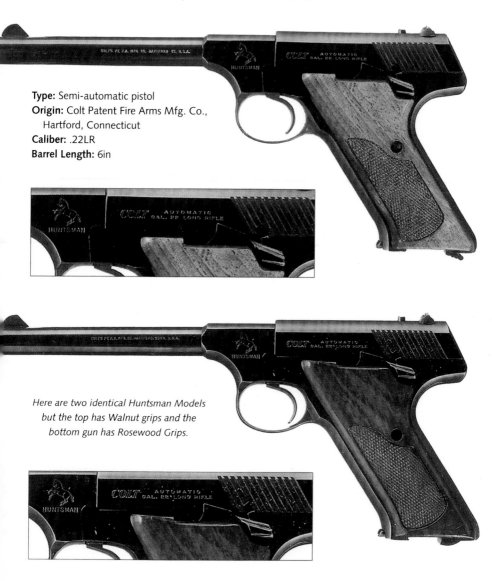

Type: Semi-automatic pistol
Origin: Colt Patent Fire Arms Mfg. Co.,
   Hartford, Connecticut
Caliber: .22LR
Barrel Length: 6in

Here are two identical Huntsman Models but the top has Walnut grips and the bottom gun has Rosewood Grips.

Both guns are marked "Colt Automatic Cal .22 Long Rifle," as well as the prancing colt and the word "Huntsman."

Woodsman Semi-Automatic Pistols

The "Woodsman" proper was divided into three production runs: First Series 1927-47; Second Series 1947-55; and Third Series 1955-1977. Within each of those series, there were three models: Target, Sport, and Match Target, and in the Second and Third Series only, additional economy models, designated Challenger, Huntsman, and Targetsman. Seen here is a variety of Woodsman models, but it should be noted that, in addition to the variations seem here, there were also differences in barrel length and more minor characteristics.

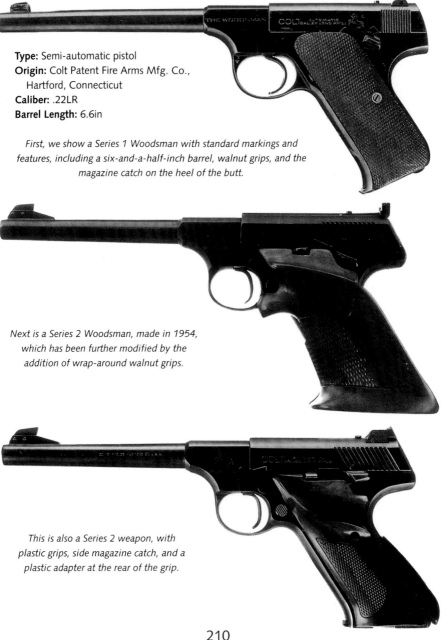

Type: Semi-automatic pistol
Origin: Colt Patent Fire Arms Mfg. Co., Hartford, Connecticut
Caliber: .22LR
Barrel Length: 6.6in

First, we show a Series 1 Woodsman with standard markings and features, including a six-and-a-half-inch barrel, walnut grips, and the magazine catch on the heel of the butt.

Next is a Series 2 Woodsman, made in 1954, which has been further modified by the addition of wrap-around walnut grips.

This is also a Series 2 weapon, with plastic grips, side magazine catch, and a plastic adapter at the rear of the grip.

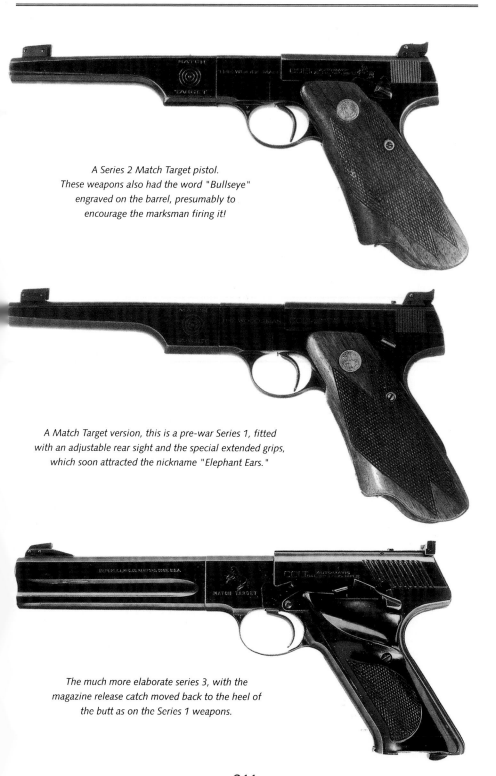

A Series 2 Match Target pistol.
These weapons also had the word "Bullseye"
engraved on the barrel, presumably to
encourage the marksman firing it!

A Match Target version, this is a pre-war Series 1, fitted
with an adjustable rear sight and the special extended grips,
which soon attracted the nickname "Elephant Ears."

The much more elaborate series 3, with the
magazine release catch moved back to the heel of
the butt as on the Series 1 weapons.

Colt All American Model 2000

The All American Model 2000 was designed by Colt to achieve a return to the police market in the United States. It was produced only in 9mm, had white-dot fixed sights and the magazine (and, thus, also the butt) was larger than usual, holding fifteen rounds. It was not a success and remained in production only until 1993.

Type: Semi-automatic pistol
Origin: Colt Patent Fire Arms Mfg. Co.,
   Hartford, Connecticut
Caliber: 9mm
Barrel Length: 4.5in

Charles Daly M1911A1

An M1911Al marketed under the Charles Daly label (part of KBI Inc. of Harrisburg, Pennsylvania). This company produces three basic models, all of which include an extended hi-rise beavertail grip safety, combat trigger, combat hammer, beveled magazine housing, modified ejection port, dovetailed front and dovetailed snag-free low profile rear sight. There are three standards of finish; Field, Empire, and Target. Three barrel lengths were also available; five-inch (with an eight round magazine); five-inch (with an eight-round magazine) and three-point-six-inch (with a six-round magazine)

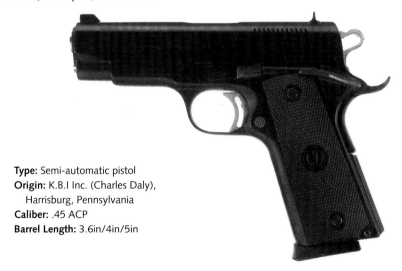

Type: Semi-automatic pistol
Origin: K.B.I Inc. (Charles Daly),
   Harrisburg, Pennsylvania
Caliber: .45 ACP
Barrel Length: 3.6in/4in/5in

Dardick Model 1500

This was a most unusual weapon, based on patents held by New York inventor, David Dardick, which, in effect, combined the rotating cylinder of a revolver with the magazine feed of an automatic. The rounds were conventional commercial rounds (e.g., .38 Special, 9mm Parabellum, .22LR) that were loaded into trochoidal-shaped carriers known as "trounds." The Dardick was marketed in two versions; Model 1100 with a small butt and eleven-round magazine, and the Model 1500 (seen here). This had a larger butt and a fifteen-round magazine.

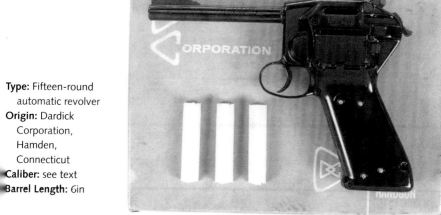

Type: Fifteen-round automatic revolver
Origin: Dardick Corporation, Hamden, Connecticut
Caliber: see text
Barrel Length: 6in

Essex M1911A1

While John M. Browning pioneered the 1911 in all its forms, the Essex Arms Corp of Island Pond, Vermont, was one of the first companies to pioneer an aftermarket frame and slide. Since the original patents of the M1911A1 have long since expired, and its popularity means that there is an ongoing demand, Essex Arms now markets a number of versions based on the company's own frames. The gun shown is an example of the blued finish with white ivory grips.

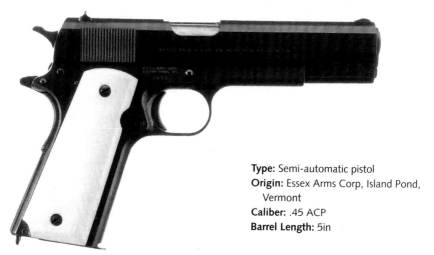

Type: Semi-automatic pistol
Origin: Essex Arms Corp, Island Pond, Vermont
Caliber: .45 ACP
Barrel Length: 5in

Grendel P10

The P10 appeared in 1988 and was intended to be a really compact, semiautomatic handgun. It made considerable use of polymers to lighten the design, but its most unusual feature was that the butt served as a fixed magazine with the eleven rounds of ammunition being loaded from a stripper clip inserted through the top of the receiver. The P12, appeared in 1991 reverted to a conventional detachable box magazine, reducing capacity to ten rounds, but this, too, had problems and went out of production in 1995.

Type: Semi-automatic pistol
Origin: Grendel Inc.,
    Rockledge, Florida
Caliber: .38
Barrel Length: 3in

Grendel P30

The P30 was another original Grendel design, chambered for .22 WMR cartridge and was available in two versions, with five-inch (P30) and eight-inch (P30L) barrels. Both models were single-action and hammerless, had a polymer black frame; fixed front and rear sight, and held the unusually large number of thirty rounds in a conventional detachable box magazine. They appeared on the market in 1990 and were withdrawn in 1994. As a result they are now rare

Type: .22 Semi-automatic pistol
Origin: Grendel Inc., Rockledge, Florid
Caliber: .22 WMRF
Barrel Length: 5in

L.A.R. Grizzly Mark I

L.A.R. Manufacturing produces a series of handguns under the Grizzly name. The Grizzly Mark 1 is produced in .45 ACP, 10mm or .45 Winchester Magnum, and a variety of barrel lengths: 5.4, 6.5, 8, and 10 inches. The gun seen here is the 6.5-inch, 0.45 Winchester version. Various finishes are also available, such as this matt nickel, as well as mountings for telescopic sights and a compensator, but all have adjustable sights and an ambidextrous safety catch.

Type: Semi-automatic pistol
Origin: L.A.R. Manufacturing, West Jordan, Utah
Caliber: .45 Winchester
Barrel Length: 6.5in

High Standard

The High Standard Mfg. Corp. has a complicated history. Founded in 1926 at New Haven to produce engineering equipment, it acquired the assets of the recently defunct Hartford Arms Co. in 1932 and started producing that company's pistols. The corporation then developed its own designs and significant sales of .22 caliber pistols were made to the US Government who trained hundreds of thousands of servicemen in World War Two using High Standard pistols. During the war, the company also produced hundreds of thousands of .50 caliber machine guns in addition to various pistols for the military. By the 1950s, the High Standard .22 pistol was the gun of choice on the NRA pistol competition circuit. The company also began to manufacture private label handguns for the major mass merchandising chains. These included its J. C. Higgins line for Sears, Roebuck Company. After the war, the company moved to Hamden, Connecticut. It was bought and sold several times, and moved to East Hertford, Connecticut in 1977. Things remained relatively stable until 1982 when the shooting sports industry experienced a major decline,

quickly followed by further decline in 1983. Sales of rifles, shotguns, and revolvers were elusive and sales of target pistols alone could not sustain the business. A new company purchased the company's trademarks and assets in 1993. The new owners set up the business in Houston, Texas, which continues to trade.

During its first phase of business, between 1926 and 1984, the High Standard Corporation produced a large number of pistols in a complicated combination of numbers and names. Early models were designated by a letter; e.g. Model C, Model H-D, etc. In 1951 came named models, each name indicating the role or standard of finish; e.g. Supermatic, Olympic, Field King, etc. After this came seven numbered series (100, 101, 102, 103, 104, 106 and 107), but the final series was designated "SH." Within each of these series, the models carried on the identifying name as before, some of which continued from one series to another (e.g., Supermatic and Olympic), although new names were sometimes introduced (e.g. the "Victor" in Series 104) and old ones were discontinued.

215

High Standard Models A and B

High Standard's first weapons products, the Models A and B, were Hartford Arms designs but carried the new company's name. These two differed only in that the Model A had adjustable sights, while in the Model B they were fixed. High Standard produced both designs from 1932 to 1942, during which time some 65,000 units were made. Both were chambered for the .22LR cartridge and were available in two different barrel lengths: 4.5 inches and 6.75 inches.

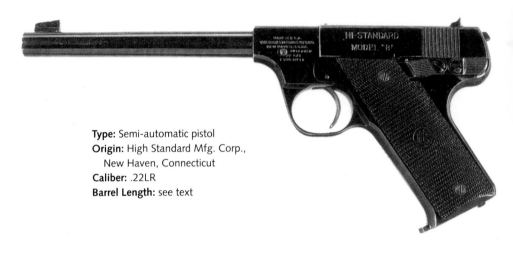

Type: Semi-automatic pistol
Origin: High Standard Mfg. Corp.,
   New Haven, Connecticut
Caliber: .22LR
Barrel Length: see text

High Standard Model H-B

This 1948-1949 Model HB Semi-Auto has a barrel length of 6.75 inches. It also has a blade front sight, a Dovetail rear sight, an exterior hammer (this is the main distinguishing feature from the Model B), left thumb safety catch, checkered hardwood grips, and a ten-round magazine for the .22 Long Rifle cartridge.

Type: Semi-automatic pistol
Origin: High Standard Mfg. Corp.,
   New Haven, Connecticut
Caliber: .22LR
Barrel Length: 6.75in

High Standard Models D and H-D

The Model D was introduced in 1938 and was generally similar to the Model A, but with a heavier barrel which, as before, was available in either 4.5 inch or 6.75 inch lengths. The Model H-D was identical to the Model D in every respect, except that it had a hammer and an adjusted safety catch. We show three pistols.

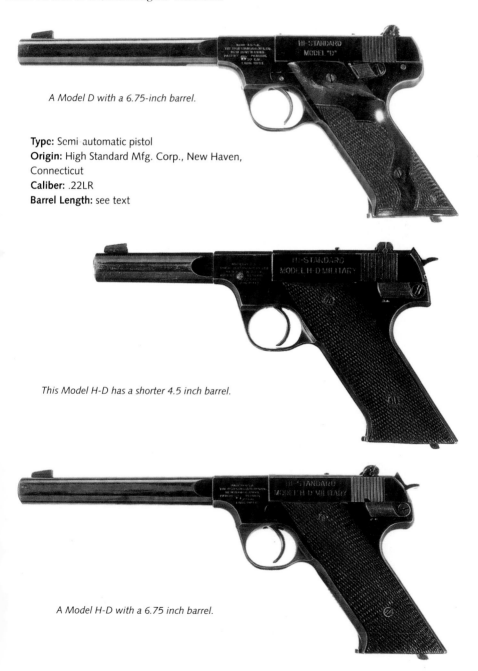

A Model D with a 6.75-inch barrel.

Type: Semi-automatic pistol
Origin: High Standard Mfg. Corp., New Haven, Connecticut
Caliber: .22LR
Barrel Length: see text

This Model H-D has a shorter 4.5 inch barrel.

A Model H-D with a 6.75 inch barrel.

High Standard Model E

The Model E was a development of the Model D, but with an even heavier and more substantial barrel. Like the Model D, the barrel was available in either 4.5 inch or 6.75 inch lengths. Some 2,000 Model Es were produced in 1940 and 1941.

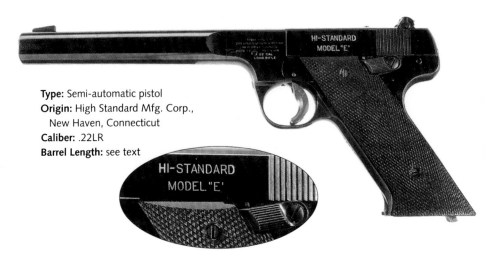

Type: Semi-automatic pistol
Origin: High Standard Mfg. Corp.,
    New Haven, Connecticut
Caliber: .22LR
Barrel Length: see text

High Standard Model G-B

The G-series weapons appeared following World War Two and, while visually similar to the pre-war models, they incorporated some changes in construction, which enabled both the slide and the barrel to be removed. The original Model G, introduced in 1947, was chambered for the 9mm Short cartridge; the first High Standard weapon made for this round, and had only a five-inch barrel. This was followed two years later by the Model G-B, which reverted to .22 caliber and was available with either 4.5 inch or 6.75 inch barrels.

Type: Semi-automatic pistol
Origin: High Standard Mfg. Corp.,
    New Haven, Connecticut
Caliber: .22LR
Barrel Length: see text

High Standard Olympic

The Olympic was developed from the G-E and was, in fact, often referred to as the Model G-O. It was chambered for the .22 Short and had a lighter slide. It was sold with either the 4.5 or 6.75 inch barrel, or with a combination of the two. The barrel was released by pressing on a catch at the front of the trigger-guard.

Type: Semi-automatic pistol
Origin: High Standard Mfg. Corp.,
    New Haven, Connecticut
Caliber: .22 Short
Barrel Length: see text

High Standard Supermatic/Supermatic Military

The Supermatic range first appeared in 1951 as a replacement for the G-series and was, in essence, a development of the Olympic and eventually numbered five models. The Supermatic featured aids for target shooting, including balance weights, a slide stop, and micrometer sights, but with similar parallel-sided barrels with an under rib to the G series which apart from aiding cooling, were also used to secure the barrel weights. Three different barrel lengths were available, in 6.75, 8, and 10 inches. The pistol we show is an original Supermatic but with removable weights fitted under the barrel.

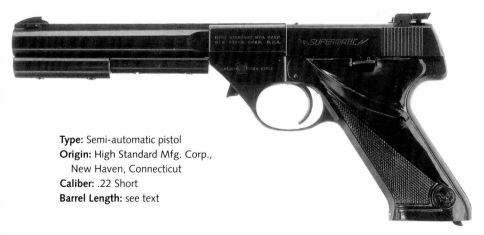

Type: Semi-automatic pistol
Origin: High Standard Mfg. Corp.,
    New Haven, Connecticut
Caliber: .22 Short
Barrel Length: see text

High Standard Field King

The Supermatic Trophy was an expensive weapon (its 1950 price was no less than $112) so High Standard developed a less sophisticated range for their 1950 catalogue. This comprised two models, the Sport King and the Field King, both chambered for .22LR and with ten-round magazines. Both were also available with either 4.5 or 6.75 inch barrels. The Field King was the slightly more expensive gun of the two, having heavier barrels, together with an adjustable backsight. Neither model had ribbed barrels or add-on weights.

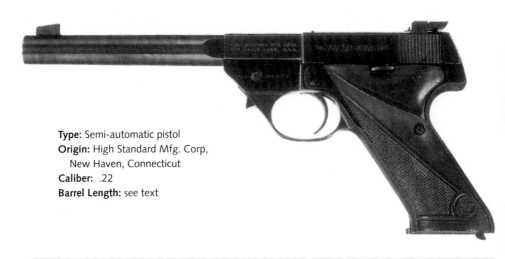

Type: Semi-automatic pistol
Origin: High Standard Mfg. Corp,
    New Haven, Connecticut
Caliber: .22
Barrel Length: see text

High Standard Supermatic S-101

The Series 100 designs were developed into the Series 101, which were produced between 1954 and 1957. The series consisted of: Supermatic, Olympic, Field King, and Duramatic models. The Supermatic S-101, seen here, has a ten-round box magazine and a heavy 6.75 inch barrel with weight. There is also a muzzle brake with one vent on either side of the foresight.

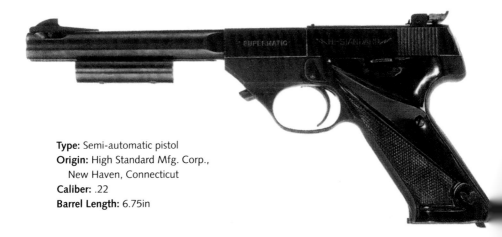

Type: Semi-automatic pistol
Origin: High Standard Mfg. Corp.,
    New Haven, Connecticut
Caliber: .22
Barrel Length: 6.75in

High Standard Series 102 Model Supermatic Tournament

The Series 102 range was produced between 1957 and 1960, and consisted of Supermatic Trophy, Citation, Tournament, Olympic (including Standard, ISU, and ISU Trophy models), Sport, Lite King, and Sharpshooter.

The weapon shown here is the Series 102 Supermatic complete with its original carrying case. The white label clearly shows the takedown button, used to release the barrel.

Type: Semi-automatic pistol
Origin: High Standard Mfg. Corp, New Haven, Connecticut
Caliber: .22
Barrel Length: 4.5, 5, or 6.75in

High Standard Series 103 Model Sport King

High Standard's Series 103 models were in production from 1960 to 1963 and differed very little from the 102 series We show a pistol with a 6.75 inch barrel which is a second model without the hold open breech and brown thumb rest grips.

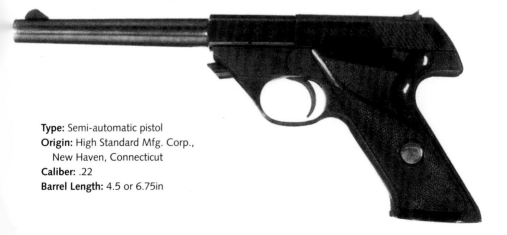

Type: Semi-automatic pistol
Origin: High Standard Mfg. Corp., New Haven, Connecticut
Caliber: .22
Barrel Length: 4.5 or 6.75in

High Standard Series 107 Model Victor

The Victor was introduced in 1970 and combined the G-type frame with a new slab-sided barrel, topped by a heavy rib, which was continued to the rear of the weapon to carry the backsight. The barrel came in two lengths, 4.5 and 5.5 inch. They were either ventilated or solid, while both types carried an under rib upon which the weights could be mounted. Shown here is a 104 series Victor with 5.5 inch barrel.

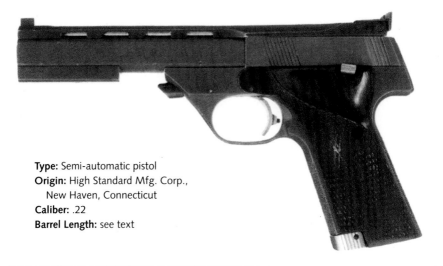

Type: Semi-automatic pistol
Origin: High Standard Mfg. Corp.,
New Haven, Connecticut
Caliber: .22
Barrel Length: see text

Ithaca M1911A1

The Ithaca Arms Co was one of many companies to produce the legendary and ever-popular M1911A1. What makes this particular weapon important is that it was carried in combat by Lieutenant-Colonel Lyman Goff, who is seen in the photograph (standing, second from right).

Colonel Goff was Deputy Commander of the 491st Bombardment Group of the Eighth Air Force in England during World War Two and is seen here with his crew and their B-24 Liberator bomber "Unconditional Surrender."

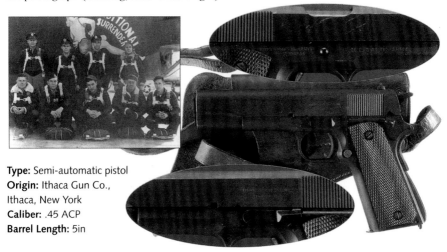

Type: Semi-automatic pistol
Origin: Ithaca Gun Co.,
Ithaca, New York
Caliber: .45 ACP
Barrel Length: 5in

Kimber M1911A1

Kimber originated in Oregon in 1979 where it manufactured some 60,000 rifles for twelve years until it was forced to close in 1991. It reopened under new management in 1993 and in 1995 added new-build M1911A1s to its product line. In 1997, it moved to New York where it is still located. Seen on this page are two of the many variations of the M1911A1 produced by the company.

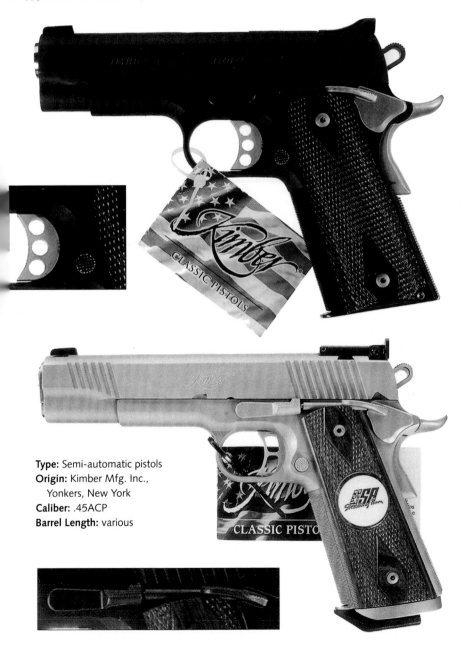

Type: Semi-automatic pistols
Origin: Kimber Mfg. Inc.,
Yonkers, New York
Caliber: .45ACP
Barrel Length: various

Lewis Pistol

This pistol is a prototype of a design by Colonel Isaac Newton Lewis (1858-1931). Lewis was both a professional soldier in the US army and a prolific inventor. His fame is mainly due to the Lewis light machine gun, the finest weapon of its type to see service in World War One. He designed this pistol in 1917 or 1918 and took out patents in 1920 and 21. It was designed for "shock action" in trench warfare, but was not accepted for service.

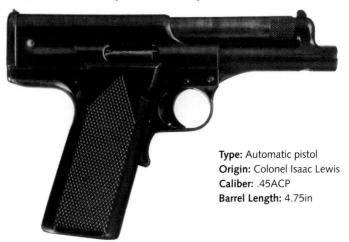

Type: Automatic pistol
Origin: Colonel Isaac Lewis
Caliber: .45ACP
Barrel Length: 4.75in

Mainhardt-Biehl MBA Gyrojet

Robert Mainhardt and Art Biehl's 1960 take on the future of pistol design was this lightweight device. Looking like a conventional automatic pistol, it was, in fact, closer in concept to a rocket launcher. The 13mm projectile was about one-and-a-half inches long. It had a conventional solid "bullet" at the front, over a tubular casing holding the rocket propellant. Underpowered and inaccurate, the Gyrojet wasn't even as effective as conventional cartridge pistols, and certainly didn't offer any advantage over them. wasn't a success.

Type: Semi-automatic rocket
   projectile pistol
Origin: Mainhardt-Biehl
Caliber: 13mm
Barrel Length: 5in

Para-Ordnance P14.45

The P14.45 is one of a number of M1911A1 clones manufactured by Canadian company, Para-Ordnance. All these products have an action similar to that of the original; i.e., blowback operation combined with a Browning locked-breech system. The Para-Ordnance models do, however, have some differences from the original, including a wider butt, for the fourteen-round magazine, and in addition to the usual grip and manual safety, have a firing-pin safety as well. The pistols are available with aluminum alloy, carbon steel, or stainless steel frames.

Type: Semi-automatic pistol
Origin: Para-Ordnance Mfg. Inc.,
  Scarborough, Ontario, Canada
Caliber: .45 ACP
Barrel Length: 5in

Phoenix Pistol

The origins of this rather undistinguished weapon are somewhat obscure. It is marked "PHOENIX. LOWELL. MASS. USA PATENT" but there was no known US gunsmith of that name. It is most probable that this was the name of an importer and that the weapon was manufactured elsewhere, most probably in Belgium by Robar of Liege. Its Caliber is .25 ACP (6.35mm) and the weapon is quite small, with a barrel length of just 2.1 inches.

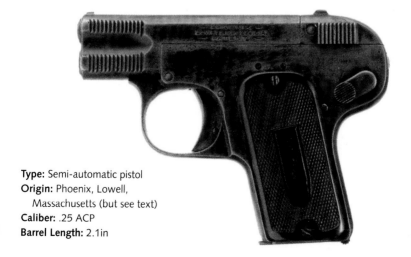

Type: Semi-automatic pistol
Origin: Phoenix, Lowell,
  Massachusetts (but see text)
Caliber: .25 ACP
Barrel Length: 2.1in

Remington M1911

With America's entry into World War One, massive orders for weapons were placed. One of the many recipients being Remington, which was awarded a contract for 150,000 Colt Model 1911 auto-loading pistols, with first delivery on June 1, 1918. In the event, Remington did not make the first delivery until August 1918, not long before the end of the war on November 11 resulted in suspension of the contract on December 17. A few more were produced but the final total was 21,677.

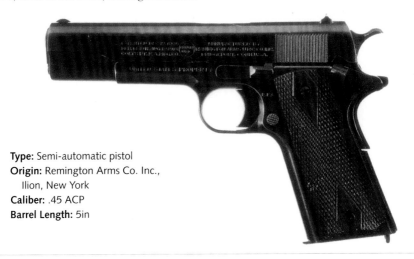

Type: Semi-automatic pistol
Origin: Remington Arms Co. Inc.,
Ilion, New York
Caliber: .45 ACP
Barrel Length: 5in

Remington Model 51

Remington's first company autoloader was designed by J.D. Petersen. The gun appeared on the market in 1919 as the Model 51 and was available in two versions. The main model was chambered for .38 Auto, with a seven-round magazine, while the .32ACP version, with an eight-round magazine, was made in much smaller numbers. The mechanism used a combination delayed blowback/recoil system, in which when the cartridge was fired the slide and breechblock moved back together very briefly, before the block stopped and unlocked, allowing the slide to continue to the rear.

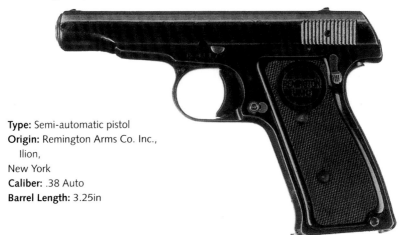

Type: Semi-automatic pistol
Origin: Remington Arms Co. Inc.,
Ilion,
New York
Caliber: .38 Auto
Barrel Length: 3.25in

Remington Model XP-100 Long-Range Target Pistol

The XP-100 series started with Remington's early 1960s decision to produce a high-powered, bolt-action, varmint pistol, chambered for a newly-developed .221 Remington "Fireball" centerfire cartridge. The first model was the single shot XP-100 (seen here with fitted scope). The company claimed that it "shoots faster, flatter, farther and tighter than any handgun in history." Since then, a number of variations have been produced featuring different sights, calibers, and stocks.

Type: Single-shot bolt-action pistol
Origin: Remington Arms Co. Inc., Ilion, New York
Caliber: .221 Remington
Barrel Length: 14.5in

Ruger Mark I Target Pistol

William B. Ruger and Alexander Sturm set up in business in 1949 to sell their "Standard Model." This was a .22 caliber, 4.75-inch barrel, blowback, semi-automatic pistol, whose physical appearance deliberately reflected that of the legendary Luger. This was a major success and led to a more accurate target model with the same frame and receiver, but a much longer 6.9in barrel, and adjustable, competition sights; this was introduced in 1951 and remained in production until 1982. The example shown here is an early weapon, with the Ruger red eagle medallion on the left grip; this device was changed to black on Alexander Sturm's death in 1951.

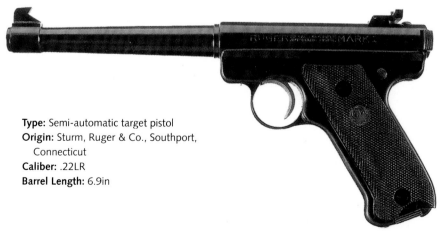

Type: Semi-automatic target pistol
Origin: Sturm, Ruger & Co., Southport, Connecticut
Caliber: .22LR
Barrel Length: 6.9in

Ruger Mark II Target Pistol

The Ruger Mark II was introduced in 1982. It retained the appearance of the original Mark I, but included some significant improvements, including a redesigned safety, magazine capacity Increased to ten rounds, bolt-stop thumb-piece, and small grooves to improve the grip on the bolt. As with the Mark I there was a parallel Mark II Target model, with the same mechanical characteristics, but with a variety of target-type barrels and adjustable sights. This example has the 5.5-inch bull barrel.

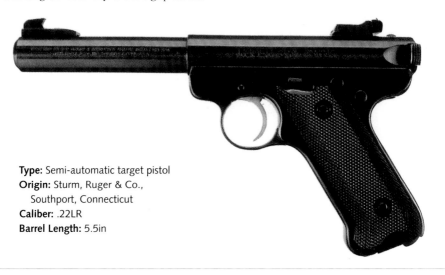

Type: Semi-automatic target pistol
Origin: Sturm, Ruger & Co.,
    Southport, Connecticut
Caliber: .22LR
Barrel Length: 5.5in

Ruger P85

The P85, a very contemporary looking pistol which appeared in 1985, is a double-action, locked breech automatic, employing the Browning swinging-link lock, but with changes developed by Ruger to ensure it is thoroughly reliable and accurate. The frame is fabricated from specially-hardened light alloy, there is an external hammer and the large ambidextrous safety catch, which is mounted on the slide, locks the firing-pin, blocks the hammer, and disconnects the trigger.

Type: Semi-automatic pistol
Origin: Sturm, Ruger & Co.,
    Southport, Connecticut
Caliber: 9mm Parabellum
Barrel Length: 4.5in

Ruger P89

The P89 is a recoil operated, locked breech semi-automatic pistol. It utilizes a 1911 style tilting barrel. The gun has an aluminum frame, with a steel slide and polycarbonate grip panels. Safety options such as the "D" model offers a decock only mode which leaves the hammer down in a safe position but is ready to fire with a double action trigger pull. The limited run P89X model came with a second barrel and recoil spring assembly that allowed conversion between 9mm and .30 Luger calibers.

Type: Semi-automatic pistol
Origin: Sturm, Ruger & Co.,
  Southport, Connecticut
Caliber: 9mm Parabellum
Barrel Length: 4.5in

Ruger P90

The P90 was launched very soon after the P89. Initially available only in stainless steel, it was chambered in .45 ACP, and has a magazine capacity of 8 rounds with the same high quality hard coated aircraft quality aluminum frame, steel slide and polycarbonate grip panels. We show a blued steel example here. The gun weighs 34 ounces and is 7.75 long overall. It is available in "Decocker" or Manual safety modes.

Type: Semi-automatic pistol
Origin: Sturm, Ruger & Co.,
  Southport, Connecticut
Caliber: .45ACP
Barrel Length: 4.5in

Ruger P95

The P95 was a revolutionary design. It used the P93's slide and barrel, but changed to a linkless design, intended to transfer energy to the frame less abruptly, reducing the felt recoil. The frame material was changed from aluminum to polyurethane resin based on Dow Chemical's "Isoplast." This reduced the weight of the pistol by four ounces. Unlike any other polymer frame handgun on the market at the time, the P95 had no metal inserts in the frame. The standard finish is blued with black polycarbonate, the gun show has a Insight M3 Flashlight fitted.

Type: Semi-automatic pistol
Origin: Sturm, Ruger & Co., Southport, Connecticut
Caliber: 9mm
Barrel Length: 4.5in

Ruger P345

The Ruger Model 345 features a compounded polymer frame, which is filled with long strand fiberglass filler. The Camblock frame design is designed to reduce felt recoil. The slide and frame are slimmer than on previous models and there is an optional Picatinny rail for lighting and sight accessories. The standard sights are a Dovetailed 3-dot system. The gun weighs twenty-nine ounces and comes with an eight-round magazine for the .45 caliber ammunition. The safety options are Manual or Decocker.

Type: Semi-automatic pistol
Origin: Sturm, Ruger & Co., Southport, Connecticut
Caliber: .45ACP
Barrel Length: 4.5in

Ruger P944

The P944 was a replacement for the P91 model and the P94, which have now disappeared from the company's catalog. As a direct descendant of those models it retains a metal construction with aluminum frames and steel slides. It has a slightly shorter barrel at 4.2 inches and weighs 33 ounces. The gun's main claim to fame is that it is chambered for the .40 S&W round and has an eleven-shot magazine. It is available with the Manual or Decocker safety systems, the latter being designated the P944D.

Type: Semi-automatic pistol
Origin: Sturm, Ruger & Co.,
    Southport, Connecticut
Caliber: .40 S&W
Barrel Length: 4.2in

Savage Model 1907

The design of this weapon originated with Major Elbert H. Searle, whose patent included the use of the bullet's torque to twist the barrel to unlock the breech, and a magazine with staggered rounds, increasing capacity compared to contemporary models. Although the pistol worked well, the supposed use of torque was often disputed, and many experts claimed that it was, in reality, a delayed blowback system. Searle sold his patent to Savage, resulting in the Model 1907. The example shown here is the .32 caliber, 3.75-inch model. There was also a .38 version with a 4.25-inch barrel.

Type: Semi-automatic pistol
Origin: Savage Arms Corp., Utica,
New York
Caliber: .32
Barrel Length: 3.6in

Savage Model 1907 Test

Savage developed a special version of the Model 1907, chambered for the .45in ACP cartridge, which was entered in the competition for the US army's standard automatic. The prototypes survived the army's initial trials and some 290 were then produced between 1900 and 1911, which were issued to the 3rd, 6th, and 11th Cavalry for field trials in competition with the Colt-Browning design. The army selected the latter, which was put into production as the Ml911 and the trial batch of Savage pistols were returned to the company for disposal.

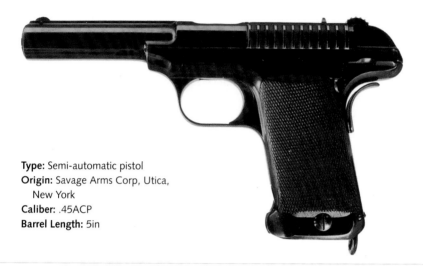

Type: Semi-automatic pistol
Origin: Savage Arms Corp, Utica, New York
Caliber: .45ACP
Barrel Length: 5in

Savage Model 1915

The Model 1915, also known as the "hammerless gun" featured a hidden cocking-piece, grip safety, and a hold-open device which locked the slide in the open position after the last round in the magazine had been fired. A total of 10,400 Model 1915s was produced in .32 and .38 versions (one of the latter is shown here) but it was not a great success.

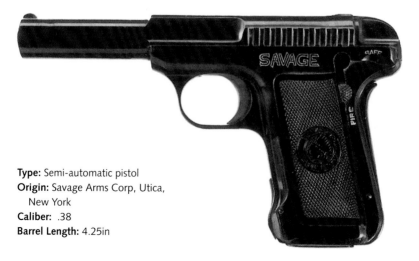

Type: Semi-automatic pistol
Origin: Savage Arms Corp, Utica, New York
Caliber: .38
Barrel Length: 4.25in

Savage Model 1917

The lack of success of the Model 1915 resulted in a new design only two years later. The visible cocking spur of the original Model 1907 was restored, the grip safety deleted and the shape of the grip improved. As before, however, there were two models: .32 caliber with 3.6-inch barrel, and .38 caliber with 4.25-inch barrel. The Model 1917 remained in production until 1928. An example of the .32 caliber version with the 3.6-inch barrel is shown here.

Type: Semi-automatic pistol
Origin: Savage Arms Corp, Utica, New York
Caliber: .32ACP/.38ACP
Barrel Length: 3.6 and 4.25in

Sheridan Tip-Up Single-Shot Pistol

Sheridan Products normally produced air-guns and gas-guns, but made this single essay into conventional pistols in 1953. It was a single-shot weapon designed to look like an automatic and was made of plastic and steel pressings. Since it fired .22 rounds it was clearly not a toy, but it was of little real use other than for not-too-serious target practise. It had the unofficial title of "the Knockabout" and remained in production until 1963.

Type: Tip-up single-shot pistol
Origin: Sheridan Products Inc., Racine, Wisconsin
Caliber: .22LR
Barrel Length: 5in

Smith & Wesson Automatic Model of 1913

Smith & Wesson had continuing and outstanding success with revolvers and hesitated for many years before attempting to move into the automatic field. The result was this pistol, which appeared in 1913. It was chambered for the specially developed rimless .35 S&W Automatic cartridge, and based (under license) on patents held by a Belgian, Charles Clement of Liege. The weapon employed a simple, if unusual, blowback system, with the recoil spring above the barrel and a grip safety located immediately below the trigger guard. The magazine held seven rounds.

Type: Semi-automatic pistol
Origin: Smith & Wesson, Springfield,
   Massachusetts
Caliber: .35 S&W automatic
Barrel Length: 3.5in

Smith & Wesson Automatic Model of 1924

Realising that the .35 Automatic and its ammunition were never going to be a commercial success, Smith & Wesson had another try, but this time using the much more readily available .32 ACP round. The designers also simplified the operation of the gun and smartened its appearance, but the result was even more dismal with only about one thousand being produced. One consequence of this small production run is that this weapon is eagerly sought by today's collectors, who will pay a high price for an example in excellent condition.

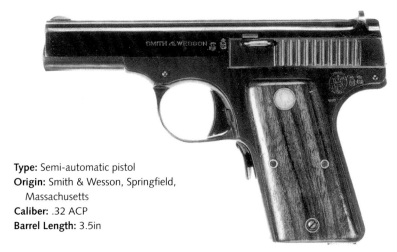

Type: Semi-automatic pistol
Origin: Smith & Wesson, Springfield,
   Massachusetts
Caliber: .32 ACP
Barrel Length: 3.5in

Smith & Wesson Model 39

After their experiences with the .35 and .32 automatics, Smith & Wesson waited until 1957 before introducing a new model, but this proved to be a winner and the first in a long line. The Model 39 was the first double-action automatic to be produced in the United States. It fired 9mm Parabellum and was selected for service with the US navy and air force, as well as with the Special Forces. Most of those produced had steel frames, but the example seen here was one of only 927 with an aluminum frame.

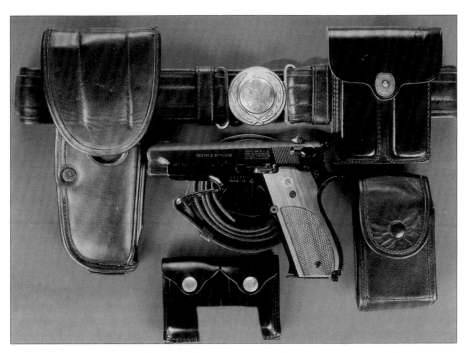

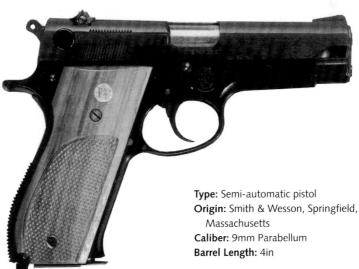

Type: Semi-automatic pistol
Origin: Smith & Wesson, Springfield, Massachusetts
Caliber: 9mm Parabellum
Barrel Length: 4in

Smith & Wesson Model 41

The Model 41 was a totally new design, introduced in 1957 for US National Match Course, as well as UTT Standard Pistol, Standard Handgun and Ladies competitions. The weapon has a grip set at the same angle as that of .45 automatics, which houses a ten-round magazine.

Various barrel lengths are available (7.375, 5.5, and 5 inches). With the five-and-a-half-inch barrel, the gun weighed forty-one ounces. Both fore- and rear sights are fully adjustable, the latter being mounted on a rib extending rearwards from the barrel, rather than on the slide.

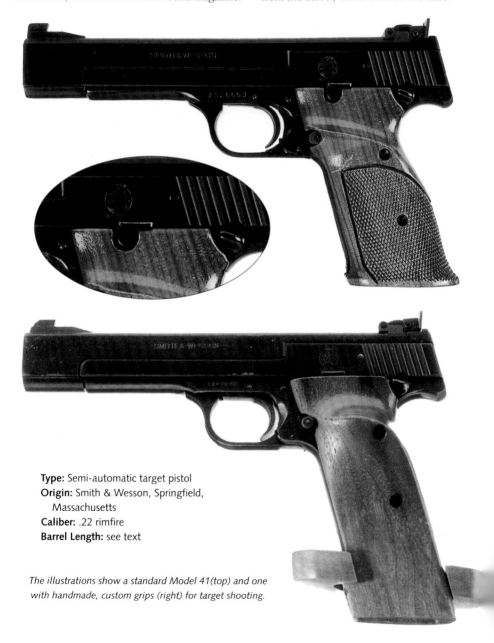

Type: Semi-automatic target pistol
Origin: Smith & Wesson, Springfield,
    Massachusetts
Caliber: .22 rimfire
Barrel Length: see text

The illustrations show a standard Model 41(top) and one with handmade, custom grips (right) for target shooting.

Smith & Wesson Model 59

The Model 59 was generally similar in design to the Model 39, being of 9mm caliber, but with a wider anodized aluminum frame (to accommodate a double-stack magazine holding fourteen rounds,) a straight backstrap, a magazine disconnect (the pistol will not fire unless a magazine is in place,) and a blued carbon steel slide that carries the manual safety. The grip is of three pieces made of two nylon panels joined by a metal backstrap. It was in production from 1971 to 1982.

Type: Semi-automatic pistol
Origin: Smith & Wesson, Springfield, Massachusetts
Caliber: 9mm Parabellum
Barrel Length: 4in

Smith & Wesson Model 459

The Smith & Wesson Model 459 was an updated version of the Model 59 with adjustable sights improved sights, marginally longer barrel (4.1-inches) and an alloy frame. The Model 559 (not shown) had a stainless steel frame, but was otherwise identical to the 459, with checkered nylon grips and a squared-off trigger guard with serrations. This model was discontinued in 1988. 803 units were produced in a brush finish with special grips made to FBI specifications.

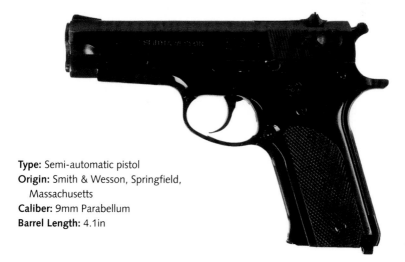

Type: Semi-automatic pistol
Origin: Smith & Wesson, Springfield, Massachusetts
Caliber: 9mm Parabellum
Barrel Length: 4.1in

Smith & Wesson Model 61

The Model 61, also known as "The Escort," is the only pocket automatic ever to be marketed by Smith & Wesson. A very small and handy design, it was chambered for the .22LR cartridge and had a five-round magazine. The barrel was 1.1 inches in length. The gun was available in two finishes, nickel, or blue (as seen here). It remained in production for a mere four years.

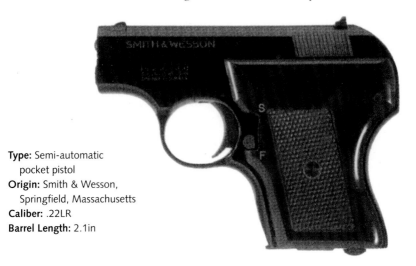

Type: Semi-automatic
   pocket pistol
Origin: Smith & Wesson,
   Springfield, Massachusetts
Caliber: .22LR
Barrel Length: 2.1in

Smith & Wesson Model 3914

Smith & Wesson revamped their existing range of 9mm automatics in 1989. The lead model was the 3904, which had a four-inch barrel, eight-round magazine, squared trigger guard to facilitate two-hand use, and an alloy frame. The Model 3906 was identical except that it was made of stainless steel. Also introduced was the Model 3914, seen here, which was slightly smaller than the Model 3904, with a three-and-a-half-inch barrel and a reduced overall length. It had an alloy frame and blued carbon steel slide, and an eight-round magazine.

Type: Semi-automatic pistol
Origin: Smith & Wesson,
   Springfield, Massachusetts
Caliber: 9mm Parabellum
Barrel Length: 3.5in

Smith & Wesson Model 1066

The Model 1006 is a full-size weapon chambered for the 10mm cartridge and a nine-round magazine. Both frame and slide were made of stainless steel. The slightly smaller Model 1066 complemented this version, as seen here, which had a 4.25-inch barrel, black plastic grips, and white-dot sights.

Type: Semi-automatic pistol
Origin: Smith & Wesson, Springfield, Massachusetts
Caliber: 10mm
Barrel Length: 4.25in

Smith & Wesson Model 4506

The Smith & Wesson Model 4506 was a new version of the .45 ACP pistol with a five-inch barrel and an eight-round magazine. It is a heavy gun weighing three pounds when loaded. The example shown here is the original Model 4506, later models had rounded trigger guards. The gun has a stainless steel finish, white-dot sights, and black Delrin grips. It was produced from 1988 to 1999.

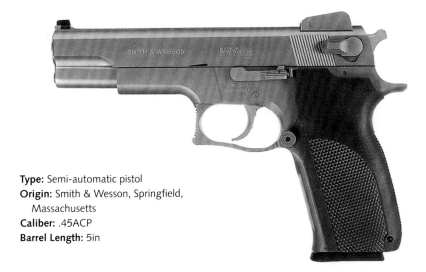

Type: Semi-automatic pistol
Origin: Smith & Wesson, Springfield, Massachusetts
Caliber: .45ACP
Barrel Length: 5in

239

Smith & Wesson Model 745

The International Practical Shooting Confederation (IPSC) was officially founded in May 1976 and Smith & Wesson marked its tenth anniversary with a special Model 745-IPSC, which was engraved with the dates and the IPSC logo on the right side of the slide. Some 5,000 of these were produced. The type was then included in the company catalog, but without the engraving, as seen here. The Model 745 was a single-action only weapon with fully adjustable target sights, stainless steel frame, and an eight-round magazine. Production lasted from 1986 to 1990.

Type: Semi-automatic pistol
Origin: Smith & Wesson,
　　　Springfield, Massachusetts
Caliber: .45 ACP
Barrel Length: 5in

Standard Arms of Nevada Model SA-9

This tiny pistol has an overall length of only six inches and weighs only fourteen ounces. It is 9mm Parabellum caliber, double-action only, of sub-compact design, with a ten-shot magazine, 3.1-inch barrel, and black polymer frame with matte black steel slide. Standard Arms of Nevada manufactured the weapon between 1999 and 2000. James Waldof, the former owner of Lorcin Engineering Inc., established the company in 1999.

Type: Semi-automatic
　　　pistol
Origin: Standard Arms
　　　of Nevada,
　　　Reno, Nevada
Caliber: 9mm
Barrel Length: 3.1in

Stevens No. 10 Target Pistol

This single-shot pistol was deliberately styled to look like an automatic, with a heavy, squared-off receiver, angled grip, and long, exposed barrel. In fact, there was a prominent release catch on the left side of the weapon which when pushed forward enabled the barrel to be pivoted forward for reloading. On closing the barrel, the catch, which was mounted on a cam, drew the barrel back towards the breech. The round, knurled knob on the rear of the weapon is the cocking-piece.

Type: Single-shot target pistol
Origin: Stevens Arms Co, Chicopee Falls, Massachusetts
Caliber: .22 LR
Barrel Length: 5in

Thompson/Center Contender

Kenneth Thompson and Warren Center founded this company in 1966 to produce firearms of the very highest quality. The original pistol range was based on the Contender, a single-shot weapon with a tip-up barrel and an external hammer. The barrels are either ten or fourteen inches long and are available in a wide variety of chamberings. Seen here is the basic weapon mounting a .22 WMR barrel, with an extra barrel in .44 MAG. The grip is made from walnut and the fore-end is made from American black walnut, with various lengths available to suit the barrel length.

Type: Single-shot target pistol
Origin: Thompson/Center Arms, Rochester, New Hampshire
Caliber: see text
Barrel Length: see text

241

Warner Infallible

The Warner Arms Corporation was set up in 1912, primarily to market weapons made for them by other companies in the United States and abroad. Warner bought the rights for a pistol designed by Andrew Fyrberg, which was later manufactured and marketed under the Davis-

Warner name as "The Infallible," as seen here. This proved to be a complete misnomer, as it proved to be particularly fault-prone, sometimes dangerously so. In addition, it had a crude-looking cast-iron frame and was not comfortable to hold. Unsurprisingly, it did not sell well.

Type: Semi-automatic pistol
Origin: Warner Arms Corporation, Brooklyn, New York, and Norwich, Connecticut
Caliber: .32ACP
Barrel Length: 3.25in

Wildey Survivor

This range of pistols was developed by W. J. "Wildey" Moore and has an adjustable gas system, which can be easily configured for differing loads. Two rounds, the .45 Winchester Magnum and 9mm Winchester Magnum were developed specially for these weapons. The pistol is gas-operated and has a

three-lug rotating bolt. The patented gas system is adjusted using the ring ahead of the piston and users report that, despite its power, the pistol is comfortable to use. The version shown here is chambered for the .45 Winchester Magnum round, has a 5in barrel, and has a stainless steel finish.

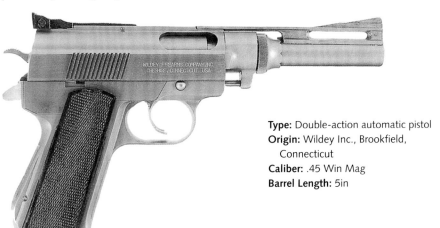

Type: Double-action automatic pistol
Origin: Wildey Inc., Brookfield, Connecticut
Caliber: .45 Win Mag
Barrel Length: 5in

Modern Revolvers

Korth Revolvers

Korth Vertriebs-GmbH was established in 1954 in Ratzeburg, in the state of Holstein in northern Germany. The company started to produce revolvers to its own design in the 1970s. There is, in effect, just one design; a conventional solid-frame, double-action weapon with a sideways swinging fluted cylinder and a cylinder-release catch. Most unusually, this is mounted alongside the hammer. All have a double action trigger with three adjustable let-off regulating points. The guns are offered with a variety of calibers, interchangeable barrels, cylinders, and various patterns of grip, but all are made to a very high standard of engineering and finish.

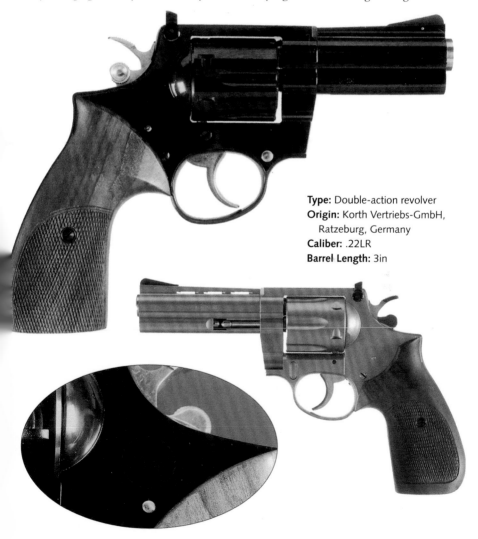

Type: Double-action revolver
Origin: Korth Vertriebs-GmbH,
   Ratzeburg, Germany
Caliber: .22LR
Barrel Length: 3in

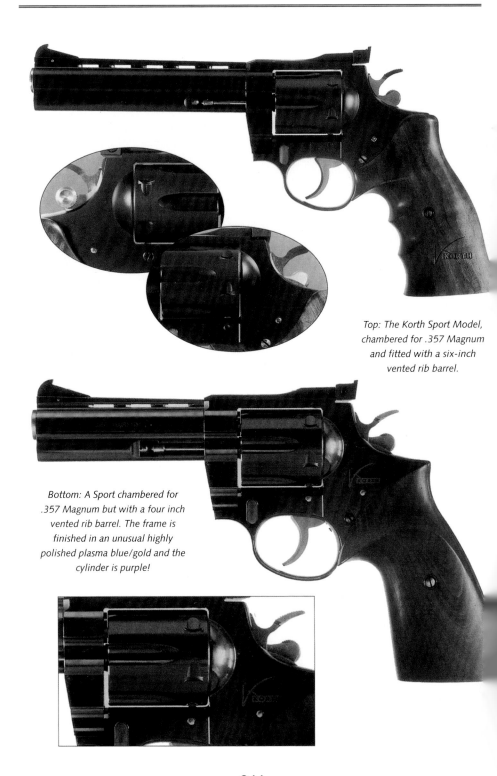

Top: The Korth Sport Model,
chambered for .357 Magnum
and fitted with a six-inch
vented rib barrel.

Bottom: A Sport chambered for
.357 Magnum but with a four inch
vented rib barrel. The frame is
finished in an unusual highly
polished plasma blue/gold and the
cylinder is purple!

Mateba Model 6 Semi-Automatic Revolver

It does not matter how well established some aspects of design may be, there will always be somebody who will challenge them. Sometimes even stand them completely on their head, as, quite literally, has been done in this case. Thus, in the Mateba Model 6, the barrel aligns with the bottom, rather than the top, cylinder; it is the front sight that is adjustable, while the rear sight is fixed; and although it has a revolving cylinder, it is, in fact, a semi-automatic weapon.

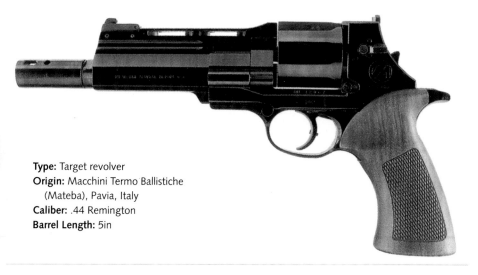

Type: Target revolver
Origin: Macchini Termo Ballistiche
   (Mateba), Pavia, Italy
Caliber: .44 Remington
Barrel Length: 5in

Uberti 1848 Colt Whitneyville

In 1959, Aldo Uberti founded A. Uberti, S.r.l. in the gun making center of Gardone Val Trompia in the Italian Alps and began making replicas of Civil War-era cap-and-ball revolvers. Uberti then expanded into replicas of classic black powder lever-action rifles, cowboy six-shooters, and big game rifles. Not only are the Uberti guns exact replicas down to the finest detail, but with modern machinery and materials, the company claims that they are actually better than the originals.

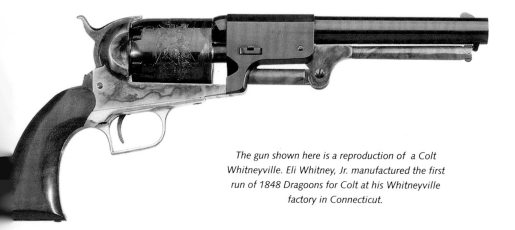

The gun shown here is a reproduction of a Colt Whitneyville. Eli Whitney, Jr. manufactured the first run of 1848 Dragoons for Colt at his Whitneyville factory in Connecticut.

Nambu Meiji 26th Year Service Revolver

In the late nineteenth century, Japan's primary preoccupation was with catching up with the West, from which it had been cut-off for many centuries. The government was determined that the country should be self-sufficient and groups of officers were tasked with achieving this. One such group assembled as many Western revolvers as possible and then studied them carefully before producing a weapon, which incorporated the best ideas from Europe and the United States. They culled ideas from Colt, Nagant, and others. This gun was the outcome.

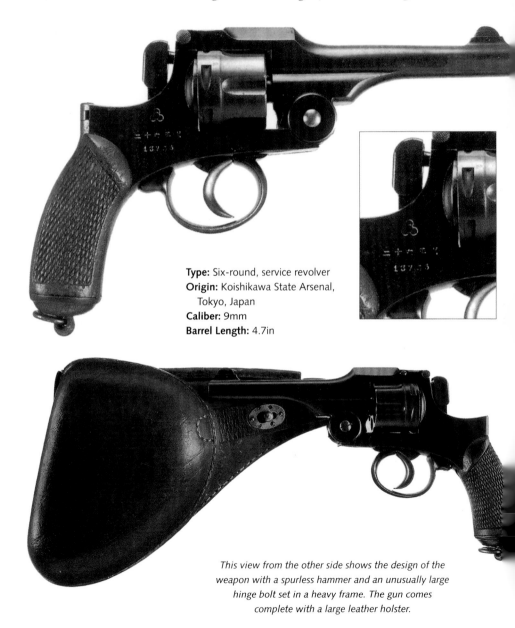

Type: Six-round, service revolver
Origin: Koishikawa State Arsenal, Tokyo, Japan
Caliber: 9mm
Barrel Length: 4.7in

This view from the other side shows the design of the weapon with a spurless hammer and an unusually large hinge bolt set in a heavy frame. The gun comes complete with a large leather holster.

Nagant M1895 Gas-Seal Revolver

The design and production rights to the Nagant patented gas-seal revolver were purchased by the Imperial Russian government in 1895 and deliveries started from the Tula Arsenal in 1899. Production continued following the Revolution and the establishment of the USSR in 1918, and throughout World War Two, ending only in 1945. The stopping power of the high-velocity 7.62mm bullet was not particularly great, but the cylinder housed seven rounds and the weapon was extremely reliable, making it very popular with its users.

Type: Seven-round service revolver
Origin: Tula State Arsenal, Russia/USSR
Caliber: 7.62mm
Barrel Length: 4.3in

Husqvarna-Nagant Ml887 Service Revolver

In 1887, the Swedish Army ran trials between the Swiss Model 1882 and a new Nagant weapon, which was won by the latter. This was then put into production at the Husqvarna factory as the Husqvarna-Nagant M1887 and remained in production until 1905. The M1887 was chambered for the 7.5 x 22R Nagant cartridge and had a six-round fluted cylinder. It remained in front-line service for many years and was then placed in reserve, with the last being disposed of as late as 1958.

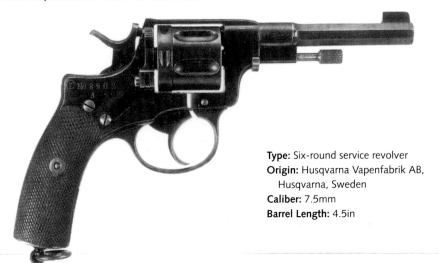

Type: Six-round service revolver
Origin: Husqvarna Vapenfabrik AB,
    Husqvarna, Sweden
Caliber: 7.5mm
Barrel Length: 4.5in

Webley Mark II Service Revolver

The Webley Mark I entered service in 1887 and remained in wide-scale use in the British and Imperial forces for many years, being periodically upgraded. The production successor to the Mark I was the Mark II, first issued in 1894, which differed from the Mark I in having a new hammer with a larger spur, a revised butt and a modified recoil shield. Like the earlier version, the Mark I was chambered for the .455 Webley round and had a six-round fluted cylinder.

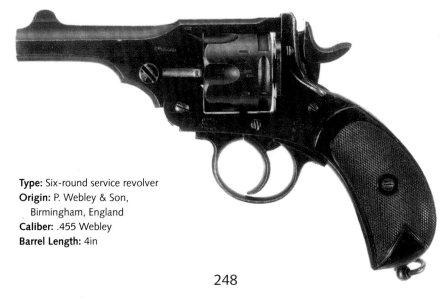

Type: Six-round service revolver
Origin: P. Webley & Son,
    Birmingham, England
Caliber: .455 Webley
Barrel Length: 4in

Enfield No. 2 Mark 1 and Mark 1* Revolver

Following the experiences of World War One the British Army decided that a smaller caliber than they had previously used would be preferable and .38in was eventually selected. This still had effective stopping power, but could be fired from a weapon that was smaller, lighter, and easier to fire. The revolver developed for this round was the Enfield No 2 Mk 1, in essence, a smaller version of the old Webley & Scott Mk VI, which began to reach troops in 1932 and was produced in very large numbers.

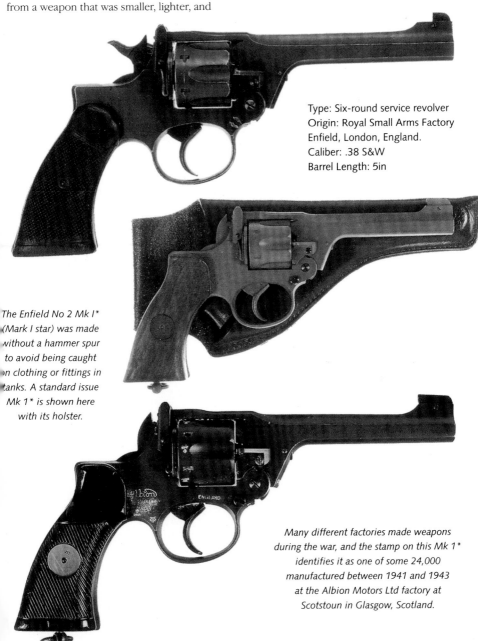

Type: Six-round service revolver
Origin: Royal Small Arms Factory
Enfield, London, England.
Caliber: .38 S&W
Barrel Length: 5in

The Enfield No 2 Mk I (Mark I star) was made without a hammer spur to avoid being caught on clothing or fittings in tanks. A standard issue Mk 1* is shown here with its holster.*

Many different factories made weapons during the war, and the stamp on this Mk 1 identifies it as one of some 24,000 manufactured between 1941 and 1943 at the Albion Motors Ltd factory at Scotstoun in Glasgow, Scotland.*

Webley & Scott Mark IV Service Revolver

Webley & Scott was the main supplier of revolvers to the British Army and the Mark IV, which was approved in 1899, continued that tradition. It was being issued as the British Army deployed to South Africa to take part in the Boer War, which resulted in the popular nickname, the "Boer War model." The Mark IV was, in reality, little different in overall design from the Mark III, but was fabricated from higher-grade steel and the hammer spur was made wider for ease of handling.

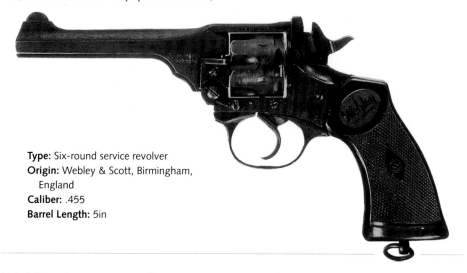

Type: Six-round service revolver
Origin: Webley & Scott, Birmingham, England
Caliber: .455
Barrel Length: 5in

Webley & Scott Mark VI Service Revolver

The Mark VI was the last Webley & Scott revolver to be accepted for service by the British Army and was also the best. It did not differ very greatly from its predecessors except that the butt was of a more "squared-off" shape in contrast to the earlier "bird beak" designs. It was a hinged-frame design with a substantial, stirrup-type barrel catch, which also incorporated the rear sight. It did excellent work in the trenches of World War One, standing up well to the dirty and damp conditions, and was particularly useful in trench raids.

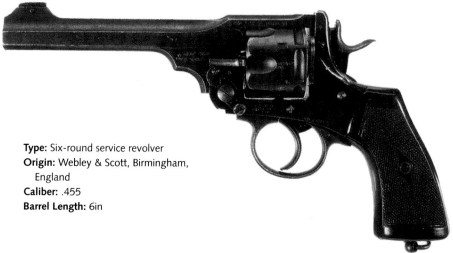

Type: Six-round service revolver
Origin: Webley & Scott, Birmingham, England
Caliber: .455
Barrel Length: 6in

Webley-Fosbery Automatic Revolver

Semi-automatic pistols were just beginning to appear when Colonel Fosbery (1832 - 1907) devised a revolver that cocked the hammer and rotated the cylinder by sliding the action, cylinder, and barrel assembly back on the frame. Fosbery patented his invention 1895 and further improvements were patented in 1896. Fosbery took his design to Webley & Scott Revolver and Arms Co., the primary manufacturer of service pistols for the British Army. Webley further developed the design and the Webley-Fosbery Automatic Revolver was introduced at the matches at Bisley of July 1900.

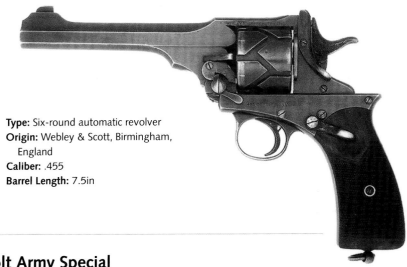

Type: Six-round automatic revolver
Origin: Webley & Scott, Birmingham, England
Caliber: .455
Barrel Length: 7.5in

Colt Army Special

The Army Special was an improved version of the New Army Revolver, and was introduced in 1908. It had a heavier frame, the cylinder rotation was changed to clockwise, and it was given a more "modern" appearance, for example, by sloping the front face of the frame. It was produced with a 4, 4.5, 5, or 6-inch barrel, and chambered for .32-20, .38 Colt, .38 S&W, or .41 Colt. This example has a five-inch barrel and is made for .32-20.

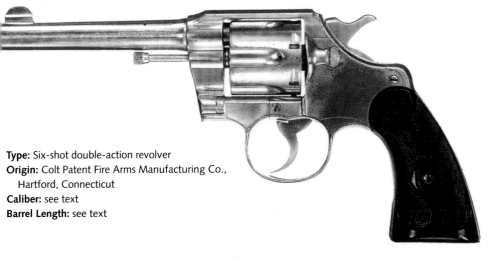

Type: Six-shot double-action revolver
Origin: Colt Patent Fire Arms Manufacturing Co., Hartford, Connecticut
Caliber: see text
Barrel Length: see text

Colt US Army Model 1917

This was developed from the New Service model and was produced only in .45 caliber (rimless) and with a 5.5 inch barrel. The main difference to the New Service model was the ammunition loading/ejection system, which involved loading in two clips of three rounds.

When the Army contract ended, Colt used the spares in the factory to produce some 1,000 for the civilian market. The only difference between the two types is that the Army revolver has its designation stamped on the butt; the civilian version does not.

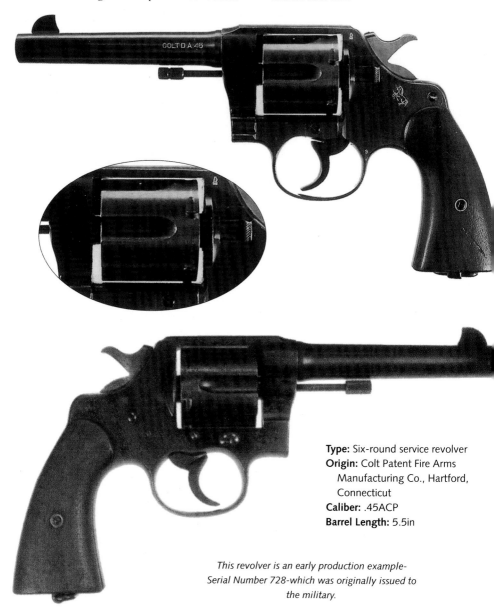

Type: Six-round service revolver
Origin: Colt Patent Fire Arms
  Manufacturing Co., Hartford,
  Connecticut
Caliber: .45ACP
Barrel Length: 5.5in

This revolver is an early production example-Serial Number 728-which was originally issued to the military.

Colt Official Police

The Official Police model was introduced by Colt in 1927 and was, in effect, a minor updating of the 1908 Army Special. Modifications included a wider, square-shaped backsight notch, and a darker blue coloring of the metalwork. Concerning calibers, .38 was available throughout its life, while .41 Colt was available until 1932, and .32-20 until 1942, while .22 OR was introduced in 1930. Barrel lengths were 2, 4, 5, and 6 inches. The model remained in production until 1969, during which time some 400,000 were sold.

Type: Six-round double-action revolver
Origin: Colt Patent Fire Arms
  Manufacturing Co., Hartford,
  Connecticut
Caliber: see text
Barrel Length: see text

This is a standard model that the owner has modified by installing a powerful scope and changing the grips.

Colt Anaconda

The Anaconda was introduced in 1990 chambered in .44 Magnum, but with four, six, or eight-inch barrel lengths. The gun was machined from satin-finish stainless steel, and it was fitted with black neoprene grips with finger grooves. In 1993, a new model chambered for the .45 Colt entered the catalog with either a six inch or eight inch barrel. Then, in 1986 a further model entered the range, which is completely finished in Realtree camouflage and has an eight-inch barrel. Seen here is an Anaconda with a four-inch barrel, firing the .44 Magnum round.

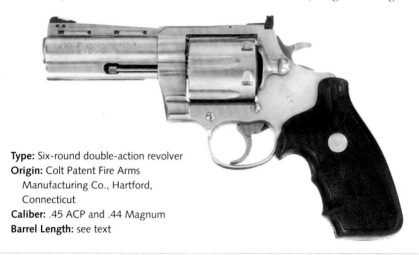

Type: Six-round double-action revolver
Origin: Colt Patent Fire Arms
　　Manufacturing Co., Hartford,
　　Connecticut
Caliber: .45 ACP and .44 Magnum
Barrel Length: see text

Colt Cobra

The Cobra was developed from the Detective Special, but with an alloy frame, which reduced the weight from twenty-two to fifteen ounces, and was in production from 1950 to 1973. It was available in .22 LR, .32, or .38 Special, and most of those produced had a two-inch barrel. A variant was the "Aircrew man Special" which weighed a mere eleven ounces, but was never sold commercially. Shown here is an excellent example of the Cobra, chambered for .38 Special, and with a two-inch barrel, nickel-plated finish and walnut grips.

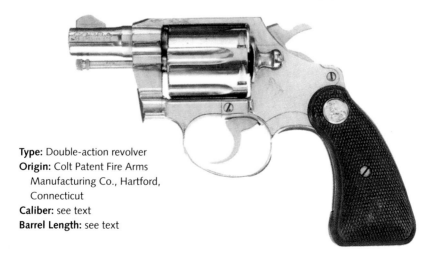

Type: Double-action revolver
Origin: Colt Patent Fire Arms
　　Manufacturing Co., Hartford,
　　Connecticut
Caliber: see text
Barrel Length: see text

Colt Commando (1942)

The Colt Commando's dramatic name disguises its rather more prosaic purpose, which was to equip security guards and other security men at defense factories. It was, in fact, the 1939 .38 Official Police revolver with a four inch barrel (although a few were produced with six inch barrels).

Type: Double-action revolver
Origin: Colt Patent Fire Arms
    Manufacturing Co., Hartford,
    Connecticut
Caliber: .38
Barrel Length: 4in

Colt Diamondback

The Diamondback was introduced in 1966 and remained in production for twenty years. It was based on the short frame of the Detective Special, but with the Python's vented rib, shrouded ejector rod and sighting system. Three barrel lengths were available (2.5, 4, or 6 inches) and two calibers (.22LR and .38 Special). The example shown here has a blue finish, vented-rib barrel, adjustable rear sight and walnut grips with the Colt medallion.

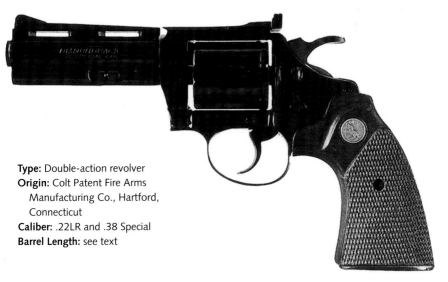

Type: Double-action revolver
Origin: Colt Patent Fire Arms
    Manufacturing Co., Hartford,
    Connecticut
Caliber: .22LR and .38 Special
Barrel Length: see text

Colt Police Positive

In 1905, Colt introduced its positive-lock mechanism, an additional safety feature which was designed to prevent the firing-pin from striking the cartridge unless the hammer was in the fully cocked position. To make it clear to customers that a revolver incorporated this new device the name "Positive" was added to the name, and so when the lock was added to the New Police Model, the latter became the Police Positive. It was chambered for .32, and 2.5, 4, 5, and 6-inch barrels were available.

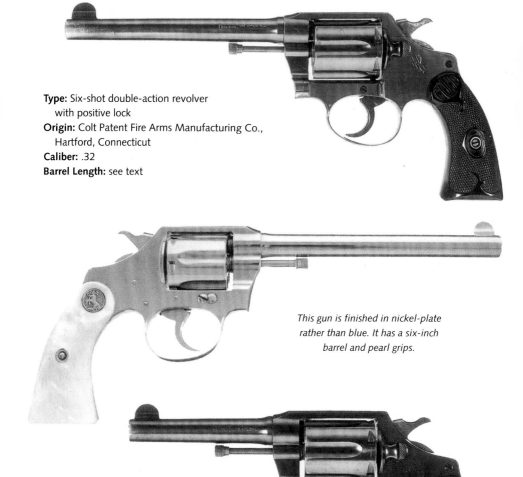

Type: Six-shot double-action revolver
  with positive lock
Origin: Colt Patent Fire Arms Manufacturing Co.,
  Hartford, Connecticut
Caliber: .32
Barrel Length: see text

This gun is finished in nickel-plate rather than blue. It has a six-inch barrel and pearl grips.

This .38 Special with a four-inch barrel was made especially for the Railway Express Agency.

Colt Python Double-Action Revolver

The Python was introduced as a "top-of-the-range" model in 1955 and was Colt's first totally new design since the early 1900s. It featured a heavy barrel with a vented rib (which is stippled to prevent reflections). All models are chambered for .357 Magnum, with 2.5, 4, 6, or 8 inch barrels (a 3 inch barrel had been discontinued). A variety of finishes were available, ranging from royal blue, through matte, to a highly polished stainless steel, this was designated "the Ultimate." The one shown here has a 6 inch barrel and is in the basic blue finish, with molded rubber grips.

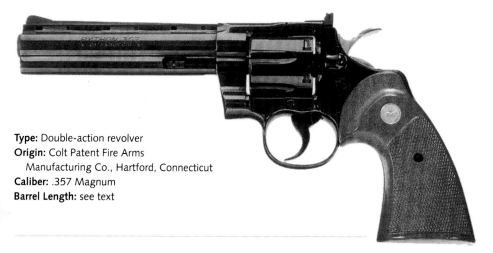

Type: Double-action revolver
Origin: Colt Patent Fire Arms
    Manufacturing Co., Hartford, Connecticut
Caliber: .357 Magnum
Barrel Length: see text

Phillips & Rodgers Model 47

This most unusual revolver was designed by Jonathan Rodgers, who noticed that he had to carry a number of different caliber revolvers to his competition shoots and decided to do something about it. The result is this weapon that can handle any of 25 different cartridges in the .38/9mm, .357 range. Barrel lengths vary between two-and-a-half and six inches. The cylinder is made from especially hardened, very high quality MilSpec 4330 vanadium steel, which makes it double the strength of normal revolver cylinders. Within the chambers, there are special springs to hold rimless cartridges in place.

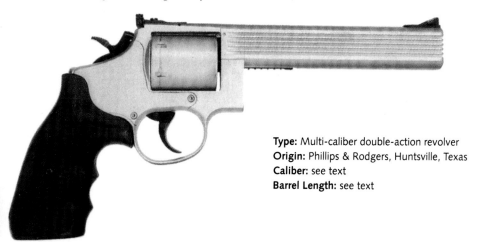

Type: Multi-caliber double-action revolver
Origin: Phillips & Rodgers, Huntsville, Texas
Caliber: see text
Barrel Length: see text

Ruger

Sturm, Ruger & Company was founded by William B. Ruger and Alexander McCormick Sturm in 1949 in a small rented machine shop in Southport, Connecticut. Just prior to their partnership, Bill Ruger had successfully designed his first .22 pistol in his garage, based on a captured Japanese Nambu that he acquired from a returning US Marine, at the close of World War Two. This first firearm produced by Ruger, the Standard .22 Automatic, was so successful that it launched the entire company, and has become the world's favorite .22 pistol. William Ruger's guns are not so much inventions, as they are refinements and improvements of other designs, which combined with state-of-the-art manufacturing techniques result in a better product. Ruger firearms is the nation's fourth largest firearms manufacturer, and the only one producing firearms in all four market segments: rifles, shotguns, pistols, and revolvers.

Ruger is a dominant player in the .22 rimfire rifle market in the US with the Ruger10/22. The 10/22 is popular due to it being relatively inexpensive and of good quality as well as the wealth of aftermarket accessories and parts available for it. In fact, the manufacturers claim that it is possible to build a 10/22 using only aftermarket parts, which are available to customers at very affordable prices.

Ruger similarly dominates the .22 rimfire semi automatic pistol market with the Ruger Mark III Like the 10/22, the MkIII is extremely well supported with a variety of good aftermarket accessories. Ruger Casting has plants in Newpor New Hampshire and Prescott, Arizona making ferrous, ductile iron and commercial titanium castings. Sturm, Ruger stock has been publicly traded since 1969, and became a New York Stock Exchange company in 1990. After Alex Sturm's death in 1951. William B. Ruger continued to direct the company until his death in 2002.

From 1949 through 2004, Ruger manufacture over twenty million firearms, and currently satis the requirement for guns of all kinds and purposes from hunting to law enforcement.

Ruger Bisley

Inspired by the 1894 Colt Bisley "Flat-top" this classic single-action Ruger pistol combines modern engineering with old style panache. The wide top strap accommodates an adjustable competition back sight. This particular gun has a blued frame and rosewood grips. Like the original Colt, the Ruger Bisley has the comfortable steeper grip shape that remains firmly in the palm of the hand while firing and reduces felt recoil. The gun is chambered for .45 Colt ammunition, and has the original's maximum barrel length of seven-and-a-half-inches.

Type: Single-action target revolver
Origin: Sturm, Ruger & Co., Southport, Connecticut
Caliber: .45 Colt
Barrel Length: 7.5in

Ruger Super Blackhawk Bisley Hunter

This full sized single-action revolver is designed to exploit the potential of the .44 Magnum cartridge for sporting uses. The gun utilizes the flat top Bisley frame and its heavy, ribbed 7.5 inch barrel is ready machined to accept Ruger 1 inch scope rings which are included in the basic price of the weapon. It comes standard with fixed sights, the front sight having a "Day-Glo" button for added visibility. It is finished in satin stainless with contrasting black laminate grips.

Type: Single-action target/sporting revolver
Origin: Sturm, Ruger & Co., Southport, Connecticut
Caliber: .44 Magnum
Barrel Length: 7.5in

Ruger Blackhawk

The Ruger Blackhawk is a six-shot, single-action revolver based on the iconic Colt 1873. Colt had very unwisely discontinued their gun prior to World War Two and failed to benefit from a buoyant market for "Cowboy" guns in the 1950s. Ruger introduced the Blackhawk in 1955 and although it bore a strong resemblance to the Colt, it scored over the old model by using more modern technology. For example it had coil springs instead of leaf springs. It was originally chambered for the .357 Magnum round but this was soon joined by a .44 Magnum version.

Type: Single-action revolver
Origin: Sturm, Ruger & Co., Southport, Connecticut
Caliber: .357 Magnum
Barrel Length: 4.63in

Ruger GP 100

The GP 100 is a medium sized double-action revolver introduced in 1985. The six round cylinder has Ruger's triple locking mechanism which secures it at the front, rear, and bottom of the frame. Chambered for the .357 Magnum cartridge, the gun can also utilize the less powerful, .38 Special. The GP 100 is strongly made with extra steel in crucial areas and no side plates. The example shown here is the stainless steel version with a four-inch barrel and rubber grips with rosewood inserts.

Type: Double-action revolver
Origin: Sturm, Ruger & Co., Southport, Connecticut
Caliber: .357 Magnum
Barrel Length: 4in

Ruger SP 101

The Ruger SP101 is a smaller frame counterpart to the GP101, both guns being marketed as replacements for the company's long standing and successful Security Six series of revolvers. The gun is very concealable at just seven inches long and weighing just twenty-five ounces in the 2.25-inch barreled version shown here. The cylinder holds five rounds of .357 Magnum ammunition. Our example has a spurless hammer but spurred versions are available. Finished in satin stainless steel with black rubber grips with synthetic inserts.

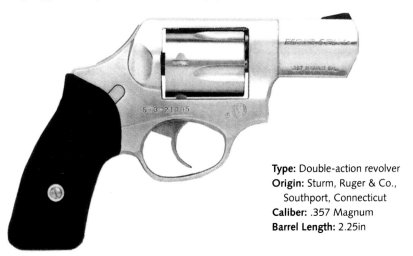

Type: Double-action revolver
Origin: Sturm, Ruger & Co., Southport, Connecticut
Caliber: .357 Magnum
Barrel Length: 2.25in

Ruger Blackhawk 50th Anniversary .44 Magnum "Flattop"

In 2006, Ruger celebrated fifty years of their Blackhawk .44 Magnum by producing a limited edition, which combined the best of Ruger's new design features with the revolver's most popular original features. The action incorporates Ruger's key-activated action lock, which disables the hammer for extra safety, and also features Ruger's newly patented reverse indexing pawl for easier loading and unloading. The top of the revolver's barrel is engraved and gold filled with the words, "50 Years Of .44 Magnum 1956 to 2006."

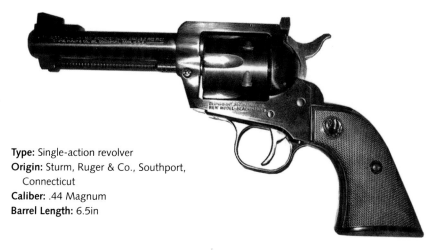

Type: Single-action revolver
Origin: Sturm, Ruger & Co., Southport, Connecticut
Caliber: .44 Magnum
Barrel Length: 6.5in

Ruger Model 117 Security Six Revolver

The Ruger line of revolvers started with the Single-Six model in 1953, which was an original Ruger design, but with the general visual impact of a Colt Single-Action Army. In 1970, the company turned to double-action revolvers with the weapon shown here, the Model 117, which was chambered for .357 Magnum and produced with 2.75, 4, or 6-inch barrels. The weapon was originally named the "Security Six" but this was later changed to "Service-Six." The model shown here is a 2.75-inch version with blue finish, walnut grips, and adjustable rear sight.

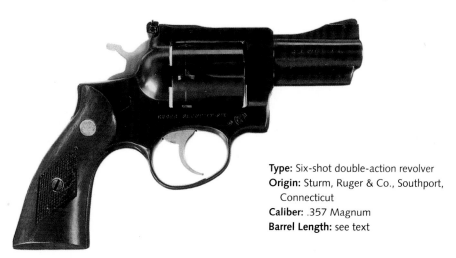

Type: Six-shot double-action revolver
Origin: Sturm, Ruger & Co., Southport, Connecticut
Caliber: .357 Magnum
Barrel Length: see text

Ruger New Bearcat

The New Bearcat is intended for campers and hikers where its lighter weight (twenty-four ounces) makes it easily portable. The .22 LR ammunition combines reasonable power with accuracy and reliability for the trail. The design is based on a Remington single-action from the 1860s and features a one-piece cylinder frame for extra rigidity. The gun incorporates new features like Ruger's transfer bar mechanism, giving both smooth operation and safety against accidental discharge. The example shown has blued finish and rosewood grips.

Type: Six-shot double-action revolver
Origin: Sturm, Ruger & Co., Southport, Connecticut
Caliber: .22LR
Barrel Length: 4in

Ruger New Model Super Blackhawk

When a gun maker has an iconic gun in its range, the best thing they can do is to carry on developing its potential. One such gun is the Ruger Blackhawk. A lot of the gun's appeal is its simple construction combined with great looks. Throw in a strengthened frame, a specialized grip, an adjustable rear sight, and add .44 Magnum ammunition, and you have a superb all round revolver for target range, campsite or trail. The example shown is with blued finish and traditional rosewood grips.

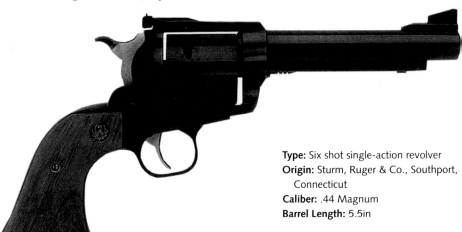

Type: Six shot single-action revolver
Origin: Sturm, Ruger & Co., Southport, Connecticut
Caliber: .44 Magnum
Barrel Length: 5.5in

Ruger New Model Single Six

The Single Six, first released in 1953 is currently produced as the New Model Single Six. The term "New Model" simply means that this model includes Ruger's transfer bar mechanism for increased safety, allowing the gun to be carried safely with all six chambers loaded. Ruger provides the transfer bar safety upgrade free of charge for owners of any old model Single Six. The New Model Single Six is currently chambered in .22 LR,.22 Magnum and .17HMR. Our example is in satin stainless finish and has a 6.5 inch barrel.

Type: Six shot single-action revolver
Origin: Sturm, Ruger & Co., Southport, Connecticut
Caliber: .22 LR/Mag
Barrel Length: 6.5in

Ruger Super Redhawk Alaskan

The Super Redhawk Alaskan is the ideal gun for outdoorsmen who hunt and fish in the habitat of dangerous big game. Its compact size (the two-and-a-half-inch barreled version) belies the power of its .454 Casull cartridge. The frame and particularly the top strap, has been strengthened to cope with the stresses imposed by powerful handgun calibers. The six-shot unfluted cylinder is machined from high-grade steel. The barrel is entirely contained within the extended frame as can be seen from the unusual angled shot.

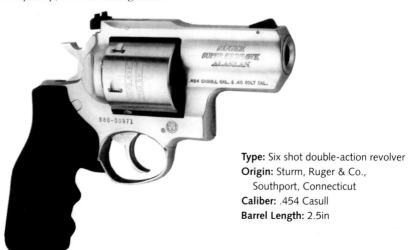

Type: Six shot double-action revolver
Origin: Sturm, Ruger & Co., Southport, Connecticut
Caliber: .454 Casull
Barrel Length: 2.5in

Ruger Redhawk

Ruger's first large bore double action revolver was the Redhawk, introduced in 1980. Influenced by the "Six" range of revolvers, it had a one-piece frame giving the strength needed to cope with heavy caliber ammunition. Other Redhawk features were a square butt grip, adjustable sights, and 5.5 and 7.5-inch barrel lengths. The Redhawk was available in blued or stainless steel (as seen here) and was primarily used by handgun hunters. Because it was designed for use with the heaviest .44 Magnum loads, it included a new latch system to firmly lock the cylinder at both front and rear.

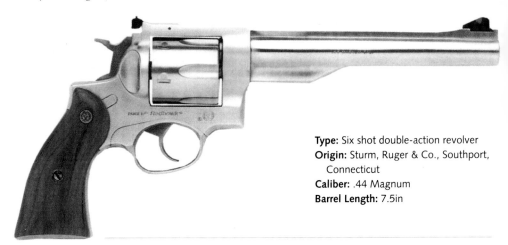

Type: Six shot double-action revolver
Origin: Sturm, Ruger & Co., Southport, Connecticut
Caliber: .44 Magnum
Barrel Length: 7.5in

Ruger New Vaquero

The Ruger Vaquero is known as "the gun that won the New West" because of its appeal to modern day cowboys and single-action target shooters. Since its introduction in 1993, it has combined the original "Old West" single-action look and feel with a modern internal mechanism and reliability. The New Vaquero includes blued, stainless steel, and engraved models in .357 Magnum and .45 Colt calibers, with barrel lengths of 4.62, 5.5, and 7.5 inches. Stainless steel New Vaqueros feature a high-gloss finish, simulating the attractive, patinated nickel-plating found on many original revolvers.

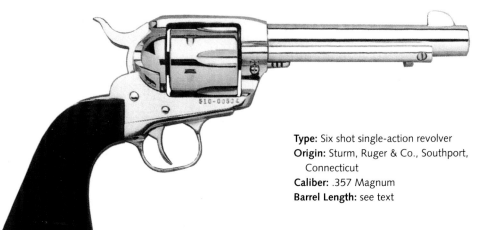

Type: Six shot single-action revolver
Origin: Sturm, Ruger & Co., Southport, Connecticut
Caliber: .357 Magnum
Barrel Length: see text

Ruger Old Army

After achieving success with his fine Single Six, and Blackhawk single-action cartridge revolvers, Ruger set out to design and produce a cap and ball revolver to appeal to the black powder shooting enthusiast and reenactor. The result is the Old Army, which is based on the three-screw Blackhawk lockwork and uses the same frame.

This is a traditional single-action revolver with a half cock hammer position with a removable cylinder and reloading rammer. The Old Army is available in satin stainless steel, gloss stainless steel, or blue (shown here) finishes; it has with fixed sights, and a 5.5 or 7.5 inch barrel.

Type: Muzzle loading cap and ball six-shot revolver
Origin: Sturm, Ruger & Co., Southport, Connecticut
Caliber: .45 BP
Barrel Length: 5.5in

Ruger New Model Single Six Hunter

The Single Six, first released in 1953, is currently produced as the New Model Single Six. There is a range of guns available, squarely aimed at the target range, campsite or trail user. The New Model Single Six Hunter Convertible (shown here) offers as a choice of cylinder allowing it to use both .17 HMR and .17 Mach 2 ammuniton. The "Hunter" designation means that it has a heavy ribbed barrel ready machined for scope rings which are part of the standard specification. Our example is in satin stainless finish and has a 7.5 inch barrel.

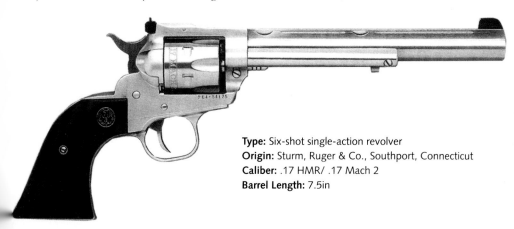

Type: Six-shot single-action revolver
Origin: Sturm, Ruger & Co., Southport, Connecticut
Caliber: .17 HMR/ .17 Mach 2
Barrel Length: 7.5in

Ruger Super Redhawk

The Super Redhawk is the culmination of the Redhawk range of full size heavy double-action Magnum revolvers, which began in 1987. Everything is in place to cater for the large caliber ammunition. The one-piece frame allows for strength and gives flexibility in grip shape. The current design incorporates extra metal in the crucial areas surrounding the confluence of barrel, frame, and top strap, which is also ready-machined for scope mounts. The fluted cylinder with offset stop notches is locked by Ruger's triple latch system. The example here is finished in satin stainless steel with plastic grips inset with rosewood.

Type: Double-action revolver
Origin: Sturm, Ruger & Co., Southport, Connecticut
Caliber: .44 Magnum
Barrel Length: 7.5in

Smith & Wesson

Horace Smith and Daniel Wesson worked very successfully together during the nineteenth century producing designs like the first cartridge revolver and guns like the Model 3 American establishing Smith & Wesson as a world leader in handgun design and manufacturing. At the age of sixty-five, Horace Smith retired from the company and sold his share of the business to Wesson, making him the sole owner of the firm. In the late 1800s, the company introduced its line of hammerless revolvers, the descendants of which are still represented in its current handgun range. In 1899, Smith & Wesson introduced what is probably the most famous revolver in the world, the .38 Military & Police or, as it is called today, the Model 10 (see facing page). This revolver has been in continual production since that year and has been used by virtually every police agency and military force around the world. Smith & Wesson's contribution to the history of handgun and cartridge development continued through the twentieth Century. The first Magnum revolver, the .357 Magnum, was introduced by the company in 1935. In 1955, the first American-made double action auto-loading pistol, the Model 39, was introduced. The Model 29, launched in 1956, chambered in .44 Magnum was immortalized by Clint Eastwood in the movie Dirty Harry. In 1965, Smith & Wesson began producing the Model 60, the world's first stainless steel revolver, launching the era of stainless steel firearms. The accomplishments of Smith & Wesson are numerous and it is difficult to understand the history of modern handguns without first understanding the history of Smith & Wesson. The company was an industry leader in 1852 when it was first founded and remains one of the pre-eminent handgun makers today with its innovations continuing into the twenty-first century.

Smith & Wesson .38 Hand-Ejector, Military & Police Model

For the first sixty years, the .38 Hand-Ejector was known as the Military & Navy Model, but when Smith & Wesson introduced a numbering system in 1958 it was re-designated the Model 10. The name "hand ejector" derived from the fact that, unlike the top-break revolvers that ejected the empty cases mechanically as the weapon was broken, in the Smith & Wesson design the cylinder-pin extension was pulled forward allowing the cylinder assembly to swing out sideways for the cases to be removed manually.

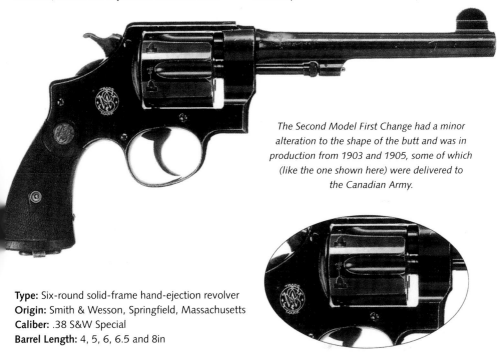

The Second Model First Change had a minor alteration to the shape of the butt and was in production from 1903 and 1905, some of which (like the one shown here) were delivered to the Canadian Army.

Type: Six-round solid-frame hand-ejection revolver
Origin: Smith & Wesson, Springfield, Massachusetts
Caliber: .38 S&W Special
Barrel Length: 4, 5, 6, 6.5 and 8in

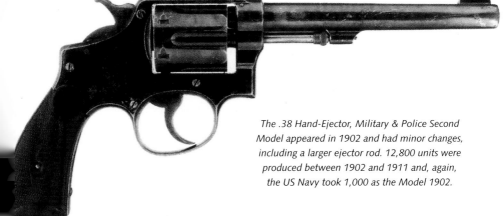

The .38 Hand-Ejector, Military & Police Second Model appeared in 1902 and had minor changes, including a larger ejector rod. 12,800 units were produced between 1902 and 1911 and, again, the US Navy took 1,000 as the Model 1902.

Smith & Wesson Model 14 (K-38 Masterpiece)

This revolver was redesignated the Model 14 in 1958. Law enforcement officers liked the K-38, but wanted a shorter barrel for pocket use. Smith & Wesson complied, introducing the new model in 1950. It had a 2 or 4 inch barrel. This was known as "K-38 Combat Masterpiece" until 1958 when it became the Model 15. This is a post-1958 K-38 model with a 6 inch barrel.

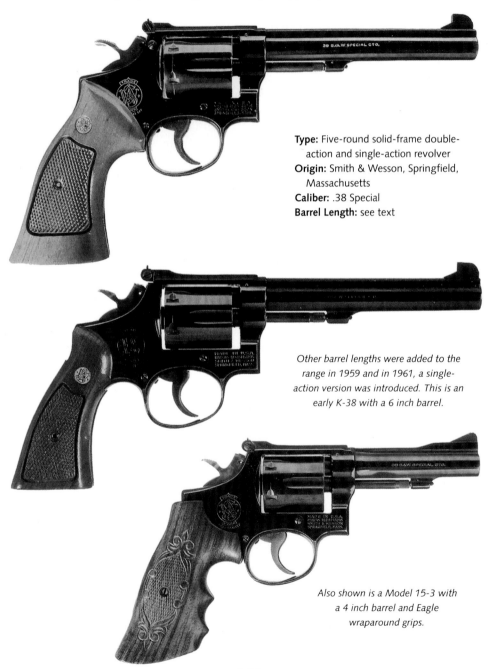

Type: Five-round solid-frame double-action and single-action revolver
Origin: Smith & Wesson, Springfield, Massachusetts
Caliber: .38 Special
Barrel Length: see text

Other barrel lengths were added to the range in 1959 and in 1961, a single-action version was introduced. This is an early K-38 with a 6 inch barrel.

Also shown is a Model 15-3 with a 4 inch barrel and Eagle wraparound grips.

Smith & Wesson Model 29

The very popular Model 29 is one of the most powerful production handguns in the world and, with an empty weight of 47 ounces, is also one of the heaviest. It was produced to take maximum advantage of the newly designed .44 Magnum round and came onto the market in 1956, with four and 6.5 inch barrels.

The 8.4 inch barrel was added in 1957, while the 4 inch version was dropped in 1993. There was also a 5 inch barrel version, of which precisely 500 were made in 1958 only. We show a Model 29-4 with a 4 inch barrel and unfluted cylinder.

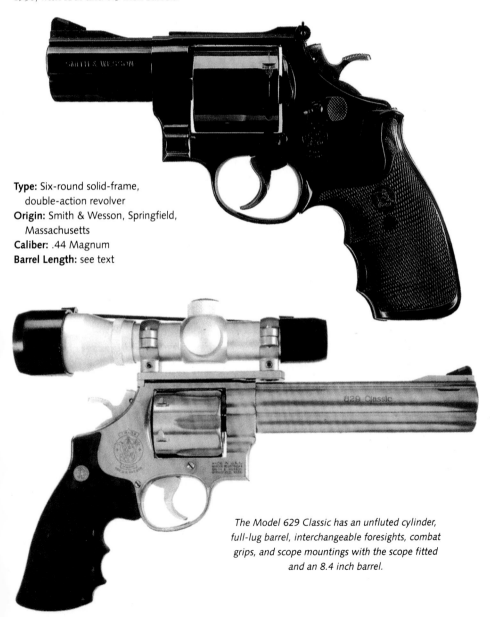

Type: Six-round solid-frame, double-action revolver
Origin: Smith & Wesson, Springfield, Massachusetts
Caliber: .44 Magnum
Barrel Length: see text

The Model 629 Classic has an unfluted cylinder, full-lug barrel, interchangeable foresights, combat grips, and scope mountings with the scope fitted and an 8.4 inch barrel.

271